THOMAS NORTON
1532–1584
and
THOMAS SACKVILLE
1536–1608
THOMAS KYD
1558–1594
THOMAS PRESTON
c. 1537–1598

Minor
Elizabethan Tragedies

Edited by T. W. Craik
Professor of English, University of Dundee

J. M. Dent & Sons Ltd   London

Contents

The Argument of the Tragedy

GORBODUC, King of Britain, divided his realm in his life time to his sons, Ferrex and Porrex. The sons fell to dissension. The younger killed the elder. The mother, that more dearly loved the elder, for revenge killed the younger. The people, moved with the cruelty of the fact, rose in rebellion, and slew both father and mother. The nobility assembled, and most terribly destroyed the rebels; and afterwards, for want of issue of the Prince, whereby the succession of the crown became uncertain, they fell to civil war, in which both they and many of their issues were slain, and the land for a long time almost desolate and miserably wasted.

The Names of the Speakers

GORBODUC, *King of Great Britain.*
VIDENA, *Queen, and wife to King Gorboduc*
FERREX, *Elder son to King Gorboduc.*
PORREX, *Younger son to King Gorboduc.*
CLOTYN, *Duke of Cornwall.*
FERGUS, *Duke of Albany.*
MANDUD, *Duke of Logris.*
GWENARD, *Duke of Camberland.*
EUBULUS, *Secretary to the King.*
AROSTUS, *a Counsellor to the King.*
DORDAN, *a Counsellor assigned by the King to his eldest son, Ferrex.*
PHILANDER, *a Counsellor assigned by the King to his youngest son, Porrex. Both being of the old king's council before.*
HERMON, *a Parasite remaining with Ferrex.*
TYNDAR, *a Parasite remaining with Porrex.*
NUNTIUS, *a Messenger of the elder brother's death.*
NUNTIUS, *a Messenger of Duke Fergus rising in arms.*
MARCELLA, *a Lady of the Queen's privy-chamber.*
CHORUS, *four ancient and sage men of Britain.]*

The Names of the Speakers: Some are "British", others "classical". Gorboduc, Videna (Iuden in Geoffrey, Widen in Fabyan's *Chronicle*), Ferrex, Porrex and Clotyn are from Geoffrey's story. The dukes' names are all British and suggest their respective regions. The counsellor Dordan, and the parasites Hermon and Tyndar, have names adapted from epic poetry (Dardanus, Harmonides, Tyndarus) but are related not at all to the characters who bore those names, merely to the tradition that Britons descended from Trojans. The name Hermon also occurs in Plutarch. The three advisers in I. ii have Greek-derived names suiting their advice: Arostus (weak), Philander (benign), Eubulus (prudent).

Introduction

The major Elizabethan tragedies are those of Marlowe and Shakespeare. Shakespeare's 'tragic period' mostly lies just beyond Elizabeth's reign, in the first five years of James's: the only tragedies he had written by 1603 were *Titus Andronicus, Romeo and Juliet, Julius Caesar* and *Hamlet*, apart from his tragic history plays, notably *Richard II* and *Richard III*. Marlowe, who died in 1593, had devoted himself wholly to tragedy of one kind or another—*Dido*, the two *Tamburlaine* plays, *The Jew of Malta, The Massacre at Paris, Edward II* and *Doctor Faustus*.

From Marlowe's plays and the earlier tragedies of Shakespeare (not to mention his later ones) it can be seen that 'Elizabethan tragedy' includes various kinds of tragic play. When their Elizabethan contemporaries and precursors are also considered, the kinds become even more diverse. The diversity may be explained by a short account of the origins of Elizabethan tragedy, taking note of both content and form.

Medieval tragedy was not dramatic but narrative: a 'tragedy' was the story of the fall of a great man, usually told as part of a series. Boccaccio compiled the first such collection about 1360, under the title *De Casibus Virorum Illustrium*; Chaucer, Lydgate and others followed, and in 1559 appeared *A Mirror for Magistrates*, bringing the catalogue up to date with examples from quite recent English history. Moral lessons were taught by all these narratives, either the grave warning that no trust can be placed in fortune or worldly things, or the severe warning that crime and error bring their own punishments.

Also in 1559 there was published the first English translation of one of Seneca's tragedies, the rest following at intervals until they were collected in 1581. Seneca's subjects were violent incidents from classical mythology—for example, Atreus' revenge on his brother Thyestes by serving up the latter's own children to him at a banquet of ostensible reconciliation—displaying violent passions of rage and grief; he expressed these passions eloquently, supplied moral reflections for the Chorus, and constructed his plays in the classical manner, observing the dramatic unities and narrating the violent actions by means of the characters' speeches.

The native English dramatic tradition was completely different from Seneca's practice. The miracles, with their biblical subjects, were essentially transpositions of narrative into dramatic speech and action, and this is what English secular drama essentially continued to be, dramatizing the whole story (instead of beginning at the crisis) and showing all the physical action (instead of reporting it). Furthermore, comic elements might be admitted to serious plays: they were not infrequent in the miracles, and in the moralities they were usual because of the opportunities offered by the temptation scenes to the Vice and his companions. This feature of the moralities encouraged playwrights to introduce something like double plotting, with the alternation of different groups of characters; the conditions of performance, among them the doubling of parts by members of the small professional troupes of the sixteenth century, further encouraged this tendency. Direct address to the audience, both in serious and in comic scenes, was a characteristic of the native tradition.

Elizabethan tragedy is a river fed by these three streams, whose merging is usually as complete as the metaphor suggests. Even *Gorboduc*, a fundamentally Senecan tragedy, is not Senecan all through, but is connected with the *de casibus* tradition and also with the theatrical traditions of the sententious morality, the elaborate court masque, and the allegorical public show. Other Elizabethan tragedies display, in varying degrees, a more complex mingling of influences upon their content and their form. The fact which should be stressed at once is that Elizabethan tragedy was eclectic and empirical: it took its materials wherever it found them, and it handled them with a view to practical effectiveness rather than theoretical correctness or consistency. It is always essentially theatrical drama, written for performance under specific conditions.

Of these four Elizabethan tragedies, the first two, *Gorboduc* and *Cambises*, belong to the 1560s; the others belong to the late 1580s and early 1590s, by which time the London public theatres were firmly established (the first of them having been built in 1576). Accordingly these two later tragedies, in spite of their differences, have much in common, especially with regard to literary and theatrical technique; the two earlier ones, on the contrary, have hardly any common features of technique at all.

Gorboduc (the only one of the four plays which can be accurately dated) was first performed on 6 January 1562 at the Inner Temple. Its authors were two students there, both still in their twenties, Thomas Norton writing the first three acts and Thomas Sackville the last two. The occasion was the final banquet of the Christmas festivities, and the play was sumptuously presented, but (since the Elizabethans often took their pleasures seriously) it was also composed with gravity and on a subject of great public concern. This important theme is national security and the dangers of civil war, a theme very topical when Queen Elizabeth had only recently succeeded to her sister Mary and their brother Edward, and when the succession to herself was unsettled. Several of her council attended the first performance, and a second performance was given in her presence at Whitehall later that month by royal command.

The source of the plot is the British pseudo-history written by Geoffrey of Monmouth and repeated by the later chroniclers. This tells a simple story of two brothers' rivalry for the future succession, the younger's plot to assassinate the elder, the elder's flight to France and return with an army, his death in the battle that followed, the queen's murder of the survivor by hacking him in pieces (with the aid of her women) while he slept in his tent, and a subsequent civil strife between five kings. In adapting this story the dramatists have developed both its political and its tragic potentialities. Political morals are drawn from Gorboduc's unwise division of his kingdom during his lifetime, the sons' readiness to give ear to bad counsellors, the people's regicidal rebellion, and Fergus's ambitious attempt to usurp the vacant throne—all additions to the source. Tragic emotions are stirred by Videna's jealous love for her firstborn son (given the emphasis of the all-important opening scene) and her revengeful passion when he is killed, by Gorboduc's dismay at the news of the deaths of both his sons (events in which he sees fulfilled the grim destiny allotted to his 'fatal line' by the angry gods), and by Marcella's pathetic narration of Porrex's murder by his own mother. This combination of political thinking with tragic feeling is the essence of the play, a feature of which is that the political calamity is fully as tragic as the personal:

> God for his mercy! what a tide of woes
> Comes rushing on this woeful land at once!

York's exclamation (*Richard II*, II. ii. 98–9) shows how *Gorboduc* points the way towards Shakespeare's tragic histories. Yet it is very far from Shakespearean in its technique. Its structure is thoroughly Senecan, with its division into five acts terminated by choric speeches, its use of messengers to report the violent deeds that must not be shown, and its limitation of the action to dialogues between the minimal number of persons. Admittedly (as Sir Philip Sidney noticed in his *Defence of Poesy*) it does not strictly observe the unities of place and time—nor, he might have added, that of action, since all the major characters are dead by the end of the fourth act. However, these breaches of the classical laws are forced upon the authors by their story and their political theme: their concern with a settled succession dictates the plot's continuance into the fifth act, and, as for their story, one would think that so many fatal strokes and counterstrokes were better not attempted within one revolution of the sun and in a single place. It may surely be said that, with these reservations, it is as Senecan a play as the authors can make it. The allegorical dumb shows, it is true, are not from Seneca: they derive either from *intermedii* interspersed in Italian plays, or (more probably) from court masques and city pageants. The debates about policy, with the balancing of good against bad advice, owe something to the morality conflict between virtue and vice for the mind of the central figure (and in performance could hardly avoid reminding the spectators of such stage conflicts, though by the 1560s it was more usual for persuaders to alternate than to coincide); even so, there are Senecan instances of such balancing, and the eloquent style always inclines the play towards the classical rather than the native tradition.

Cambises, on the contrary, is thoroughly repugnant to classical form and style. It was probably written shortly before its publication (*c.* 1570, without date), and bears the name of Thomas Preston as author. This may have been the Thomas Preston who had a distinguished career at Cambridge, disputing and acting before the Queen there in 1564, and finally becoming master of a college. If so, he was a learned man writing popular drama (there is precedent for this, notably in the robust anti-Catholic plays of John Bale in the 1530s). Nothing is known of the play's actors or audiences, but the fact that

its characters are distributed (not quite correctly) among eight 'men'
(the last two, who play women and children, being presumably boys)
suggests that it was intended for a professional troupe, not amateurs
like the performers of *Gorboduc*.

The story is from Persian history, the ultimate source being
Herodotus, and the immediate source Richard Taverner, who recounts
it in his prose work *The Garden of Wisdom* (1539). Preston, following
this version closely, dramatizes it in the manner of a moral interlude.
The career of the tyrant is presented as a tragedy of retribution. Cambises begins his reign well, fighting a victorious war and executing an
unjust judge who has mismanaged the realm in his absence. There-
after he steeply deteriorates. He becomes a drunkard, and when a lord
reproves him for this fault he shoots the lord's young son to prove
the steadiness of his hand. He murders his brother Smerdis for fear he
should inherit the kingdom and eclipse his memory, marries his first
cousin in defiance of religious prohibition, and murders her in her
turn because she dares lament his brother's death. Finally divine
vengeance overtakes him: while mounting his horse he accidentally
falls on his own sword.

Cambises is much more a mixture than *Gorboduc*. At first sight it is a
sensational entertainment devoid of tragic dignity. All the violence is
shown: the judge is flayed (with a false skin), imitation blood (vinegar
in a bladder) flows from Smerdis's wounds, the child's heart is cut out
to show the arrow transfixing it, and Cambises makes his final entry
with the sword sticking in his side, bleeding, and dies on stage. There
is equally violent knockabout comedy between soldiers, women and
rustics, egged on by a morality Vice, Ambidexter, who is in the play
mostly as a mischief-maker and commentator, although he does also do
a little encouraging of the judge and the king in their wickedness. Yet
though this play follows the native tradition in telling the whole
story, staging the whole physical action, mingling serious events with
boisterous comedy, and bringing in abstractions like Shame to blow a
black trumpet, it is linked with Senecan tragedy in its carnal, bloody
and unnatural acts, and there is something of the Senecan passion and
the Senecan rhetoric in the mother's lament for her murdered child—

Is this the joy of thee I reap? O king, of tiger's brood!
O tiger's whelp, hadst thou the heart to see this child's heart-blood?

—which makes itself felt even through the ungainly couplets in fourteeners. This metre, so inferior as a tragic medium to the new blank verse of *Gorboduc*, is yet another link with Seneca, because it was the metre of the contemporary English translations. When Shakespeare made Falstaff declaim 'in King Cambises' vein' he parodied Lyly's prose and contemporary blank verse; it was in Bottom's play that he parodied *Cambises* itself:

> I feel myself a-dying now, of life bereft am I;
> Now am I dead, now am I fled, my soul is in the sky.

(The first line of this composite couplet is from *Cambises*, the second from *A Midsummer Night's Dream*.)

Cumbrous metre and cumbrous diction ('My queen and lords, to take repast, let us attempt the same') typify the serious style of *Cambises*, while decorum is observed by using loose unmetrical couplets and colloquialisms for its comic parts. One is tempted to say that comic irregular doggerel takes turns with serious regular doggerel. Even so, a first step is made towards that freedom and variety of style, as well as of subject-matter, that distinguishes Shakespearean drama. A miracle play is written in one stanza-form throughout; it is the content and diction that differ when Mak is speaking to the Shepherds and when the Angel is speaking to them. In *Gorboduc*, which is wholly written in blank verse, the question of contrast does not arise: there are no clowns, only kings. But *Gorboduc* is in this respect, as in most others, more classical than it was natural for English drama to be. Elizabethan tragedy needed *Gorboduc*, but it needed *Cambises* too, and to make both of them what they were it needed Seneca. With these materials, and the evolution of the London theatres and audiences, it was made ready for Kyd, Marlowe and Shakespeare.

Thomas Kyd's *Spanish Tragedy* (published, without date, in 1592) and Christopher Marlowe's two *Tamburlaine* plays (written in 1587-8, published in 1590) combined to form the public taste in serious drama, and most elements in their immediate successors can be traced back to one or the other dramatist. Whether Kyd's tragedy preceded or followed Marlowe's is unknown: the earliest record of its performance is in 1592 at the Rose theatre on the Bankside.

Whereas the structure of either part of *Tamburlaine* is fundamentally a biography of the hero (in which, though in almost nothing else, Marlowe's two plays recall *Cambises*), that of *The Spanish Tragedy* is a complex plot of rivalry and revenge (recalling *Gorboduc*). No source for this plot has been discovered; it may have been Kyd's invention. Seneca's influence on the treatment is marked, especially in the framework of Induction and Choruses provided by Andrea's Ghost and Revenge, and in the General's narrative of the battle (I. ii), as well as in the hero's long Latin declamation at the end of the scene where he finds his son murdered (II. iv), and his triumphant self-vindication when he has achieved his revenge.

The vehemence of Hieronimo's passions (and those of others, particularly Isabella and Bel-imperia), and the ingenuity of the plot (set in motion and sustained by Lorenzo's villainy, and brought to its catastrophe by Hieronimo's cunning revenge), chiefly account for the play's enduring popularity, combined as they are with a stage action which presents the sensational events in a genuinely dramatic way. In II. i, for example, Pedringano does not voluntarily betray Bel-imperia to Lorenzo, but is coerced at sword's point, and then sworn to secrecy 'on this cross' (the hilt of the sword). In the following scene, Bel-imperia and Horatio exchange words of love, while 'Pedringano showeth all to the Prince and Lorenzo, placing them in secret', so that the lovers' lines can be repeated with sinister inversion by the over-hearers 'above'. A short return to the public business between King and Ambassador separates this from the lovers' second meeting, at night in Hieronimo's garden. Here Pedringano, with strong dramatic irony, is posted as a faithful watchman at the garden gate; he leaves the stage announcing (aside) that he will admit their enemies, and this expectation hangs over their unsuspecting lyrical dialogue. Then, with 'Who's there? Pedringano! we are betray'd!', violence bursts out: Horatio is repeatedly stabbed ('Ay, thus, and thus: these are the fruits of love') and his body is hung up in the arbour. Bel-imperia is dragged screaming away, and the stage is left empty except for Hora-tio's hanging body. Now 'Enter Hieronimo in his shirt, etc.', and in his speech Kyd deliberately delays the expected shock of tragic recog-nition which is the true emotional climax of the scene and the act.

The whole play is handled with similar assurance. Though fault may be found with the episode of false accusation in Portugal (I. iii; III. i), with some of the mannerisms of the rhetoric, and with other features in which Kyd falls short of Shakespeare's later and greater achievement, *The Spanish Tragedy* is an impressive whole. The macabre humour of Pedringano's execution while he confidently expects a non-existent pardon, and the sardonic wit of both villain

('Yet is he at the highest now he is dead', II. iv. 60) and hero ('I'll play the murderer, I warrant you', IV. i. 129), have their important part in the total effect; they correspond to the equally integral comic elements in tragedies as different from each other as *The Jew of Malta* and *Hamlet*. The extremity of passion, verging on madness, which afflicts Hieronimo is also an important element in contemporary and later tragedies: Zabina's suicide speech in *1 Tamburlaine*, the hero's 'impassionate fury' at Zenocrate's death in *2 Tamburlaine*, and the outbursts of Hamlet, Othello and Lear, may be compared. Later texts of *The Spanish Tragedy* itself, from 1602 onwards, include additions (printed in italics in the present volume), one of which, the famous Painter Scene (III. xiiA), explores the poetic possibilities of such passions in an original and imaginative way. The authorship, and the date, of these additions are unknown (though Jonson was paid to write additions in 1601–2, there has been much debate as to whether these printed ones can be his); they are certainly not by Kyd, and, whether treated as additions or (more properly) as replacements, they obscure rather than improve the original plotting and characterization, and are best omitted at a first reading of the play. They do, however, show that Hieronimo's passions came to be regarded as chief of the tragedy's attractions.

Hieronimo's suffering and his revenge gave *The Spanish Tragedy* the arresting power of a tragedy of modern life. The protagonists of Seneca's plays, and those of *Gorboduc* and *Cambises*, are figures from legends and old chronicles: Hieronimo is a contemporary courtier. Although it is true to say that in the English histories of Shakespeare and Marlowe (as in the miracles too) the past lives again in terms of the present, there is still a difference between dramatizing a familiar story and dramatizing an unfamiliar one. This is evidently the case with an invented story such as Kyd's seems to be, and also with the stories which come into Elizabethan tragedy by way of narrative fiction, notably the collections of Italian *novelle*. The finest examples of this type of tragic subject are *Romeo and Juliet* and *Othello*. When, like Faustus, a man is one part history and three parts legend, his being at least a man of Marlowe's own century goes a good way towards establishing him as a contemporary when he appears as a tragic hero. The same contemporary interest attaches to figures of recent history, like the Duke of Guise in Marlowe's *Massacre at Paris*.

Arden of Feversham (first extant edition, 1592; probably written in 1591) is a domestic tragedy closely based upon the narrative given in Holinshed's *Chronicles* (1577 edition) of a murder committed in 1551. The play's title page reads:

The lamentable and true tragedy of Master Arden of Feversham in Kent. Who was most wickedly murdered by the means of his disloyal and wanton wife, who, for the love she bare to one Mosbie, hired two desperate ruffians, Black Will and Shakebag, to kill him. Wherein is showed the great malice and dissimulation of a wicked woman, the unsatiable desire of filthy lust, and the shameful end of all murderers.

This summary account suggests the general attractions of the story: realism, sensationalism, and moralism. Its details show why Holinshed thought the murder specially memorable; a series of attempts at assassination all miscarry, until finally one succeeds. Consequently, the story is one of suspense and intrigue. The anonymous playwright, who has never been identified, transposes this story into a chain of dramatic episodes which are equal in theatrical power to the scenes of *The Spanish Tragedy*: the midnight adventure at Franklin's house in London, and the murder itself, while Arden plays backgammon with his wife's lover across his own supper-table, are the peaks of this sequence. Again like Kyd, the playwright has added drama of character to drama of event. In this he has greatly improved on Holinshed's narrative, expanding the merest hints and supplying imaginative inventions of his own. For instance, in Holinshed, when the final scheme was suggested, Mosbie at first disliked its underhandedness and 'in a fury flung away' to his inn, whence Alice recalled him by messenger, 'and at his coming back she fell down on her knees to him and besought him to go through with the matter'. In the play Mosbie is given no such moral scruples, but the quarrel is developed into an important scene much earlier in the action (Scene viii, itself foreshadowed by their first dialogue in the opening scene), where it springs directly from their adulterous relationship, the social distance between them, Mosbie's self-interested distrust even of his mistress, and Alice's misgivings which are prompted partly by wounded pride and partly by genuine remorse. There is a real interest in the mutual relationships of the characters, not excluding the minor ones; and this interest works alongside an organizing power, bringing the story's raw materials into considerable dramatic unity. Alice's servant and Mosbie's sister, separate characters in the source, are combined as

Susan, and made the bone of contention between Arden's servant Michael and the painter Clarke, whose rivalry provides a comic counterpoint to the serious rivalry of Arden and Mosbie, and is completely missing from Holinshed. This comic element is present, too, in the aggressive touchiness of Black Will in his dealings with his companion ruffian Shakebag and with others (the new incidents with the Prentice and the Ferryman develop this characteristic of his, as well as particularizing what is left general in the source's 'he missed of his purpose' and 'he missed the way'). By making Black Will and Shakebag comic as well as sinister, the dramatist concentrates the full seriousness of his play upon Alice, Mosbie, and Arden himself.

The play is a two-fold tragedy in conception: a tragedy of retribution upon Alice and Mosbie, and a tragedy of pathos in Arden's betrayal and finally inevitable death. The opening scene, and the role of his friend and confidant Franklin (an invented character) throughout, make it clear that Arden was conceived as a pathetic victim, and it is made doubly clear by Alice's contrition at the end. Holinshed's statement that Arden, because Alice's wealthy relations were profitable to him, turned a blind eye to her adultery, is suppressed. Yet Holinshed's other statement, that the print of Arden's murdered body was visible for two years in a field which he had extorted from Reede's wife, is retained, given to Franklin in his epilogue, and prepared by a scene in which (again as reported in Holinshed) Reede curses Arden for withholding the land. Thus, and at some damage to the general tragic conception, the play becomes also in part a tragedy of retribution upon Arden. Probably the dramatist included this detail because it was so striking that he could not bear to leave it out, and also because he wanted to suggest as often and as forcibly as possible the hand of divine providence in the events, thereby giving them the dignity that tragedy requires; Arden's forebodings (notably his dream, Scene vi), Alice's early recognition that her fatal passion will be her ruin, and especially the circumstances by which the murder is discovered, work towards the same end. Arden's covetousness, however, remains an undigested element which the play would be better without, even though it might be argued that this particular moral flaw both increases the lifelike imperfection of moral character and also heightens the social realism.

One returns, as with *The Spanish Tragedy*, to dramatic power as the chief virtue of the piece. The combination of suspense with dramatic irony is a feature of the climaxes of both plays; the murderer's cue, 'Now I can take you' (provided by Holinshed), seems to have set the tone for the preceding dialogue at the supper-table, where in nine lines there are no less than four distinct strokes of dramatic irony:

Mosbie. Yet, Arden, I protest to thee by heaven,
    Thou ne'er shalt see me more after this night.
    I'll go to Rome rather than be forsworn.
Arden. Tush, I'll have no such vows made in my house.
Alice. Yes, I pray you, husband, let him swear;
    And, on that condition, Mosbie, pledge me here.
Mosbie. Ay, as willingly as I mean to live.
Arden. Come, Alice, is our supper ready yet?
Alice. It will by then you have play'd a game at tables.

It is hard to suppose that this dialogue was not written in the shadow of *The Spanish Tragedy* and perhaps also of *The Jew of Malta.*

The characteristic and fundamental qualities of Elizabethan tragedy are strong passions, an exciting action, and a feeling of the inevitability of the catastrophe.

In conclusion, something must be said of the stage performance for which these plays were intended, since Elizabethan drama is essentially theatrical, as has already been said and shown. *Gorboduc* and *Cambises* precede the establishment of public theatres. The setting for *Gorboduc* was a scaffold erected in a hall, first at the Inner Temple and then at Whitehall. From the fourth dumb show, in which the kings and queens driven by furies 'came forth from under the stage, as though out of hell', we may infer that there was a trap, such as is unmistakably required to represent a gulf and a grave in Gascoigne's and Kinwelmershe's *Jocasta,* performed in similar circumstances at Gray's Inn in 1566. In *Gorboduc* the physical action is restricted to these elaborate and musical dumb shows; indeed, from the second, in which a king 'placed himself in a chair of estate prepared for him', we may also infer that Gorboduc himself never sat in a throne at all, but remained standing like all the other characters. Little more use is made of stage furniture in *Cambises:* a table and seats for the banquet are provided (by a servant called Preparation, assisted by the Vice), and are later removed at the angry king's bidding (by the banqueting lords?), but apart from this the action takes place on a bare stage, and there is no call for an upper level or for stage machinery (in contrast with a contemporary and in many respects similar play, *Horestes,* which calls for a city to be taken by storm, Clytemnestra to 'speak over the wall', and Aegisthus to mount a ladder to a gallows upon which he is hanged). The play could be performed on the floor of a hall or on the most elementary indoor or outdoor scaffold. The king three times calls for appropriate sound-effects, drums for his Egyptian campaign and music for his betrothal and wedding-banquet, while the actors playing the lord and lady (later Cambises' queen) are expected to perform on lute and cittern. Much attention is paid to realistic and symbolic action, the shooting of Praxaspes' son by the king and of the king by Cupid, the murder of Smerdis and the execution of Sisamnes (the latter essentially symbolic, since his beheading is a blow in the neck and since it would be both tedious and indecent to remove all his clothes: the actors must have the false skin, a well-known and indispensable detail of the story, ready to hold up, perhaps throwing a sheet over the body).

The stage directions to *The Spanish Tragedy*, many of which are probably Kyd's own, show a firm grasp of the resources of the public theatre, even though there may be debate as to how some of them are to be obeyed—whether, for instance, Andrea's Ghost and Revenge sit above the stage or on it, and where the stage audience for Hieronimo's fatal play is placed, and how Isabella 'cuts down the arbour' (symbolic action only?). There is clearly an upper stage from which Lorenzo and Balthazar overhear the lovers, and from which Belimperia's 'letter falleth' during her imprisonment (she also appears 'at a window'). Hieronimo 'knocks up the curtain' for his play, in the course of which Horatio's body can be moved into position ready for him to exhibit it at 'See here my show, look on this spectacle' (when, if the stage audience is above, he will need to draw the body out upon a bier). There is an 'arbour' strong enough to take Horatio's weight, a gallows for Pedringano to ascend (evidently by ladder, for the hangman finally 'turns him off'), and a 'stake' to which Alexandro is bound. A banquet is held, graced with a dumb show provided by Hieronimo, and a supernatural dumb show is witnessed by Andrea's Ghost and Revenge.

With *Arden of Feversham* we revert to simpler stage effects, as befits the realism of this domestic tragedy. No upper stage is required, and no machinery except the shutter that breaks Black Will's head (a portable stall brought on at the start of the scene?). Shakebag's fall into the ditch need not involve a trap, though that would help the effect. A feature of this play is the way the action will shift, in the course of a single scene, from the outside to the inside of a house. This happens in the first scene when Alice says 'Husband, sit down; your breakfast will be cold'; he obeys, and at least Mosbie also sits down. Seats and perhaps a table are required at this point. Again, Scene xiv begins in some indeterminate place outdoors with a conversation between Black Will, Shakebag and Greene, who are joined, first by Alice and Michael, and then by Mosbie; by the time Mosbie and Greene leave, the place has somehow become the inside of Arden's house, for Alice begins showing the ruffians the counting-house where they are to hide. For the game at tables, Will has required a chair to be set for Mosbie and a stool with its back to the counting-house for Arden; these, and the supper-table, must be at some moment produced by somebody, and after the murder six persons sit down at the table, which, again, somebody must at some moment take away—unless the furniture was permanently on stage. The counting-house itself seems to be a discovery-space, since Arden's body is put there while the guests are in the house, and after their departure it is disclosed again (surely to the full view of the audience, like Horatio's in *The Spanish Tragedy*) and taken out to the fields; it is also displayed to Alice by the Mayor in Scene xvi, presumably as it lies in the fields, so once again a discovery is desirable. These details and others (notably a carelessness in indicating Michael's entrances and exits in the scenes with the furniture) suggest that the playwright left the minor points of staging to the actors; his own understanding of the basic elements of his stage gave them the framework within which to perform his play.

In reconstructing the stage requirements of these and other plays, indeed, it is necessary to assume that the playwrights knew their business, but it is also prudent to remember that they may not have worked out the stage technique in all its detail. If a play is fundamentally stageworthy, means can always be found to stage it.

It cannot be too often repeated that the test of all plays is theatrical performance, and it is especially the test of Elizabethan tragedies, in which so much use is made of rhetoric or of stage action, or of both. Many difficulties which are excogitated by the analytical reader are not present at all to the spectator who witnesses the plays moment by dramatic moment: this is true of Shakespeare (*Hamlet* in particular springs to mind), and is therefore not an admission that the plays will not bear critical analysis, merely that the wrong kind of analysis is inappropriate. To say so should be a truism, but in practice many readers approach Elizabethan plays with demands of verisimilitude and consistency which belong rather to the novel than to the drama, and, if to drama, then to realistic plays rather than to romantic ones. Analogies between different arts can easily be exaggerated, but it may be suggested that the dramatic situations of Verdi's *Rigoletto* or *Il Trovatore*, heightened by emotional music and reinforced with strong theatrical spectacle, take the spectator's feelings by storm in the same way as the great scenes of *Arden of Feversham* or *The Spanish Tragedy*. If these plays are approached by way of Italian tragic opera, or by way of the more melodramatic events of Dickens's novels (such as Krook's spontaneous combustion in *Bleak House*, or the plunge to death of Headstone and Riderhood in *Our Mutual Friend*), they make a similar emotional impact. Even in the reading, the effect of these two plays in particular ought to be partly physical: the excitement of them should be felt on the pulses, and a reader who feels nothing of this kind would do well to abandon them and read something else to which he is temperamentally more adapted. This strong and simple emotional response is only the beginning of one's understanding of Elizabethan tragedy (which requires to be seen in the light of its origins and development), but without it there can be no understanding at all

1974.   T. W. CRAIK.

Note on the Text

I have taken as copy texts for the plays in this volume the following sixteenth-century editions:

Gorboduc. Q2. John Day, n.d., 1570? (First authorized edition.)

Cambises. Q1. John Allde, n.d., 1570?

The Spanish Tragedy. Q1. Edward Allde for Edward White, n.d., 1592.
Q4. W[illiam] W[hite] for Thomas Pavier, 1602. (For the additions.)

Arden of Feversham. Q1. For Edward White, 1592.

I have consulted also the other editions, early and modern, listed in the following Bibliographical Note.

Stage directions, divisions into acts and scenes, and lists of *dramatis personae* are from the copy texts unless enclosed in square brackets, when they are editorial.

Spelling and punctuation are modernized. Old forms of words are normally replaced by their modern equivalents (egal by equal, murther by murder, randon by random, mought by might, scinder'd by sunder'd, etc.); but occasionally they are retained for aesthetic reasons (handkercher in *The Spanish Tragedy*) and always when they are necessary to the metre ('In any case be not too jealous'; 'May beg me from the gallows of the shrieve', *Arden of Feversham*, i. 48, 168) or to the rhyme ('otherwise'/'advise', for 'advice', *Cambises*, 648–9). Also in the interests of metre, I have distinguished the two pronunciations of final 'ed' as ''d' and 'èd' in the verse passages, using the form 'ed' throughout in the prose. In so doing, the metre and not the copy text has been my guide when the two conflict. It is often necessary, when the two pronunciations occur in the same line, to indicate which is long and which is short ('Inflam'd the parchèd earth with heaven's fire', *Gorboduc*, I. ii. 387). I have not, however, attempted to show in the

text how other words should be accented. The reader's experience of
Elizabethan language and Elizabethan verse must dictate his different
stresses in 'In your own kingdom triumphs over you' (*Gorboduc*,
II. i. 110) and 'In which sweet silence such as we triumph' (*Arden of
Feversham*, v. 5), and so on.

Q stands for the copy text; when the readings of more than one
quarto are contrasted they are indicated by number, as Q1, Q2, etc.;
when a quarto not listed in the Bibliographical Note is cited, it is
cited from a modern editor's textual apparatus.

Important emendations are indicated in the footnotes by giving the
rejected reading of the copy text. Editorial insertions in the text are
enclosed in square brackets. There has not been room for a full textual
apparatus listing the minor corrections of the copy text, and recording
editorial readings and conjectures which have not been followed in
this edition. New readings introduced in this edition are indicated by
my initial in parenthesis (C). Changes from the line-divisions of the
copy texts are not indicated.

I am glad to acknowledge my debts to the earlier editors of these
plays and to the authors of the critical works mentioned in the Bibliographical Note, and I also wish to thank G. R. Proudfoot, M. R. G.
Spiller, K. M. Sturgess, and M. L. Wine for discussing particular
points with me. I gratefully dedicate this edition to my teacher, Enid
Welsford.

Select Bibliography

WORKS

Gorboduc. Thomas Norton (1532–84) and Thomas Sackville (1536–1608).

Early Editions.   Q1. William Griffith, 1565; Q2. John Day, n.d., 1570?

Modern Editions.   J. M. Manly, *Specimens of the Pre-Shaksperean Drama,* II, 1897; J. W. Cunliffe, *Early English Classical Tragedies,* 1912; J. Q. Adams, *Chief Pre-Shakespearean Dramas,* 1924; A. K. McIlwraith, *Five Elizabethan Tragedies,* 1938; I. B. Cauthen (Regents Renaissance Drama), 1970.

Cambises. Thomas Preston (c. 1537–98).

Early Editions.   Q1. John Allde, n.d., 1570? Q2. Edward Allde, n.d., 1585?

Modern Editions.   J. M. Manly, *Specimens of the Pre-Shaksperean Drama,* II, 1897; J. Q. Adams, *Chief Pre-Shakespearean Dramas,* 1924.

The Spanish Tragedy. Thomas Kyd (1558–94).

Early Editions.   Q1. Edward Allde for Edward White, n.d., 1592; Q4. W[illiam] W[hite] for Thomas Pavier, 1602.

Modern Editions.   J. M. Manly, *Specimens of the Pre-Shaksperean Drama,* II, 1897; F. S. Boas, *The Works of Thomas Kyd,* 1901; W. W. Greg and F. S. Boas (Malone Society Reprints), 1925 (Q4); A. K. McIlwraith, *Five Elizabethan Tragedies,* 1938; W. W. Greg and D. N. Smith (Malone Society Reprints), 1949 (Q1); P. Edwards (The Revels Plays), 1959; A. S. Cairncross (Regents Renaissance Drama), 1967; J. R. Mulryne (New Mermaid Dramatists), 1970.

Arden of Feversham. [Anonymous.]

Early Edition.   Q1. For Edward White, 1592.

Modern Editions.   K. Warnke and L. Proescholdt, *Pseudo-Shakespearian Plays,* 1888; R. Bayne (The Temple Dramatists), 1897; C. F. Tucker Brooke, *The Shakespeare Apocrypha,* 1908; A. K. McIlwraith, *Five Elizabethan Tragedies,* 1938; H. Macdonald and D. N. Smith (Malone Society Reprints), 1947; K. Sturgess, *Three Elizabethan Domestic Tragedies,* 1969.

BIOGRAPHY AND CRITICISM

Barish, J. A. '*The Spanish Tragedy*, or the Pleasures and Perils of Rhetoric'. In *Elizabethan Theatre* (*Stratford-upon-Avon Studies*, 9). 1966.

Bradbrook, M. C. *Themes and Conventions of Elizabethan Tragedy*. 1935.

Chambers, E. K. *The Elizabethan Stage*. 4 vols. 1923.

Clemen, W. H. *English Tragedy before Shakespeare: the Development of Dramatic Speech*. 1961.

Doran, M. *Endeavors of Art: a Study of Form in Elizabethan Drama*. 1954.

Edwards, P. *Thomas Kyd and Early Elizabethan Tragedy* (*Writers and their Work*, 192). 1966.

Farnham, W. E. *The Medieval Heritage of Elizabethan Tragedy*. 1936.

Freeman, A. *Thomas Kyd, Facts and Problems*. 1967.

Murray, P. B. *Thomas Kyd*. 1969.

Wickham, G. *Early English Stages, 1300 to 1660*; Vol. 2, *1576 to 1660*, *Part I*. 1963.

Gorboduc

Gorboduc

THE ORDER OF THE DUMB SHOW BEFORE THE FIRST ACT, AND THE SIGNIFICATION THEREOF.

First, the music of violins began to play, during which came in upon the stage six wild men, clothed in leaves. Of whom the first bare in his neck a fagot of small sticks, which they all, both severally and together, assayed with all their strength to break; but it could not be broken by them. At the length, one of them plucked out one of the sticks, and brake it: and the rest plucking out all the other sticks, one after another, did easily break them, the same being severed; which being conjoined, they had before attempted in vain. After they had this done, they departed the stage, and the music ceased. Hereby was signified, that a state knit in unity doth continue strong against all force, but being divided, is easily destroyed; as befell upon Duke Gorboduc dividing his land to his two sons, which he before held in monarchy; and upon the dissension of the brethren, to whom it was divided.

ACT I

SCENE I

VIDENA.   FERREX.

Vid. The silent night that brings the quiet pause,
    From painful travails of the weary day,
    Prolongs my careful thoughts, and makes me blame
    The slow Aurore, that so for love or shame
    Doth long delay to show her blushing face;
    And now the day renews my grieffull plaint.
Fer. My gracious lady, and my mother dear,
    Pardon my grief for your so grievèd mind
    To ask what cause tormenteth so your heart.
Vid. So great a wrong and so unjust despite,   10
    Without all cause against all course of kind!

3

Fer. Such causeless wrong, and so unjust despite,
    May have redress, or, at the least, revenge.
Vid. Neither, my son; such is the froward will,
    The person such, such my mishap and thine.
Fer. Mine know I none, but grief for your distress.
Vid. Yes; mine for thine, my son. A father? no:
    In kind a father, not in kindliness.
Fer. My father? Why? I know nothing at all,
    Wherein I have misdone unto his grace. 20
Vid. Therefore the more unkind to thee and me.
    For, knowing well, my son, the tender love
    That I have ever borne, and bear to thee,
    He, griev'd thereat, is not content alone
    To spoil me of thy sight, my chiefest joy,
    But thee of thy birth-right and heritage,
    Causeless, unkindly, and in wrongful wise,
    Against all law and right, he will bereave:
    Half of his kingdom he will give away.
Fer. To whom?
Vid.   Even to Porrex, his younger son; 30
    Whose growing pride I do so sore suspect,
    That, being rais'd to equal rule with thee,
    Methinks I see his envious heart to swell,
    Fill'd with disdain and with ambitious hope.
    The end the gods do know, whose altars I
    Full oft have made in vain of cattle slain
    To send the sacred smoke to Heaven's throne,
    For thee, my son, if things do so succeed,
    As now my jealous mind misdeemeth sore.
Fer. Madam, leave care and careful plaint for me. 40
    Just hath my father been to every wight:
    His first injustice he will not extend
    To me, I trust, that give no cause thereof;
    My brother's pride shall hurt himself, not me.
Vid. So grant the gods! But yet, thy father so
    Hath firmly fixèd his unmovèd mind,
    That plaints and prayers can no whit avail;

25 *To spoil me of thy sight* (R. Dodsley, *Old Plays*, 1744.)] To spoil thee of my sight Q.

  For those have I assay'd, but even this day
  He will endeavour to procure assent
  Of all his council to his fond device.   50
Fer. Their ancestors from race to race have borne
  True faith to my forefathers and their seed:
  I trust they eke will bear the like to me.
Vid. There resteth all. But if they fail thereof,
  And if the end bring forth an ill success,
  On them and theirs the mischief shall befall,
  And so I pray the gods requite it them;
  And so they will, for so is wont to be,
  When lords and trusted rulers under kings,
  To please the present fancy of the prince,   60
  With wrong transpose the course of governance;
  Murders, mischief, or civil sword at length,
  Or mutual treason, or a just revenge,
  When right succeeding line returns again,
  By Jove's just judgment and deservèd wrath,
  Brings them to cruel and reproachful death,
  And roots their names and kindreds from the earth.
Fer. Mother, content you, you shall see the end.
Vid. The end! thy end I fear: Jove end me first! [*Exeunt.*]

SCENE II

GORBODUC. AROSTUS. PHILANDER. EUBULUS.

Gor. My lords, whose grave advice and faithful aid
  Have long upheld my honour and my realm,
  And brought me to this age from tender years,
  Guiding so great estate with great renown:
  Now more importeth me than erst to use
  Your faith and wisdom, whereby yet I reign;
  That when by death my life and rule shall cease,
  The kingdom yet may with unbroken course
  Have certain prince, by whose undoubted right
  Your wealth and peace may stand in quiet stay; 10

And eke that they whom nature hath prepar'd
In time to take my place in princely seat,
While in their father's time their pliant youth
Yields to the frame of skilful governance,
May so be taught and train'd in noble arts,
As what their fathers, which have reign'd before,
Have with great fame derivèd down to them,
With honour they may leave unto their seed;
And not be thought, for their unworthy life,
And for their lawless swerving out of kind,　　　　　20
Worthy to lose what law and kind them gave;
But that they may preserve the common peace,
The cause that first began and still maintains
The lineal course of kings' inheritance,
For me, for mine, for you, and for the state
Whereof both I and you have charge and care.
Thus do I mean to use your wonted faith
To me and mine, and to your native land.
My lords, be plain, without all wry respect,
Or poisonous craft to speak in pleasing wise,　　　　30
Lest as the blame of ill-succeeding things
Shall light on you, so light the harms also.

Aros. Your good acceptance so, most noble king,
Of such our faithfulness, as heretofore
We have employ'd in duties to your grace
And to this realm, whose worthy head you are,
Well proves, that neither you mistrust at all,
Nor we shall need in boasting wise to show
Our truth to you, nor yet our wakeful care
For you, for yours, and for our native land.　　　　40
Wherefore, O king, I speak as one for all,
Sith all as one do bear you equal faith:
Doubt not to use our counsels and our aids,
Whose honours, goods, and lives are whole avow'd,
To serve, to aid, and to defend your grace.

Gor. My lords, I thank you all. This is the case:
Ye know, the gods, who have the sovereign care
For kings, for kingdoms, and for common weals,
Gave me two sons in my more lusty age,

Who now, in my decaying years, are grown   50
Well towards riper state of mind and strength,
To take in hand some greater princely charge.
As yet they live and spend their hopeful days
With me, and with their mother, here in court.
Their age now asketh other place and trade,
And mine also doth ask another change,
Theirs to more travail, mine to greater ease.
When fatal death shall end my mortal life,
My purpose is to leave unto them twain
The realm divided in two sundry parts.   60
The one, Ferrex, mine elder son, shall have,
The other shall the younger, Porrex, rule.
That both my purpose may more firmly stand,
And eke that they may better rule their charge,
I mean forthwith to place them in the same;
That in my life they may both learn to rule,
And I may joy to see their ruling well.
This is, in sum, what I would have ye weigh:
First, whether ye allow my whole device,
And think it good for me, for them, for you,   70
And for our country, mother of us all:
And if ye like it and allow it well,
Then, for their guiding and their governance,
Show forth such [further] means of circumstance,
As ye think meet to be both known and kept.
Lo, this is all; now tell me your advice.
Aros. And this is much, and asketh great advice:
But for my part, my sovereign lord and king,
This do I think. Your majesty doth know,
How under you, in justice and in peace,   80
Great wealth and honour long we have enjoy'd:
So as we cannot seem with greedy minds
To wish for change of prince or governance:
But if we like your purpose and device,
Our liking must be deemèd to proceed

---

74 [*further*] (C). Compare 141. Manly suggests "Show forth [to me]" or
'Show forth [, I pray]'.

Of rightful reason, and of heedful care,
Not for ourselves, but for the common state,
Sith our own state doth need no better change.
I think in all as erst your grace hath said:
First, when you shall unload your aged mind　　　　90
Of heavy care and troubles manifold,
And lay the same upon my lords, your sons,
Whose growing years may bear the burden long,
(And long I pray the gods to grant it so)
And in your life, while you shall so behold
Their rule, their virtues, and their noble deeds,
Such as their kind behighteth to us all,
Great be the profits that shall grow thereof;
Your age in quiet shall the longer last,
Your lasting age shall be their longer stay.　　　　100
For cares of kings, that rule as you have rul'd,
For public wealth, and not for private joy,
Do waste man's life and hasten crooked age,
With furrow'd face, and with enfeebl'd limbs,
To draw on creeping death a swifter pace.
They two, yet young, shall bear the parted reign
With greater ease than one, now old, alone
Can wield the whole, for whom much harder is
With lessen'd strength the double weight to bear.
Your eye, your counsel, and the grave regard　　　　110
Of father, yea, of such a father's name,
Now at beginning of their sunder'd reign,
When is the hazard of their whole success,
Shall bridle so their force of youthful heats,
And so restrain the rage of insolence,
Which most assails the young and noble minds,
And so shall guide and train in temper'd stay
Their yet green bending wits with reverent awe.
As now inur'd with virtues at the first,
Custom, O king, shall bring delightfulness;　　　　120
By use of virtue, vice shall grow in hate.

---

111 *father* Q2] fathers Q1. This is also possible, punctuating "Of father's—
yea, of such a father's—name" (so Adams).

But if you so dispose it that the day
Which ends your life shall first begin their reign,
Great is the peril what will be the end,
When such beginning of such liberties,
Void of such stays as in your life do lie,
Shall leave them free to random of their will,
An open prey to traitorous flattery,
The greatest pestilence of noble youth:
Which peril shall be past, if in your life,   130
Their temper'd youth with aged father's awe
Be brought in ure of skilful stayedness;
And in your life, their lives disposèd so
Shall length your noble life in joyfulness.
Thus think I that your grace hath wisely thought,
And that your tender care of common weal
Hath bred this thought, so to divide your land,
And plant your sons to bear the present rule,
While you yet live to see their ruling well,
That you may longer live by joy therein.   140
What further means behooveful are and meet,
At greater leisure may your grace devise,
When all have said, and when we be agreed
If this be best, to part the realm in twain,
And place your sons in present government:
Whereof, as I have plainly said my mind,
So would I hear the rest of all my lords.
Phil. In part I think as hath been said before;
In part, again, my mind is otherwise.
As for dividing of this realm in twain,   150
And lotting out the same in equal parts
To either of my lords, your grace's sons,
That think I best for this your realm's behoof,
For profit and advancement of your sons,
And for your comfort and your honour eke:
But so to place them while your life do last,
To yield to them your royal governance,
To be above them only in the name
Of father, not in kingly state also,
I think not good for you, for them, nor us.   160

This kingdom, since the bloody civil field
Where Morgan slain did yield his conquer'd part
Unto his cousin's sword in Camberland,
Containeth all that whilom did suffice
Three noble sons of your forefather Brute;
So your two sons it may suffice also,
The mo the stronger, if they 'gree in one.
The smaller compass that the realm doth hold,
The easier is the sway thereof to wield,
The nearer justice to the wrongèd poor,　　　　　　　170
The smaller charge, and yet enough for one.
And when the region is divided so
That brethren be the lords of either part,
Such strength doth nature knit between them both,
In sundry bodies by conjoinèd love,
That, not as two, but one of doubl'd force,
Each is to other as a sure defence.
The nobleness and glory of the one
Doth sharp the courage of the other's mind
With virtuous envy to contend for praise.　　　　　　180
And such an equalness hath nature made
Between the brethren of one father's seed,
As an unkindly wrong it seems to be
To throw the brother subject under feet
Of him whose peer he is by course of kind;
And Nature, that did make this equalness,
Oft so repineth at so great a wrong
That oft she raiseth up a grudging grief
In younger brethren at the elder's state,
Whereby both towns and kingdoms have been raz'd,　　190
And famous stocks of royal blood destroy'd:
The brother, that should be the brother's aid,

---

161 *the bloody civil field:* Cordelia's nephews Morgan and Cunedag rebelled against her and divided her kingdom. Afterwards Morgan invaded Cunedag's share and was killed. *See* III. i. 182.

164–5 See note on *The Names of the Speakers.* The legendary Brutus was the great-grandson of Aeneas, and founded Britain as his ancestor had founded Rome after the fall of Troy. Hence the allusions to the Britons as latter-day Trojans, II. ii. 76–7 and III. i. 1–10.

And have a wakeful care for his defence,
Gapes for his death, and blames the lingering years
That draw not forth his end with faster course;
And oft, impatient of so long delays,
With hateful slaughter he prevents the fates,
And heaps a just reward for brother's blood
With endless vengeance on his stock for aye.
Such mischiefs here are wisely met withal,   200
If equal state may nourish equal love,
Where none hath cause to grudge at other's good.
But now the head to stoop beneath them both,
Ne kind, ne reason, ne good order bears.
And oft it hath been seen, where nature's course
Hath been perverted in disorder'd wise,
When fathers cease to know that they should rule,
The children cease to know they should obey;
And often overkindly tenderness
Is mother of unkindly stubbornness.   210
I speak not this in envy or reproach,
As if I grudg'd the glory of your sons,
Whose honour I beseech the gods increase:
Nor yet as if I thought there did remain
So filthy cankers in their noble breasts,
Whom I esteem (which is their greatest praise)
Undoubted children of so good a king.
Only I mean to show by certain rules,
Which kind hath graft within the mind of man,
That Nature hath her order and her course,   220
Which (being broken) doth corrupt the state
Of minds and things, ev'n in the best of all.
My lords, your sons, may learn to rule of you.
Your own example in your noble court
Is fittest guider of their youthful years.
If you desire to see some present joy
By sight of their well ruling in your life,
See them obey, so shall you see them rule:
Whoso obeyeth not with humbleness
Will rule with outrage and with insolence.   230
Long may they rule, I do beseech the gods,

But long may they learn, ere they begin to rule.
If kind and fates would suffer, I would wish
Them aged princes, and immortal kings.
Wherefore, most noble king, I well assent
Between your sons that you divide your realm,
And as in kind, so match them in degree.
But while the gods prolong your royal life,
Prolong your reign; for thereto live you here,
And therefore have the gods so long forborne　　　240
To join you to themselves, that still you might
Be prince and father of our common weal.
They, when they see your children ripe to rule,
Will make them room, and will remove you hence,
That yours, in right ensuing of your life,
May rightly honour your immortal name.

Eub. Your wonted true regard of faithful hearts
Makes me, O king, the bolder to presume
To speak what I conceive within my breast;
Although the same do not agree at all　　　　　250
With that which other here my lords have said,
Nor which yourself have seemèd best to like.
Pardon I crave, and that my words be deem'd
To flow from hearty zeal unto your grace,
And to the safety of your common weal.
To part your realm unto my lords, your sons,
I think not good for you, ne yet for them,
But worst of all for this our native land.
Within one land, one single rule is best:
Divided reigns do make divided hearts;　　　　260
But peace preserves the country and the prince.
Such is in man the greedy mind to reign,
So great is his desire to climb aloft,
In worldly stage the stateliest parts to bear,
That faith and justice, and all kindly love,
Do yield unto desire of sovereignty,

232 *But long may they learn:* Q's "But", sometimes omitted on metrical
grounds, is necessary. Perhaps "they" is wrongly repeated from 231; but
it is best to take the lines as a balanced pair, contrasted by the extra-
metrical "But".

Where equal state doth raise an equal hope
To win the thing that either would attain.
Your grace remembereth how in passèd years,
The mighty Brute, first prince of all this land,   270
Possess'd the same, and rul'd it well in one:
He, thinking that the compass did suffice
For his three sons three kingdoms eke to make,
Cut it in three, as you would now in twain.
But how much British blood hath since been spilt,
To join again the sunder'd unity,
What princes slain before their timely hour,
What waste of towns and people in the land,
What treasons heap'd on murders and on spoils,
Whose just revenge ev'n yet is scarcely ceas'd,   280
Ruthful remembrance is yet raw in mind.
The gods forbid the like to chance again:
And you, O king, give not the cause thereof.
My lord Ferrex, your elder son, perhaps
(Whom kind and custom gives a rightful hope
To be your heir, and to succeed your reign)
Shall think that he doth suffer greater wrong
Than he perchance will bear, if power serve.
Porrex, the younger, so uprais'd in state,
Perhaps in courage will be rais'd also.   290
If flattery then, which fails not to assail
The tender minds of yet unskilful youth,
In one shall kindle and increase disdain,
And envy in the other's heart inflame,
This fire shall waste their love, their lives, their land,
And ruthful ruin shall destroy them both.
I wish not this, O king, so to befall,
But fear the thing that I do most abhor.
Give no beginning to so dreadful end.
Keep them in order and obedience,   300
And let them both by now obeying you
Learn such behaviour as beseems their state:
The elder, mildness in his governance,
The younger, a yielding contentedness.
And keep them near unto your presence still,

That they, restrainèd by the awe of you,
May live in compass of well temper'd stay,
And pass the perils of their youthful years.
Your aged life draws on to feebler time,
Wherein you shall less able be to bear   310
The travails that in youth you have sustain'd
Both in your person's and your realm's defence.
If planting now your sons in further parts,
You send them further from your present reach,
Less shall you know how they themselves demean:
Traitorous corrupters of their pliant youth
Shall have unspied a much more free access;
And if ambition and inflam'd disdain
Shall arm the one, the other, or them both
To civil war, or to usurping pride,   320
Late shall you rue that you ne reck'd before.
Good is I grant of all to hope the best,
But not to live still dreadless of the worst.
So trust the one that th' other be foreseen.
Arm not unskilfulness with princely power.
But you that long have wisely rul'd the reins
Of royalty within your noble realm,
So hold them, while the gods, for our avails,
Shall stretch the thread of your prolongèd days.
Too soon he clomb into the flaming car,   330
Whose want of skill did set the earth on fire.
Time, and example of your noble grace,
Shall teach your sons both to obey and rule.
When time hath taught them, time shall make them place,
The place that now is full: and so I pray
Long it remain, to comfort of us all.
Gor. I take your faithful hearts in thankful part:
But sith I see no cause to draw my mind
To fear the nature of my loving sons,
Or to misdeem that envy or disdain   340
Can there work hate, where nature planteth love,
In one self purpose do I still abide.
My love extendeth equally to both,

330 *Too soon he clomb:* Phaeton. See 385–7 and II. i. 204.

My land sufficeth for them both also.
Humber shall part the marches of their realms:
The southern part the elder shall possess,
The northern shall Porrex, the younger, rule.
In quiet I will pass mine aged days,
Free from the travail and the painful cares
That hasten age upon the worthiest kings.　　　　350
But lest the fraud that ye do seem to fear,
Of flattering tongues, corrupt their tender youth,
And writhe them to the ways of youthful lust,
To climbing pride, or to revenging hate,
Or to neglecting of their careful charge
Lewdly to live in wanton recklessness,
Or to oppressing of the rightful cause,
Or not to wreak the wrongs done to the poor,
To tread down truth, or favour false deceit,
I mean to join to either of my sons　　　　360
Some one of those, whose long approvèd faith
And wisdom tried, may well assure my heart
That mining fraud shall find no way to creep
Into their fencèd ears with grave advice.
This is the end; and so I pray you all
To bear my sons the love and loyalty
That I have found within your faithful breasts.
Aros. You, nor your sons, my sovereign lord, shall want
Our faith and service, while our hearts do last.　　*[Exeunt.]*

CHORUS.

When settled stay doth hold the royal throne　　　　370
　　In steadfast place, by known and doubtless right,
And chiefly when descent on one alone
　　Makes single and unparted reign to light,
Each change of course unjoints the whole estate,
And yields it thrall to ruin by debate.

The strength that, knit by fast accord in one,
　　Against all foreign power of mighty foes

Could of itself defend itself alone,
   Disjoinèd once, the former force doth lose.
The sticks, that sunder'd brake so soon in twain,   380
In fagot bound attempted were in vain.

Oft tender mind that leads the partial eye
   Of erring parents in their children's love,
Destroys the wrongly lovèd child thereby.
   This doth the proud son of Apollo prove,
Who, rashly set in chariot of his sire,
Inflam'd the parchèd earth with heaven's fire.

And this great king that doth divide his land,
   And change the course of his descending crown,
And yields the reign into his children's hand,   390
   From blissful state of joy and great renown
A mirror shall become to princes all,
To learn to shun the cause of such a fall.

380 *The sticks:* expounding the first dumb show. The choruses at the ends
    of Acts II, III and IV similarly recall their dumb shows.
392 *A mirror: A Mirror for Magistrates* was published in 1559 (see Intro-
    duction). Compare *Cambises,* 469.

THE ORDER AND SIGNIFICATION OF THE DUMB
SHOW BEFORE THE SECOND ACT.

*First, the music of cornets began to play, during which came in upon
the stage a king accompanied with a number of his nobility and
gentlemen. And after he had placed himself in a chair of estate
prepared for him, there came and kneeled before him a grave and
aged gentleman, and offered up unto him a cup of wine in a glass,
which the king refused. After him comes a brave and lusty young
gentleman, and presents the king with a cup of gold filled with
poison, which the king accepted, and drinking the same, immediately fell down dead upon the stage, and so was carried
thence away by his lords and gentlemen, and then the music ceased.
Hereby was signified, that as glass by nature holdeth no poison, but
is clear and may easily be seen through, ne boweth by any art; so
a faithful counsellor holdeth no treason, but is plain and open, ne
yieldeth to any indiscreet affection, but giveth wholesome counsel,
which the ill advised prince refuseth. The delightful gold filled with
poison betokeneth flattery, which under fair seeming of pleasant
words beareth deadly poison, which destroyeth the prince that
receiveth it. As befell in the two brethren, Ferrex and Porrex, who,
refusing the wholesome advice of grave counsellors, credited these
young parasites, and brought to themselves death and destruction
thereby.*

ACT II
SCENE I

FERREX. HERMON. DORDAN.

Fer. I marvel much what reason led the king
My father, thus, without all my desert,
To reave me half the kingdom, which by course
Of law and nature should remain to me.

Dumb show 17 *destroyeth* Q1] destroyed Q2.

17

Her. If you with stubborn and untamèd pride
       Had stood against him in rebelling wise
       Or if, with grudging mind, you had envied
       So slow a sliding of his aged years,
       Or sought before your time to haste the course
       Of fatal death upon his royal head,   10
       Or stain'd your stock with murder of your kin,
       Some face of reason might perhaps have seem'd
       To yield some likely cause to spoil ye thus.
Fer. The wreakful gods pour on my cursèd head
       Eternal plagues and never-dying woes,
       The hellish prince adjudge my damnèd ghost
       To Tantale's thirst, or proud Ixion's wheel,
       Or cruel gripe to gnaw my growing heart,
       To during torments and unquenchèd flames,
       If ever I conceiv'd so foul a thought,   20
       To wish his end of life, or yet of reign.
Dor. Ne yet your father, O most noble prince,
       Did ever think so foul a thing of you;
       For he, with more than father's tender love,
       While yet the fates do lend him life to rule
       (Who long might live to see your ruling well),
       To you, my lord, and to his other son,
       Lo, he resigns his realm and royalty;
       Which never would so wise a prince have done,
       If he had once misdeem'd that in your heart   30
       There ever lodgèd so unkind a thought.
       But tender love, my lord, and settled trust
       Of your good nature, and your noble mind,
       Made him to place you thus in royal throne,
       And now to give you half his realm to guide;
       Yea, and that half which, in abounding store
       Of things that serve to make a wealthy realm,
       In stately cities, and in fruitful soil,
       In temperate breathing of the milder heaven,
       In things of needful use, which friendly sea   40
       Transports by traffic from the foreign parts,

14–21 The punishments of Tantalus, Ixion and Tityus in the underworld are
often mentioned in Seneca's plays.

In flowing wealth, in honour, and in force,
Doth pass the double value of the part
That Porrex hath allotted to his reign.
Such is your case, such is your father's love.

Fer. Ah love, my friends! Love wrongs not whom he loves.

Dor. Ne yet he wrongeth you, that giveth you
So large a reign, ere that the course of time
Bring you to kingdom by descended right,
Which time perhaps might end your time before.   50

Fer. Is this no wrong, say you, to reave from me
My native right of half so great a realm,
And thus to match his younger son with me
In equal power, and in as great degree?
Yea, and what son? The son whose swelling pride
Would never yield one point of reverence,
When I the elder and apparent heir
Stood in the likelihood to possess the whole;
Yea, and that son which from his childish age
Envieth mine honour, and doth hate my life.   60
What will he now do, when his pride, his rage,
The mindful malice of his grudging heart
Is arm'd with force, with wealth, and kingly state?

Her. Was this not wrong, yea, ill advisèd wrong,
To give so mad a man so sharp a sword,
To so great peril of so great mishap,
Wide open thus to set so large a way?

Dor. Alas, my lord, what griefful thing is this,
That of your brother you can think so ill!
I never saw him utter likely sign,   70
Whereby a man might see or once misdeem
Such hate of you, ne such unyielding pride.
Ill is their counsel, shameful be their end,
That raising such mistrustful fear in you,
Sowing the seed of such unkindly hate,
Travail by treason to destroy you both.
Wise is your brother, and of noble hope,
Worthy to wield a large and mighty realm.
So much a stronger friend have you thereby,
Whose strength is your strength if you 'gree in one.   80

Her. If Nature and the Gods had pinchèd so
    Their flowing bounty and their noble gifts
    Of princely qualities from you, my lord,
    And pour'd them all at once in wasteful wise
    Upon your father's younger son alone,
    Perhaps there be, that in your prejudice
    Would say that birth should yield to worthiness.
    But sith in each good gift and princely art
    Ye are his match, and in the chief of all
    In mildness and in sober governance   90
    Ye far surmount; and sith there is in you
    Sufficing skill and hopeful towardness
    To wield the whole, and match your elder's praise;
    I see no cause why ye should lose the half,
    Ne would I wish you yield to such a loss,
    Lest your mild sufferance of so great a wrong,
    Be deemèd cowardice and simple dread,
    Which shall give courage to the fiery head
    Of your young brother to invade the whole.
    While yet therefore sticks in the people's mind   100
    The loathèd wrong of your disheritance;
    And ere your brother have, by settled power,
    By guileful cloak of an alluring show,
    Got him some force and favour in the realm;
    And while the noble queen, your mother, lives,
    To work and practise all for your avail;
    Attempt redress by arms, and wreak yourself
    Upon his life that gaineth by your loss,
    Who now to shame of you, and grief of us,
    In your own kingdom triumphs over you.   110
    Show now your courage meet for kingly state,
    That they which have avow'd to spend their goods,
    Their lands, their lives and honours in your cause,
    May be the bolder to maintain your part,
    When they do see that coward fear in you
    Shall not betray ne fail their faithful hearts.
    If once the death of Porrex end the strife,
    And pay the price of his usurpèd reign,
    Your mother shall persuade the angry king,

The lords, your friends, eke shall appease his rage.   120
For they be wise, and well they can foresee
That ere long time your aged father's death
Will bring a time when you shall well requite
Their friendly favour, or their hateful spite,
Yea, or their slackness to advance your cause.
"Wise men do not so hang on passing state
Of present princes, chiefly in their age,
But they will further cast their reaching eye,
To view and weigh the times and reigns to come."
Ne is it likely, though the king be wroth,   130
That he yet will, or that the realm will bear,
Extreme revenge upon his only son:
Or, if he would, what one is he that dare
Be minister to such an enterprise?
And here you be now placèd in your own,
Amid your friends, your vassals, and your strength:
We shall defend and keep your person safe,
Till either counsel turn his tender mind,
Or age or sorrow end his weary days.
But if the fear of gods, and secret grudge   140
Of nature's law, repining at the fact,
Withhold your courage from so great attempt,
Know ye, that lust of kingdoms hath no law.
The gods do bear and well allow in kings
The things [that] they abhor in rascal routs.
"When kings on slender quarrels run to wars,
And then in cruel and unkindly wise
Command thefts, rapes, murders of innocents,
The spoil of towns, ruins of mighty realms,
Think you such princes do suppose themselves   150
Subject to laws of kind, and fear of gods?"
Murders and violent thefts in private men
Are heinous crimes, and full of foul reproach;
Yet none offence, but deck'd with glorious name
Of noble conquests in the hands of kings.
But if you like not yet so hot device,

126–9 Quotation marks draw attention to "sentences" (*sententiae*, maxims), whether moral or, as here, immoral.

Ne list to take such vantage of the time,
But, though with peril of your own estate,
You will not be the first that shall invade,
Assemble yet your force for your defence,   160
And for your safety stand upon your guard.

Dor. O heaven! was there ever heard or known
So wicked counsel to a noble prince?
Let me, my lord, disclose unto your grace
This heinous tale, what mischief it contains;
Your father's death, your brother's, and your own,
Your present murder, and eternal shame.
Hear me, O king, and suffer not to sink
So high a treason in your princely breast.

Fer. The mighty gods forbid that ever I   170
Should once conceive such mischief in my heart.
Although my brother hath bereft my realm,
And bear, perhaps, to me an hateful mind,
Shall I revenge it with his death therefore?
Or shall I so destroy my father's life
That gave me life? The gods forbid, I say.
Cease you to speak so any more to me;
Ne you, my friend, with answer once repeat
So foul a tale. In silence let it die.
What lord or subject shall have hope at all,   180
That under me they safely shall enjoy
Their goods, their honours, lands, and liberties,
With whom neither one only brother dear,
Ne father dearer, could enjoy their lives?
But, sith I fear my younger brother's rage,
And sith, perhaps, some other man may give
Some like advice, to move his grudging head
At mine estate (which counsel may perchance
Take greater force with him, than this with me),
I will in secret so prepare myself,   190
As, if his malice or his lust to reign
Break forth in arms or sudden violence,
I may withstand his rage and keep mine own.

                                        [*Exeunt Ferrex and Hermon.*]

Dor. I fear the fatal time now draweth on,

When civil hate shall end the noble line
Of famous Brute, and of his royal seed.
Great Jove, defend the mischiefs now at hand!
O that the secretary's wise advice
Had erst been heard, when he besought the king
Not to divide his land, nor send his sons   200
To further parts from presence of his court,
Ne yet to yield to them his governance.
Lo, such are they now in the royal throne
As was rash Phaeton in Phœbus' car;
Ne then the fiery steeds did draw the flame
With wilder random through the kindled skies,
Than traitorous counsel now will whirl about
The youthful heads of these unskilful kings.
But I hereof their father will inform;
The reverence of him perhaps shall stay   210
The growing mischiefs, while they yet are green.
If this help not, then woe unto themselves,
The prince, the people, the divided land!   [*Exit.*]

SCENE II

PORREX. TYNDAR. PHILANDER.

Por. And is it thus? and doth he so prepare
Against his brother as his mortal foe?
And now, while yet his aged father lives?
Neither regards he him, nor fears he me?
War would he have? and he shall have it so.
Tyn. I saw, myself, the great preparèd store
Of horse, of armour, and of weapons there:
Ne bring I to my lord reported tales,
Without the ground of seen and searchèd truth.
Lo, secret quarrels run about his court,   10
To bring the name of you, my lord, in hate.
Each man, almost, can now debate the cause,
And ask a reason of so great a wrong,
Why he, so noble and so wise a prince,

Is, as unworthy, reft his heritage,
And why the king, misled by crafty means,
Divided thus his land from course of right.
The wiser sort hold down their griefful heads;
Each man withdraws from talk and company
Of those that have been known to favour you.   20
To hide the mischief of their meaning there,
Rumours are spread of your preparing here.
The rascal numbers of unskilful sort
Are filled with monstrous tales of you and yours.
In secret I was counsell'd by my friends
To haste me thence, and brought you, as you know,
Letters from those that both can truly tell,
And would not write unless they knew it well.

Phil. My lord, yet ere you move unkindly war,
Send to your brother, to demand the cause.   30
Perhaps some traitorous tales have fill'd his ears
With false reports against your noble grace;
Which, once disclos'd, shall end the growing strife,
That else, not stay'd with wise foresight in time,
Shall hazard both your kingdoms and your lives.
Send to your father eke, he shall appease
Your kindled minds, and rid you of this fear.

Por. Rid me of fear! I fear him not at all;
Ne will to him, ne to my father send.
If danger were for one to tarry there,   40
Think ye it safety to return again?
In mischiefs such as Ferrex now intends,
The wonted courteous laws to messengers
Are not observ'd, which in just war they use.
Shall I so hazard any one of mine?
Shall I betray my trusty friends to him,
That have disclos'd his treason unto me?
Let him entreat that fears; I fear him not.
Or shall I to the king, my father, send?
Yea, and send now, while such a mother lives,   50
That loves my brother, and that hateth me?
Shall I give leisure, by my fond delays,
To Ferrex to oppress me all unware?

I will not; but I will invade his realm,
And seek the traitor prince within his court.
Mischief for mischief is a due reward.
His wretched head shall pay the worthy price
Of this his treason and his hate to me.
Shall I abide, and treat, and send, and pray,
And hold my yielden throat to traitor's knife,   60
While I, with valiant mind and conquering force,
Might rid myself of foes, and win a realm?
Yet rather, when I have the wretch's head,
Then to the king, my father, will I send.
The bootless case may yet appease his wrath:
If not, I will defend me as I may.

                              [*Exeunt Porrex and Tyndar.*]

Phil. Lo, here the end of these two youthful kings!
The father's death! the ruin of their realms!
" O most unhappy state of counsellors,
That light on so unhappy lords and times   70
That neither can their good advice be heard,
Yet must they bear the blames of ill success."
But I will to the king, their father, haste,
Ere this mischief come to the likely end;
That, if the mindful wrath of wreakful gods
(Since mighty Ilion's fall not yet appeas'd
With these poor remnants of the Trojan name)
Have not determin'd by unmovèd fate,
Out of this realm to raze the British line,
By good advice, by awe of father's name,   80
By force of wiser lords, this kindled hate
May yet be quench'd ere it consume us all.   [*Exit.*]

CHORUS

When youth, not bridled with a guiding stay,
    Is left to random of their own delight,
And wields whole realms by force of sovereign sway,
    Great is the danger of unmaster'd might,
Lest skilless rage throw down, with headlong fall,
Their lands, their states, their lives, themselves and all.

When growing pride doth fill the swelling breast,
   And greedy lust doth raise the climbing mind,   90
Oh, hardly may the peril be repress'd.
   Ne fear of angry gods, ne law of kind,
Ne country's care can firèd hearts restrain,
When force hath armèd envy and disdain.

When kings of foreset will neglect the rede
   Of best advice, and yield to pleasing tales
That do their fancies' noisome humour feed,
   Ne reason nor regard of right avails.
Succeeding heaps of plagues shall teach, too late,
To learn the mischiefs of misguided state.   100

Foul fall the traitor false that undermines
   The love of brethren to destroy them both.
Woe to the prince that pliant ear inclines,
   And yields his mind to poisonous tale that floweth
From flattering mouth!   And woe to wretched land,
That wastes itself with civil sword in hand!
   Lo thus it is, poison in gold to take,
   And wholesome drink in homely cup forsake.

---

92 *law of* (C)] lawes Q. A singular noun is required to correspond to "fear"
and "care". For the phrase compare IV. ii. 118.

THE ORDER AND SIGNIFICATION OF THE DUMB
SHOW BEFORE THE THIRD ACT.

*First, the music of flutes began to play, during which came in upon
the stage a company of mourners, all clad in black, betokening
death and sorrow to ensue upon the ill-advised misgovernment
and dissension of brethren, as befell upon the murder of Ferrex
by his younger brother. After the mourners had passed thrice
about the stage, they departed, and then the music ceased.*

ACT III

SCENE I

GORBODUC. EUBULUS. AROSTUS.

Gor. O cruel fates, O mindful wrath of gods,
Whose vengeance neither Simois' stainèd streams
Flowing with blood of Trojan princes slain,
Nor Phrygian fields made rank with corpses dead
Of Asian kings and lords, can yet appease;
Ne slaughter of unhappy Priam's race,
Nor Ilion's fall, made level with the soil,
Can yet suffice: but still continued rage
Pursues our lives, and from the farthest seas
Doth chase the issues of destroyèd Troy.   10
" Oh, no man happy till his end be seen."
If any flowing wealth and seeming joy
In present years might make a happy wight,
Happy was Hecuba, the woefull'st wretch
That ever liv'd to make a mirror of;

11 *Oh, no man happy till his end be seen:* an ancient saying attributed to Solon.
Its most famous use is in the final chorus of Sophocles' *Oedipus Rex*, which
also concerns a fated royal house.

27

And happy Priam, with his noble sons;
And happy I, till now, alas, I see
And feel my most unhappy wretchedness.
Behold, my lords, read ye this letter here;
Lo, it contains the ruin of our realm,   20
If timely speed provide not hasty help.
Yet, O ye gods, if ever woeful king
Might move ye, kings of kings, wreak it on me
And on my sons, not on this guiltless realm:
Send down your wasting flames from wrathful skies,
To reave me and my sons the hateful breath.
Read, read, my lords; this is the matter why
I call'd ye now, to have your good advice.

The letter from DORDAN, *the Counsellor of the elder Prince.*

EUBULUS *readeth the letter.*

My sovereign lord, what I am loath to write,
But loathest am to see, that I am forc'd   30
By letters now to make you understand.
My lord Ferrex, your eldest son, misled
By traitorous fraud of young untemper'd wits,
Assembleth force against your younger son,
Ne can my counsel yet withdraw the heat
And furious pangs of his inflamèd head.
Disdain, saith he, of his disheritance
Arms him to wreak the great pretended wrong,
With civil sword upon his brother's life.
If present help do not restrain this rage,   40
This flame will waste your sons, your land, and you.
            Your Majesty's faithful,
               and most humble subject,
                     DORDAN.

Aros. O king, appease your grief, and stay your plaint;
     Great is the matter, and a woeful case:
     But timely knowledge may bring timely help.
     Send for them both unto your presence here:

The reverence of your honour, age, and state,
Your grave advice, the awe of father's name,   50
Shall quickly knit again this broken peace.
And if in either of my lords, your sons,
Be such untamèd and unyielding pride,
As will not bend unto your noble hests;
If Ferrex, the elder son, can bear no peer,
Or Porrex, not content, aspires to more
Than you him gave above his native right,
Join with the juster side; so shall you force
Them to agree, and hold the land in stay.

Eub. What meaneth this?　Lo, yonder comes in haste   60
Philander from my lord your younger son.

[*Enter* PHILANDER.]

Gor. The gods send joyful news!
Phil.   The mighty Jove
Preserve your majesty, O noble king.
Gor. Philander, welcome: but how doth my son?
Phil. Your son, sir, lives, and healthy I him left.
But yet, O king, the want of lustful health
Could not be half so griefful to your grace,
As these most wretched tidings that I bring.
Gor. O heavens, yet more? no end of woes to me?
Phil. Tyndar, O king, came lately from the court   70
Of Ferrex, to my lord your younger son,
And made report of great preparèd store
For war, and saith that it is wholly meant
Against Porrex, for high disdain that he
Lives now a king, and equal in degree
With him that claimeth to succeed the whole,
As by due title of descending right.
Porrex is now so set on flaming fire,
Partly with kindled rage of cruel wrath,
Partly with hope to gain a realm thereby,   80
That he in haste prepareth to invade

62 The first line to be divided between two speakers in the play.

His brother's land, and with unkindly war
Threatens the murder of your elder son;
Ne could I him persuade, that first he should
Send to his brother to demand the cause,
Nor yet to you to stay this hateful strife:
Wherefore sith there no more I can be heard,
I come myself now to inform your grace,
And to beseech you, as you love the life
And safety of your children and your realm,
Now to employ your wisdom and your force   90
To stay this mischief ere it be too late.

Gor. Are they in arms? would he not send to me?
Is this the honour of a father's name?
In vain we travail to assuage their minds,
As if their hearts, whom neither brother's love,
Nor father's awe, nor kingdom's cares, can move,
Our counsels could withdraw from raging heat.
Jove slay them both, and end the cursèd line!
For though perhaps fear of such mighty force   100
As I, my lords, join'd with your noble aids,
May yet raise, shall repress their present heat,
The secret grudge and malice will remain:
The fire not quench'd, but kept in close restraint,
Fed still within, breaks forth with double flame.
Their death and mine must 'pease the angry gods.

Phil. Yield not, O king, so much to weak despair:
Your sons yet live, and long, I trust, they shall.
If fates had taken you from earthly life,
Before beginning of this civil strife,   110
Perhaps your sons in their unmaster'd youth,
Loose from regard of any living wight,
Would run on headlong, with unbridled race,
To their own death, and ruin of this realm.
But sith the gods, that have the care for kings,
Of things and times dispose the order so,
That in your life this kindled flame breaks forth,
While yet your life, your wisdom, and your power,
May stay the growing mischief, and repress
The fiery blaze of their enkindled heat,   120

It seems, and so ye ought to deem thereof,
That loving Jove hath temper'd so the time
Of this debate to happen in your days,
That you yet living may the same appease,
And add it to the glory of your age,
And they your sons may learn to live in peace.
Beware, O king, the greatest harm of all,
Lest, by your wailful plaints, your hasten'd death
Yield larger room unto their growing rage.
Preserve your life, the only hope of stay.   130
And if your highness herein list to use
Wisdom or force, counsel or knightly aid,
Lo we, our persons, powers, and lives are yours;
Use us till death, O king, we are your own.

Eub. Lo, here the peril that was erst foreseen,
When you, O king, did first divide your land,
And yield your present reign unto your sons.
But now, O noble prince, now is no time
To wail and plain, and waste your woeful life;
Now is the time for present good advice.   140
Sorrow doth dark the judgment of the wit.
" The heart unbroken, and the courage free
From feeble faintness of bootless despair,
Doth either rise to safety or renown
By noble valour of unvanquish'd mind,
Or yet doth perish in more happy sort."
Your grace may send to either of your sons
Some one both wise and noble personage,
Which with good counsel, and with weighty name
Of father, shall present before their eyes   150
Your hest, your life, your safety, and their own,
The present mischief of their deadly strife.
And in the while, assemble you the force
Which your commandment and the speedy haste

---

125 *age* (Dodsley)] latter age Q. Q's line requires improbable elision ("add't
to th'glory"); "latter" was perhaps introduced into Q1 to show that
Gorboduc's years and not his epoch were meant (and uncorrected in Q2).
146 *Or yet doth perish in more happy sort:* the stoical philosophy that death
cancels all worldly cares.

Of all my lords here present can prepare.
The terror of your mighty power shall stay
The rage of both, or yet of one at least.

[*Enter* NUNTIUS.]

Nun. O king, the greatest grief that ever prince did hear,
That ever woeful messenger did tell,
That ever wretched land hath seen before,   160
I bring to you: Porrex your younger son
With sudden force invaded hath the land
That you to Ferrex did allot to rule;
And with his own most bloody hand he hath
His brother slain, and doth possess his realm.
Gor. O heavens, send down the flames of your revenge!
Destroy, I say, with flash of wreakful fire
The traitor son, and then the wretched sire!
But let us go, that yet perhaps I may
Die with revenge, and 'pease the hateful gods.   [*Exeunt.*]

CHORUS.

The lust of kingdom knows no sacred faith,   171
    No rule of reason, no regard of right,
No kindly love, no fear of heaven's wrath;
    But with contempt of gods, and man's despite,
Through bloody slaughter doth prepare the ways
    To fatal sceptre and accursèd reign.
The son so loathes the father's lingering days,
    Ne dreads his hand in brother's blood to stain.
O wretched prince, ne dost thou yet record
    The yet fresh murders done within the land   180
Of thy forefathers, when the cruel sword
    Bereft Morgan his life with cousin's hand?
Thus fatal plagues pursue the guilty race,
    Whose murderous hand, imbru'd with guiltless blood,

158 "O king" gives the line an extra foot, but (as the opening of the speech)
    this is allowable, and there is no need to omit the "ever" (compare 159,
    160).

Asks vengeance still before the heaven's face,
  With endless mischiefs on the cursèd brood.
The wicked child thus brings to woeful sire
  The mournful plaints to waste his very life.
Thus do the cruel flames of civil fire
  Destroy the parted reign with hateful strife.   190
And hence doth spring the well from which doth flow
The dead black streams of mourning, plaints, and woe.

THE ORDER AND SIGNIFICATION OF THE DUMB
SHOW BEFORE THE FOURTH ACT

*First, the music of hautboys began to play, during which there came
forth from under the stage, as though out of hell, three furies,
Alecto, Megæra, and Tisiphone, clad in black garments
sprinkled with blood and flames, their bodies girt with snakes,
their heads spread with serpents instead of hair, the one bearing
in her hand a snake, the other a whip, and the third a burning
firebrand: each driving before them a king and a queen, which,
moved by furies, unnaturally had slain their own children. The
names of the kings and queens were these: Tantalus, Medea,
Athamas, Ino, Cambises, Althea; after that the furies and these
had passed about the stage thrice, they departed, and then the
music ceased. Hereby was signified the unnatural murders to
follow; that is to say, Porrex slain by his own mother, and of
king Gorboduc and queen Videna, killed by their own subjects.*

ACT IV

SCENE I

VIDENA *sola.*

Why should I live, and linger forth my time
In longer life to double my distress?
O me, most woeful wight, whom no mishap
Long ere this day could have bereavèd hence.
Might not these hands, by fortune or by fate,

Dumb show: Tantalus served up his son's flesh to the gods. Medea stabbed her
two sons to revenge Jason's desertion. Athamas and Ino his wife, mad-
dened by Juno, killed their elder and younger sons respectively. Althea
deliberately burned a firebrand which was to last as long as her son
Meleager's life. Cambises killed his brother, not his son (perhaps Praxaspes'
son is meant, in error).

34

Have pierc'd this breast, and life with iron reft?
Or in this palace here, where I so long
Have spent my days, could not that happy hour
Once, once have happ'd, in which these hugy frames
With death by fall might have oppressèd me?   10
Or should not this most hard and cruel soil,
So oft where I have press'd my wretched steps,
Sometime had ruth of mine accursèd life
To rend in twain, and swallow me therein?
So had my bones possessèd now in peace
Their happy grave within the closèd ground,
And greedy worms had gnawn this pinèd heart
Without my feeling pain: so should not now
This living breast remain the ruthful tomb,
Wherein my heart yielden to death is grav'd;   20
Nor dreary thoughts, with pangs of pining grief,
My doleful mind had not afflicted thus.
O my belovèd son! O my sweet child!
My dear Ferrex, my joy, my life's delight!
Is my belovèd son, is my sweet child,
My dear Ferrex, my joy, my life's delight,
Murder'd with cruel death? O hateful wretch!
O heinous traitor both to heaven and earth!
Thou, Porrex, thou this damnèd deed hast wrought;
Thou, Porrex, thou shalt dearly bye the same.   30
Traitor to kin and kind, to sire and me,
To thine own flesh, and traitor to thyself:
The gods on thee in hell shall wreak their wrath,
And here in earth this hand shall take revenge
On thee, Porrex, thou false and caitiff wight.
If after blood so eager were thy thirst,
And murd'rous mind had so possessèd thee,
If such hard heart of rock and stony flint
Liv'd in thy breast, that nothing else could like
Thy cruel tyrant's thought but death and blood,   40
Wild savage beasts, might not their slaughter serve
To feed thy greedy will, and in the midst

26 This may be an accidental repetition of 24, though it is not very likely
that so great an error was overlooked in the printing of Q2.

Of their entrails to stain thy deadly hands
With blood deserv'd, and drink thereof thy fill?
Or if nought else but death and blood of man
Might please thy lust, could none in Britain land,
Whose heart betorn out of his panting breast
With thine own hand, or work what death thou would'st,
Suffice to make a sacrifice to 'pease
That deadly mind and murderous thought in thee,   50
But he who in the selfsame womb was wrapp'd,
Where thou in dismal hour receivedst life?
Or if needs, needs thy hand must slaughter make,
Mightest thou not have reach'd a mortal wound,
And with thy sword have pierc'd this cursèd womb
That the accursèd Porrex brought to light,
And given me a just reward therefore?
So Ferrex yet sweet life might have enjoy'd,
And to his aged father comfort brought,
With some young son in whom they both might live.   60
But whereunto waste I this ruthful speech,
To thee that hast thy brother's blood thus shed?
Shall I still think that from this womb thou sprung?
That I thee bare? or take thee for my son?
No, traitor, no; I thee refuse for mine:
Murderer, I thee renounce; thou art not mine.
Never, O wretch, this womb conceivèd thee;
Nor never bode I painful throes for thee.
Changeling to me thou art, and not my child,
Nor to no wight that spark of pity knew.   70
Ruthless, unkind, monster of nature's work,
Thou never suck'd the milk of woman's breast,
But, from thy birth, the cruel tiger's teats
Have nursèd thee; nor yet of flesh and blood
Form'd is thy heart, but of hard iron wrought;
And wild and desert woods bred thee to life.
But canst thou hope to 'scape my just revenge?
Or that these hands will not be wroke on thee?
Dost thou not know that Ferrex' mother lives,
That lovèd him more dearly than herself?   80
And doth she live, and is not veng'd on thee?   [*Exit.*]

SCENE II

GORBODUC.　AROSTUS

Gor. We marvel much, whereto this ling'ring stay
　　　Falls out so long: Porrex unto our court,
　　　By order of our letters, is return'd;
　　　And Eubulus receiv'd from us behest,
　　　At his arrival here, to give him charge
　　　Before our presence straight to make repair,
　　　And yet we have no word whereof he stays.
Aros. Lo where he comes, and Eubulus with him.

　　　　　　[*Enter* EUBULUS *and* PORREX.]

Eub. According to your highness' hest to me,
　　　Here have I Porrex brought, even in such sort　　　10
　　　As from his wearied horse he did alight,
　　　For that your grace did will such haste therein.
Gor. We like and praise this speedy will in you,
　　　To work the thing that to your charge we gave.
　　　Porrex, if we so far should swerve from kind,
　　　And from those bounds which law of nature sets,
　　　As thou hast done by vile and wretched deed,
　　　In cruel murder of thy brother's life,
　　　Our present hand could stay no longer time,
　　　But straight should bathe this blade in blood of thee,　　　20
　　　As just revenge of thy detested crime.
　　　No, we should not offend the law of kind,
　　　If now this sword of ours did slay thee here:
　　　For thou hast murder'd him, whose heinous death
　　　Even nature's force doth move us to revenge
　　　By blood again; and justice forceth us
　　　To measure death for death, thy due desert.
　　　Yet sithens thou art our child, and sith as yet
　　　In this hard case what word thou canst allege
　　　For thy defence by us hath not been heard,　　　30
　　　We are content to say our will for that

4 *behest* (Dodsley)] by hest Q. (The 16th century spelling "byhest" wrongly
divided.)

Which justice bids us presently to work,
And give thee leave to use thy speech at full,
If ought thou have to lay for thine excuse.

Por. Neither, O king, I can or will deny
But that this hand from Ferrex life hath reft:
Which fact how much my doleful heart doth wail,
Oh, would it might as full appear to sight,
As inward grief doth pour it forth to me!
So yet, perhaps, if ever ruthful heart   40
Melting in tears within a manly breast,
Through deep repentance of his bloody fact,
If ever grief, if ever woeful man
Might move regret with sorrow of his fault,
I think the torment of my mournful case,
Known to your grace, as I do feel the same,
Would force even wrath herself to pity me.
But as the water, troubled with the mud,
Shows not the face which else the eye should see,
Even so your ireful mind with stirrèd thought   50
Cannot so perfectly discern my cause.
But this unhap, amongst so many heaps,
I must content me with, most wretched man,
That to myself I must reserve my woe,
In pining thoughts of mine accursèd fact,
Since I may not show here my smallest grief,
Such as it is, and as my breast endures,
Which I esteem the greatest misery
Of all mishaps that fortune now can send.
Not that I rest in hope with plaint and tears   60
To purchase life; for to the gods I clepe
For true record of this my faithful speech:
Never this heart shall have the thoughtful dread
To die the death that by your grace's doom,
By just desert, shall be pronounc'd to me;
Nor never shall this tongue once spend the speech,
Pardon to crave, or seek by suit to live.
I mean not this as though I were not touch'd
With care of dreadful death, or that I held
Life in contempt, but that I know the mind   70

Stoops to no dread, although the flesh be frail.
And for my guilt, I yield the same so great
As in myself I find a fear to sue
For grant of life.

Gor.   In vain, O wretch, thou showest
A woeful heart: Ferrex now lies in grave,
Slain by thy hand.

Por.   Yet this, O father, hear;
And then I end.   Your majesty well knows,
That when my brother Ferrex and myself
By your own hest were join'd in governance
Of this your grace's realm of Britain land,   80
I never sought nor travail'd for the same;
Nor by myself, nor by no friend I wrought,
But from your highness' will alone it sprung,
Of your most gracious goodness bent to me.
But how my brother's heart even then repin'd
With swoll'n disdain against mine equal rule,
Seeing that realm, which by descent should grow
Wholly to him, allotted half to me,
Even in your highness' court he now remains,
And with my brother then in nearest place,   90
Who can record what proof thereof was show'd,
And how my brother's envious heart appear'd.
Yet I that judgèd it my part to seek
His favour and good will, and loath to make
Your highness know the thing which should have brought
Grief to your grace, and your offence to him,
Hoping my earnest suit should soon have won
A loving heart within a brother's breast,
Wrought in that sort, that, for a pledge of love
And faithful heart, he gave to me his hand.   100
This made me think that he had banish'd quite
All rancour from his thought, and bare to me
Such hearty love as I did owe to him.
But after once we left your grace's court,
And from your highness' presence liv'd apart,
This equal rule still, still did grudge him so,
That now those envious sparks which erst lay rak'd

In living cinders of dissembling breast,
Kindled so far within his heart disdain,
That longer could he not refrain from proof   110
Of secret practice to deprive me life
By poison's force; and had bereft me so,
If mine own servant hirèd to this fact,
And mov'd by truth with hate to work the same,
In time had not bewray'd it unto me.
When thus I saw the knot of love unknit,
All honest league and faithful promise broke,
The law of kind and truth thus rent in twain,
His heart on mischief set, and in his breast
Black treason hid, then, then did I despair   120
That ever time could win him friend to me;
Then saw I how he smil'd with slaying knife
Wrapp'd under cloak, then saw I deep deceit
Lurk in his face and death prepar'd for me:
Even nature mov'd me then to hold my life
More dear to me than his, and bade this hand,
Since by his life my death must needs ensue,
And by his death my life to be preserv'd,
To shed his blood, and seek my safety so.
And wisdom willèd me without protract   130
In speedy wise to put the same in ure.
Thus have I told the cause that movèd me
To work my brother's death; and so I yield
My life, my death, to judgment of your grace.
Gor. Oh cruel wight, should any cause prevail
To make thee stain thy hands with brother's blood?
But what of thee we will resolve to do
Shall yet remain unknown. Thou in the mean
Shalt from our royal presence banish'd be,
Until our princely pleasure further shall   140
To thee be show'd. Depart therefore our sight,
Accursèd child! [*Exit Porrex.*] What cruel destiny,
What froward fate hath sorted us this chance,
That even in those, where we should comfort find,

122–3 Alluding to Chaucer's *Knight's Tale*, 1999: "The smylere with the
knyf under the cloke."

   Where our delight now in our aged days
   Should rest and be, even there our only grief
   And deepest sorrows to abridge our life,
   Most pining cares and deadly thoughts do grow?
Aros. Your grace should now, in these grave years of yours,
   Have found ere this the price of mortal joys,   150
   How short they be, how fading here in earth,
   How full of change, how brittle our estate,
   Of nothing sure, save only of the death,
   To whom both man and all the world doth owe
   Their end at last; neither shall nature's power
   In other sort against your heart prevail,
   Than as the naked hand whose stroke assays
   The armèd breast where force doth light in vain.
Gor. Many can yield right safe and grave advice
   Of patient sprite to others wrapp'd in woe,   160
   And can in speech both rule and conquer kind,
   Who, if by proof they might feel nature's force,
   Would show themselves men as they are indeed,
   Which now will needs be gods.   But what doth mean
   The sorry cheer of her that here doth come?

     [*Enter* MARCELLA.]

Mar. Oh where is ruth, or where is pity now?
   Whither is gentle heart and mercy fled?
   Are they exil'd out of our stony breasts,
   Never to make return?   Is all the world
   Drownèd in blood, and sunk in cruelty?   170
   If not in women mercy may be found,
   If not, alas, within the mother's breast,
   To her own child, to her own flesh and blood,
   If ruth be banish'd thence, if pity there
   May have no place, if there no gentle heart
   Do live and dwell, where should we seek it then?

166–266 Marcella, instead of another Nuntius (messenger), is given this
  narrative for several probable reasons: to provide variety by her sex;
  thereby to forestall the objection that the witness might have prevented the
  disaster (see 214); and by her womanly pity to emphasize the unnatural
  ruthlessness of Videna's deed.

Gor. Madam, alas, what means your woeful tale?
Mar. O silly woman I! why to this hour
  Have kind and fortune thus deferr'd my breath,
  That I should live to see this doleful day?   180
  Will ever wight believe that such hard heart
  Could rest within the cruel mother's breast,
  With her own hand to slay her only son?
  But out, alas! these eyes beheld the same:
  They saw the dreary sight, and are become
  Most ruthful records of the bloody fact.
  Porrex, alas, is by his mother slain,
  And with her hand, a woeful thing to tell,
  While slumbering on his careful bed he rests,
  His heart stabb'd in with knife is reft of life. 190
Gor. O Eubulus, oh draw this sword of ours,
  And pierce this heart with speed! O hateful light,
  O loathsome life, O sweet and welcome death!
  Dear Eubulus, work this we thee beseech!
Eub. Patient your grace; perhaps he liveth yet,
  With wound receiv'd, but not of certain death.
Gor. O let us then repair unto the place,
  And see if Porrex live, or thus be slain.
      [*Exeunt Gorboduc and Eubulus.*]
Mar. Alas, he liveth not! it is too true,
  That with these eyes, of him a peerless prince, 200
  Son to a king, and in the flower of youth,
  Even with a twink a senseless stock I saw.
Aros. O damnèd deed!
Mar.   But hear his ruthful end:
  The noble prince, pierc'd with the sudden wound,
  Out of his wretched slumber hastely start,
  Whose strength now failing straight he overthrew,
  When in the fall his eyes, even new unclos'd,
  Beheld the queen, and cried to her for help.
  We then, alas, the ladies which that time
  Did there attend, seeing that heinous deed, 210
  And hearing him oft call the wretched name
  Of mother, and to cry to her for aid
  Whose direful hand gave him the mortal wound,

Pitying, alas, (for nought else could we do)
His ruthful end, ran to the woeful bed,
Despoilèd straight his breast, and all we might
Wipèd in vain with napkins next at hand,
The sudden streams of blood that flushèd fast
Out of the gaping wound.   O what a look,
O what a ruthful steadfast eye methought   220
He fix'd upon my face, which to my death
Will never part from me, when with a braid
A deep-fet sigh he gave, and therewithal
Clasping his hands, to heaven he cast his sight;
And straight, pale death pressing within his face,
The flying ghost his mortal corpse forsook.

Aros. Never did age bring forth so vile a fact.

Mar. O hard and cruel hap, that thus assign'd
Unto so worthy a wight so wretched end:
But most hard cruel heart that could consent   230
To lend the hateful destinies that hand,
By which, alas, so heinous crime was wrought.
O queen of adamant! O marble breast!
If not the favour of his comely face,
If not his princely cheer and countenance,
His valiant active arms, his manly breast,
If not his fair and seemly personage,
His noble limbs in such proportion cast
As would have rapt a silly woman's thought,
If this might not have mov'd thy bloody heart,   240
And that most cruel hand the wretched weapon
Ev'n to let fall, and kiss'd him in the face,
With tears for ruth to reave such one by death,
Should nature yet consent to slay her son?
O mother, thou to murder thus thy child!
Even Jove with justice must with lightning flames
From heaven send down some strange revenge on thee.
Ah, noble prince, how oft have I beheld
Thee mounted on thy fierce and trampling steed,
Shining in armour bright before the tilt,   250

241 The first feminine ending in the play.

And with thy mistress' sleeve tied on thy helm,
And charge thy staff, to please thy lady's eye,
That bow'd the head-piece of thy friendly foe!
How oft in arms on horse to bend the mace,
How oft in arms on foot to break the sword,
Which never now these eyes may see again!

Aros. Madam, alas, in vain these plaints are shed;
Rather with me depart, and help to 'suage
The thoughtful griefs that in the aged king
Must needs by nature grow by death of this   260
His only son, whom he did hold so dear.

Mar. What wight is that which saw that I did see,
And could refrain to wail with plaint and tears?
Not I, alas! That heart is not in me.
But let us go, for I am griev'd anew,
To call to mind the wretched father's woe.   [*Exeunt.*]

CHORUS.

When greedy lust in royal seat to reign
    Hath reft all care of gods and eke of men,
And cruel heart, wrath, treason, and disdain,
    Within ambitious breast are lodgèd, then   270
Behold how mischief wide herself displays,
And with the brother's hand the brother slays.

When blood thus shed doth stain the heaven's face,
    Crying to Jove for vengeance of the deed,
The mighty god even moveth from his place,
    With wrath to wreak: then sends he forth with speed
The dreadful Furies, daughters of the night,
    With serpents girt, carrying the whip of ire,
With hair of stinging snakes, and shining bright
    With flames and blood, and with a brand of fire.   280
These, for revenge of wretched murder done,
Do make the mother kill her only son.

Blood asketh blood, and death must death requite:
　　Jove, by his just and everlasting doom,
Justly hath ever so requited it.
　　The times before record, and times to come
Shall find it true, and so doth present proof
Present before our eyes for our behoof.

O happy wight, that suffers not the snare
　　Of murderous mind to tangle him in blood;　　　290
And happy he, that can in time beware
　　By other's harms, and turn it to his good.
But woe to him that, fearing not to offend,
Doth serve his lust, and will not see the end.

THE ORDER AND SIGNIFICATION OF THE DUMB SHOW BEFORE THE FIFTH ACT.

First, the drums and flutes began to sound, during which there came forth upon the stage a company of harquebusiers, and of armed men, all in order of battle. These, after their pieces discharged, and that the armed men had three times marched about the stage, departed, and then the drums and flutes did cease. Hereby was signified tumults, rebellions, arms, and civil wars to follow, as fell in the realm of Great Britain, which, by the space of fifty years and more, continued in civil war between the nobility after the death of king Gorboduc and of his issues, for want of certain limitation in the succession of the crown, till the time of Dunwallo Molmutius, who reduced the land to monarchy.

ACT V

SCENE I

CLOTYN. MANDUD. GWENARD. FERGUS. EUBULUS.

Clot. Did ever age bring forth such tyrants' hearts?
    The brother hath bereft the brother's life;
    The mother, she hath dyed her cruel hands
    In blood of her own son; and now at last
    The people, lo, forgetting truth and love,
    Contemning quite both law and loyal heart,
    Even they have slain their sovereign lord and queen.
Man. Shall this their traitorous crime unpunish'd rest?
    Even yet they cease not, carried on with rage,
    In their rebellious routs, to threaten still   10
    A new bloodshed unto the prince's kin,

Dumb show: Dunwallo Molmutius. The son of Clotyn, who speaks first in this scene. He ruled for forty years.

46

To slay them all, and to uproot the race
Both of the king and queen; so are they mov'd
With Porrex' death, wherein they falsely charge
The guiltless king, without desert at all;
And traitorously have murder'd him therefore,
And eke the queen.

Gwen. Shall subjects dare with force
To work revenge upon their prince's fact?
Admit the worst that may, as sure in this
The deed was foul, the queen to slay her son,   20
Shall yet the subject seek to take the sword,
Arise against his lord, and slay his king?
O wretched state, where those rebellious hearts
Are not rent out even from their living breasts,
And with the body thrown unto the fowls,
As carrion food, for terror of the rest.

Ferg. There can no punishment be thought too great
For this so grievous crime: let speed therefore
Be us'd therein, for it behooveth so.

Eub. Ye all, my lords, I see, consent in one,   30
And I as one consent with ye in all.
I hold it more than need, with sharpest law
To punish this tumultuous bloody rage.
For nothing more may shake the common state
Than sufferance of uproars without redress;
Whereby how soon kingdoms of mighty power,
After great conquests made, and flourishing
In fame and wealth, have been to ruin brought!
I pray to Jove, that we may rather wail
Such hap in them than witness in ourselves.   40
Eke fully with the duke my mind agrees,
That no cause serves, whereby the subject may
Call to account the doings of his prince,
Much less in blood by sword to work revenge,
No more than may the hand cut off the head;

36 *soon* (C)] some Q. Misreading of "soone".
42–9 Q1. Omitted from Q2, possibly because Norton (as a strong Calvinist) disagreed with the principle of non-resistance expressed here by Sackville.

In act nor speech, no not in secret thought
The subject may rebel against his lord,
Or judge of him that sits in Cæsar's seat,
With grudging mind to damn those he mislikes.
Though kings forget to govern as they ought,   50
Yet subjects must obey as they are bound.
But now, my lords, before ye farther wade,
Or spend your speech, what sharp revenge shall fall
By justice' plague on these rebellious wights,
Methinks ye rather should first search the way
By which in time the rage of this uproar
Might be repress'd, and these great tumults ceas'd.
Even yet the life of Britain land doth hang
In traitors' balance of unequal weight.
Think not, my lords, the death of Gorboduc,   60
Nor yet Videna's blood, will cease their rage:
Even our own lives, our wives, and children dear,
Our country, dear'st of all, in danger stands
Now to be spoil'd, now, now made desolate,
And by ourselves a conquest to ensue.
For, give once sway unto the people's lusts
To rush forth on, and stay them not in time,
And as the stream that rolleth down the hill,
So will they headlong run with raging thoughts
From blood to blood, from mischief unto mo,   70
To ruin of the realm, themselves, and all:
So giddy are the common people's minds,
So glad of change, more wavering than the sea.
Ye see, my lords, what strength these rebels have,
What hugy number is assembled still:
For though the traitorous fact, for which they rose,
Be wrought and done, yet lodge they still in field;
So that how far their furies yet will stretch
Great cause we have to dread.   That we may seek
By present battle to repress their power,   80
Speed must we use to levy force therefore;
For either they forthwith will mischief work,
Or their rebellious roars forthwith will cease.
These violent things may have no lasting long.

Let us, therefore, use this for present help:
Persuade by gentle speech, and offer grace
With gift of pardon, save unto the chief;
And that upon condition that forthwith
They yield the captains of their enterprise,
To bear such guerdon of their traitorous fact   90
As may be both due vengeance to themselves,
And wholesome terror to posterity.
This shall, I think, scatter the greatest part
That now are holden with desire of home,
Wearied in field with cold of winter's nights,
And some, no doubt, stricken with dread of law.
When this is once proclaimèd, it shall make
The captains to mistrust the multitude,
Whose safety bids them to betray their heads;
And so much more, because the rascal routs,   100
In things of great and perilous attempts,
Are never trusty to the noble race.
And while we treat, and stand on terms of grace,
We shall both stay their furious rage the while,
And eke gain time, whose only help sufficeth
Withouten war to vanquish rebels' power.
In the meanwhile, make you in readiness
Such band of horsemen as ye may prepare.
Horsemen, you know, are not the commons' strength,
But are the force and store of noble men;   110
Whereby the unchosen and unarmèd sort
Of skilless rebels, whom none other power
But number makes to be of dreadful force,
With sudden brunt may quickly be oppress'd.
And if this gentle mean of proffer'd grace
With stubborn hearts cannot so far avail,
As to assuage their desperate courages;
Then do I wish such slaughter to be made,
As present age, and eke posterity,
May be adrad with horror of revenge   120
That justly then shall on these rebels fall.
This is, my lords, the sum of mine advice.
Clot. Neither this case admits debate at large,

And though it did, this speech that hath been said
Hath well abridg'd the tale I would have told.
Fully with Eubulus do I consent
In all that he hath said; and if the same
To you, my lords, may seem for best advice,
I wish that it should straight be put in ure.
Man. My lords, then let us presently depart,   130
And follow this that liketh us so well.
                    [*Exeunt Clotyn, Mandud, Gwenard, and Eubulus.*]
Ferg. If ever time to gain a kingdom here
Were offer'd man, now it is offer'd me.
The realm is reft both of their king and queen,
The offspring of the prince is slain and dead,
No issue now remains, the heir unknown,
The people are in arms and mutinies,
The nobles, they are busied how to cease
These great rebellious tumults and uproars;
And Britain land, now desert left alone   140
Amid these broils uncertain where to rest,
Offers herself unto that noble heart
That will or dare pursue to bear her crown.
Shall I, that am the Duke of Albany,
Descended from that line of noble blood,
Which hath so long flourish'd in worthy fame
Of valiant hearts, such as in noble breasts
Of right should rest above the baser sort,
Refuse to venture life to win a crown?
Whom shall I find en'mies that will withstand   150
My fact herein, if I attempt by arms
To seek the same now in these times of broil?
These dukes' [poor] power can hardly well appease
The people that already are in arms.
But if, perhaps, my force be once in field,
Is not my strength in power above the best
Of all these lords now left in Britain land?
And though they should match me with power of men,
Yet doubtful is the chance of battles join'd.

153 [*poor*] (C). The compositor wrongly supposed that "power" was written
     twice in his copy.

If victors of the field we may depart   160
Ours is the sceptre then of Great Britain;
If slain amid the plain this body lie,
Mine enemies yet shall not deny me this,
But that I died giving the noble charge
To hazard life for conquest of a crown.
Forthwith, therefore, will I in post depart
To Albany, and raise in armour there
All power I can; and here my secret friends,
By secret practice shall solicit still
To seek to win to me the people's hearts.   [*Exit.*]

SCENE II

EUBULUS *solus.*

Eub. O Jove, how are these people's hearts abus'd!
What blind fury thus headlong carries them?
That though so many books, so many rolls
Of ancient time, record what grievous plagues
Light on these rebels aye, and though so oft
Their ears have heard their aged fathers tell
What just reward these traitors still receive,
Yea, though themselves have seen deep death and blood,
By strangling cord and slaughter of the sword
To such assign'd, yet can they not beware,   10
Yet cannot stay their lewd rebellious hands;
But suffering, lo, foul treason to distain
Their wretched minds, forget their loyal heart,
Reject all truth, and rise against their prince.
A ruthful case, that those, whom duty's bond,
Whom grafted law, by nature, truth, and faith,
Bound to preserve their country and their king,
Born to defend their commonwealth and prince,
Even they should give consent thus to subvert
Thee, Britain land, and from thy womb should spring,   20

15–22 Difficult syntax. "Bound" (17) seems to be both a plural verb (govern-
ed by the nouns "bond" and "law" in 15–16) and a participle (paralleled
by "Born", 18).

O native soil, those that will needs destroy
And ruin thee, and eke themselve in fine.
For lo, when once the dukes had offer'd grace
Of pardon sweet the multitude misled
By traitorous fraud of their ungracious heads,
One sort that saw the dangerous success
Of stubborn standing in rebellious war,
And knew the difference of prince's power
From headless number of tumultuous routs,
Whom common country's care and private fear   30
Taught to repent the error of their rage,
Laid hands upon the captains of their band,
And brought them bound unto the mighty dukes.
Another sort, not trusting yet so well
The truth of pardon, or mistrusting more
Their own offence than that they could conceive
Such hope of pardon for so foul misdeed,
Or for that they their captains could not yield,
Who, fearing to be yielded, fled before,
Stole home by silence of the secret night.   40
The third unhappy and enragèd sort
Of desperate hearts, who, stain'd in princes' blood,
From traitorous furor could not be withdrawn
By love, by law, by grace, ne yet by fear,
By proffer'd life, ne yet by threaten'd death,
With minds hopeless of life, dreadless of death,
Careless of country, and aweless of God,
Stood bent to fight, as furies did them move,
With violent death to close their traitorous life:
These all by power of horsemen were oppress'd,   50
And with revenging sword slain in the field,
Or with the strangling cord hang'd on the trees,
Where yet their carrion carcases do preach
The fruits that rebels reap of their uproars,
And of the murder of their sacred prince.
But lo, where do approach the noble dukes
By whom these tumults have been thus appeas'd.

25 *their ungracious heads:* their irreligious leaders.
34 *Another* (C)] And other Q. Caught from "And", 33.

[*Enter* CLOTYN, MANDUD, GWENARD, *and* AROSTUS.]

Clot. I think the world will now at length beware
    And fear to put on arms against their prince.
Man. If not, those traitorous hearts that dare rebel,   60
    Let them behold the wide and hugy fields
    With blood and bodies spread of rebels slain;
    The lofty trees cloth'd with the corpses dead,
    That, strangled with the cord, do hang thereon.
Aros. A just reward; such as all times before
    Have ever lotted to those wretched folks.
Gwen. But what means he that cometh here so fast?

[*Enter* NUNTIUS.]

Nun. My lords, as duty and my troth doth move,
    And of my country work a care in me,
    That, if the spending of my breath avail'd   70
    To do the service that my heart desires,
    I would not shun to embrace a present death,
    So have I now, in that wherein I thought
    My travail might perform some good effect,
    Ventur'd my life to bring these tidings here.
    Fergus, the mighty duke of Albany,
    Is now in arms, and lodgeth in the field
    With twenty thousand men: hither he bends
    His speedy march, and minds to invade the crown.
    Daily he gathereth strength, and spreads abroad   80
    That to this realm no certain heir remains,
    That Britain land is left without a guide,
    That he the sceptre seeks for nothing else
    But to preserve the people and the land,
    Which now remain as ship without a stern.
    Lo, this is that which I have here to say.   [*Exit.*]
Clot. Is this his faith? and shall he falsely thus
    Abuse the vantage of unhappy times?
    O wretched land, if his outrageous pride,
    His cruel and untemper'd wilfulness,   90
    His deep dissembling shows of false pretence,
    Should once attain the crown of Britain land!
    Let us, my lords, with timely force resist

The new attempt of this our common foe,
As we would quench the flames of common fire.
Man. Though we remain without a certain prince,
    To wield the realm, or guide the wandering rule,
    Yet now the common mother of us all,
    Our native land, our country, that contains
    Our wives, our children, kindred, selves, and all   100
    That ever is or may be dear to man,
    Cries unto us to help ourselves and her.
    Let us advance our powers to repress
    This growing foe of all our liberties.
Gwen. Yea, let us so, my lords, with hasty speed.
    And ye, O gods, send us the welcome death,
    To shed our blood in field, and leave us not
    In loathsome life to linger out our days,
    To see the hugy heaps of these unhaps,
    That now roll down upon the wretched land,   110
    Where empty place of princely governance,
    No certain stay now left of doubtless heir,
    Thus leave this guideless realm an open prey
    To endless storms and waste of civil war.
Aros. That ye, my lords, do so agree in one,
    To save your country from the violent reign
    And wrongfully usurpèd tyranny
    Of him that threatens conquest of you all,
    To save your realm, and in this realm yourselves,
    From foreign thraldom of so proud a prince,   120
    Much do I praise; and I beseech the gods,
    With happy honour to requite it you.
    But, O my lords, sith now the heaven's wrath
    Hath reft this land the issue of their prince;
    Sith of the body of our late sovereign lord
    Remains no more, since the young kings be slain,
    And of the title of descended crown
    Uncertainly the divers minds do think
    Even of the learned sort, and more uncertainly
    Will partial fancy and affection deem,   130

100 *Our wives, our children, kindred, selves* (C)] Our wiues, children, kindred,
    our selues Q. Metre compels the correction of the transposition.

But most uncertainly will climbing pride
And hope of reign withdraw to sundry parts
The doubtful right and hopeful lust to reign;
When once this noble service is achiev'd
For Britain land, the mother of ye all,
When once ye have with armèd force repress'd
The proud attempts of this Albanian prince,
That threatens thraldom to your native land,
When ye shall vanquishers return from field,
And find the princely state an open prey   140
To greedy lust and to usurping power,
Then, then, my lords, if ever kindly care
Of ancient honour of your ancestors,
Of present wealth and nobless of your stocks,
Yea, of the lives and safety yet to come
Of your dear wives, your children, and yourselves,
Might move your noble hearts with gentle ruth,
Then, then, have pity on the torn estate;
Then help to salve the well-near hopeless sore;
Which ye shall do, if ye yourselves withhold   150
The slaying knife from your own mother's throat.
Her shall you save, and you, and yours in her,
If ye shall all with one assent forbear
Once to lay hand or take unto yourselves
The crown, by colour of pretended right,
Or by what other means soever it be,
Till first by common counsel of you all
In parliament, the regal diadem
Be set in certain place of governance;
In which your parliament, and in your choice,   160
Prefer the right, my lords, without respect
Of strength or friends, or whatsoever cause
That may set forward any other's part.
For right will last, and wrong cannot endure.
Right mean I his or hers, upon whose name
The people rest by mean of native line,

165 *His or hers:* The feminine possessive has been taken to refer to Lady
Katherine Grey as Elizabeth's heir-presumptive, but it may equally be
used because a queen was ruling at the time.

Or by the virtue of some former law
Already made their title to advance.
Such one, my lords, let be your chosen king,
Such one so born within your native land;   170
Such one prefer, and in no wise admit
The heavy yoke of foreign governance:
Let foreign titles yield to public wealth.
And with that heart wherewith ye now prepare
Thus to withstand the proud invading foe,
With that same heart, my lords, keep out also
Unnatural thraldom of [a] stranger's reign;
Ne suffer you, against the rules of kind,
Your mother land to serve a foreign prince.

Eub. Lo, here the end of Brutus' royal line,   180
And lo, the entry to the woeful wreck
And utter ruin of this noble realm.
The royal king and eke his sons are slain;
No ruler rests within the regal seat;
The heir, to whom the sceptre 'longs, unknown;
That to each force of foreign princes' power,
Whom vantage of our wretched state may move
By sudden arms to gain so rich a realm,
And to the proud and greedy mind at home,
Whom blinded lust to reign leads to aspire,   190
Lo, Britain realm is left an open prey,
A present spoil by conquest to ensue.
Who seeth not now how many rising minds
Do feed their thoughts with hope to reach a realm?
And who will not by force attempt to win
So great a gain, that hope persuades to have?
A simple colour shall for title serve.
Who wins the royal crown will want no right,
Nor such as shall display by long descent
A lineal race to prove him lawful king.   200
In the meanwhile these civil arms shall rage,
And thus a thousand mischiefs shall unfold,
And far and near spread thee, O Britain land;
All right and law shall cease, and he that had

177 [*a*] (C).

Nothing to-day, to-morrow shall enjoy
Great heaps of gold, and he that flow'd in wealth,
Lo, he shall be bereft of life and all;
And happiest he that then possesseth least.
The wives shall suffer rape, the maids deflower'd,
And children fatherless shall weep and wail;   210
With fire and sword thy native folk shall perish;
One kinsman shall bereave another's life,
The father shall unwitting slay the son,
The son shall slay the sire and know it not.
Women and maids the cruel soldier's sword
Shall pierce to death, and silly children lo,
That playing in the streets and fields are found,
By violent hands shall close their latter day.
Whom shall the fierce and bloody soldier
Reserve to life?   Whom shall he spare from death?   220
Even thou, O wretched mother, half alive,
Thou shalt behold thy dear and only child
Slain with the sword while he yet sucks thy breast.
Lo, guiltless blood shall thus each where be shed.
Thus shall the wasted soil yield forth no fruit,
But dearth and famine shall possess the land.
The towns shall be consum'd and burnt with fire,
The peopled cities shall wax desolate;
And thou, O Britain, whilom in renown,
Whilom in wealth and fame, shalt thus be torn,   230
Dismember'd thus, and thus be rent in twain,
Thus wasted and defac'd, spoil'd and destroy'd.
These be the fruits your civil wars will bring.
Hereto it comes when kings will not consent
To grave advice, but follow wilful will.
This is the end, when in fond princes' hearts
Flattery prevails, and sage rede hath no place.
These are the plagues, when murder is the mean
To make new heirs unto the royal crown.
Thus wreak the gods, when that the mother's wrath   240

217 *playing* Q1] play Q2.
234–5 Eubulus here (like the Chorus expounding the dumb shows) summarizes the lessons of each act of the play, each in two lines.

Nought but the blood of her own child may 'suage;
These mischiefs spring when rebels will arise
To work revenge and judge their prince's fact.
This, this ensues, when noble men do fail
In loyal truth, and subjects will be kings.
And this doth grow, when lo, unto the prince,
Whom death or sudden hap of life bereaves,
No certain heir remains, such certain heir,
As not all only is the rightful heir,
But to the realm is so made known to be,   250
And truth thereby vested in subjects' hearts,
To owe faith there where right is known to rest.
Alas, in parliament what hope can be,
When is of parliament no hope at all,
Which, though it be assembled by consent,
Yet is not likely with consent to end;
While each one for himself, or for his friend,
Against his foe, shall travail what he may;
While now the state, left open to the man
That shall with greatest force invade the same,   260
Shall fill ambitious minds with gaping hope;
When will they once with yielding hearts agree?
Or in the while, how shall the realm be us'd?
No, no: then parliament should have been holden,
And certain heirs appointed to the crown,
To stay the title of establish'd right,
And in the people plant obedience,
While yet the prince did live, whose name and power
By lawful summons and authority
Might make a parliament to be of force,   270
And might have set the state in quiet stay.
But now, O happy man whom speedy death
Deprives of life, ne is enforc'd to see
These hugy mischiefs and these miseries,
These civil wars, these murders, and these wrongs.
Of justice yet must God in fine restore
This noble crown unto the lawful heir:
For right will always live, and rise at length,
But wrong can never take deep root to last.

Cambises

The Division of the Parts

COUNSEL HUF PRAXASPES MURDER LOB THE THIRD LORD	} *For one Man.*	CAMBISES EPILOGUS	} *For one Man.*

COUNSEL
HUF
PRAXASPES } *For one Man.*
MURDER
LOB
THE THIRD LORD

CAMBISES } *For one Man.*
EPILOGUS

LORD
RUF
COMMONS' CRY } *For one Man.*
COMMONS' COMPLAINT
LORD SMERDIS
VENUS

PROLOGUE
SISAMNES
DILIGENCE
CRUELTY } *For one Man.*
HOB
PREPARATION
THE FIRST LORD

KNIGHT
SNUF
SMALL HABILITY } *For one Man.*
PROOF
EXECUTION
ATTENDANCE
SECOND LORD

AMBIDEXTER } *For one Man.*
TRIAL

MERETRIX
SHAME
OTIAN } *For one Man.*
MOTHER
LADY
QUEEN

YOUNG CHILD } *For one Man.*
CUPID

The Division of the Parts: Marian May-be-good and the Waiting-Maid are missing.
 Lady and Queen, assigned as two parts to the seventh actor, are the same
 person: this Lady cannot be the same as the Waiting-Maid, who is on stage
 with the future Queen. Marian can be given to the seventh actor, but the
 Waiting-Maid cannot be given to the eighth (who is on stage as Cupid) nor
 to the second (who is on stage as Venus), so that in fact four of the eight
 actors have to include women or children among their parts.

Cambises

[PROLOGUE]

The PROLOGUE *entereth.*

Agathon, he whose counsel wise to prince's weal extended,
By good advice unto a prince three things he hath commended:
First is that he hath government and ruleth over men;
Secondly, to rule with laws, eke justice, saith he, then;
Thirdly, that he must well conceive he may not always reign.
Lo, thus the rule unto a prince Agathon squarèd plain.
Tully the wise, whose sapience in volumes great doth tell,
Who in wisdom in that time did many men excel,
" A prince," saith he, " is of himself a plain and speaking law:
The law, a schoolmaster divine,"—this by his rule I draw.   10
The sage and witty Seneca his words thereto did frame:
" The honest exercise of kings, men will ensue the same.
But contrariwise if that a king abuse his kingly seat,
His ignomy and bitter shame in fine shall be more great."
In Persia there reign'd a king, who Cyrus hight by name,
Who did deserve, as I do read, the lasting blast of fame.
But he, when Sisters Three had wrought to shear his vital thread,
As heir due to take the crown, Cambises did proceed.
He in his youth was trainèd up, by trace of virtue's lore;
Yet (being king) did clean forget his perfect race before.   20
Then cleaving more unto his will, such vice did imitate
As one of Icarus his kind: forewarning then did hate,
Thinking that none could him dismay, ne none his fact could see;
Yet at the last a fall he took, like Icarus to be:
Else, as the fish, which oft had take the pleasant bait from hook,
In safe did spring and pierce the streams when fisher fast did
        look
To hoist up from the watery waves unto the drièd land,
Then 'scap'd, at last by subtle bait come to the fisher's hand;

22 Icarus melted his waxen wings by flying too near the sun.

Even so this King Cambises here, when he had wrought his will,
Taking delight the innocent his guiltless blood to spill,   30
Then mighty Jove would not permit to prosecute offence,
But what measure the king did mete, the same did Jove com-
      mence,
To bring to end with shame his race, two years he did not reign.
His cruelty we will dilate, and make the matter plain.
Craving that this may suffice now your patience to win,
I take my way.   Behold, I see the players coming in.

FINIS

First enter CAMBISES *the king*, KNIGHT, [LORD,] *and*
COUNSELLOR.

Camb. My counsel grave and sapient with lords of legal train,
    Attentive ears towards me bend, and mark what shall be
      sain.
    So you likewise, my valiant knight, whose manly acts
      doth fly
    By bruit of Fame, that sounding trump doth pierce the
      azure sky.
    My sapient words I say perpend, and so your skill dilate.
    You know that Mors vanquishèd hath Cyrus, that king of
      state:
    And I by due inheritance possess that princely crown,
    Ruling by sword of mighty force in place of great renown.
    You know and often have heard tell my father's worthy
      facts,
    A manly Mars's heart he bare appearing by his acts.   10
    And what? shall I to ground let fall my father's golden
      praise?
    No, no! I mean for to attempt this fame more large to
      raise.
    In that that I, his son, succeed his kingly seat as due,
    Extend your counsel unto me in that I ask of you.
    I am the king of Persia, a large and fertile soil,
    The Egyptians against us repugn, as varlets slave and vile;
    Therefore I mean with Mars's heart, with wars them to
      frequent;

Them to subdue as captives mine, this is my heart's intent.

So shall I win honour's delight, and praise of me shall go.

My counsel speak, and lordings eke:—is it not best do so?   20

Couns. O puissant king, your blissful words deserves abundant praise,

That you in this do go about your father's fame to raise.

O blissful day, that king so young such profit should conceive,

His father's praise and his to win, from those that would deceive.

Sure, my true and sovereign king, I fall before you prest,

Answer to give as duty mine, in that your grace request.

If that your heart addicted be, the Egyptians to convince,

Through Mars's aid the conquest won, then deed of happy prince

Shall pierce the skies unto the throne of the supernal seat,

And merit there a just reward, of Jupiter the great.   30

But then your grace must not turn back from this pretencèd will;

For to proceed in virtuous life, employ endeavour still.

Extinguish vice, and in that cup to drink have no delight.

To martial feats and kingly sport fix all your whole delight.

King. My counsel grave, a thousand thanks with heart I do you render,

That you my case so prosperous entirely do tender!

I will not swerve from those your steps whereto you would me train.

But now, my lord and valiant knight, with words give answer plain.

Are you content with me to go, the Mars's games to try?

Lord. Yea, peerless prince, to aid your grace, myself will live and die.   40

Knight. And I, for my hability, for fear will not turn back,

But as the ship against the rocks sustain and bide the wrack.

King. O willing hearts, a thousand thanks I render unto you.

Strike up your drums with courage great, we will march forth even now!

Couns. Permit, O king, few words to hear, my duty serves no less.

Therefore give leave to counsel thine, his mind for to express.

King. Speak on my counsel what it be, you shall have favour
mine.

Couns. Then will I speak unto your grace, as duty doth me bind.

Your grace doth mean for to attempt of war the manly art.

Your grace therein may hap receive with others for your
part   50

The dint of death—in those affairs, all persons are alike.

The heart courageous oftentimes his detriment doth seek.

It's best therefore for to permit a ruler of your land

To sit and judge with equity when things of right are scann'd.

King. My grace doth yield to this your talk; to be thus now
it shall.

My knight, therefore prepare yourself, Sisamnes for to call.

A judge he is of prudent skill, even he shall bear the sway

In absence mine, when from the land I do depart my way.

Knight. Your knight before your grace even here, himself hath
ready prest

With willing heart for to fulfil as your grace made request.

Exit. 60

Couns. Pleaseth your grace, I judge of him to be a man right fit,

For he is learnèd in the law, having the gift of wit.

In your grace's precinct I do not view for it a meeter man.

His learning is of good effect, bring proof thereof I can.

I do not know what is his life, his conscience hid from me;

I doubt not but the fear of God before his eyes to be.

Lord. Report declares he is a man that to himself is nigh,

One that favoureth much the world and too much sets thereby.

But this I say of certainty: if he your grace succeed

In your absence but for a while, he will be warn'd indeed 70

No injustice for to frequent, no partial judge to prove,

But rule all things with equity, to win your grace's love.

King. Of that he shall a warning have, my hests for to obey;

Great punishment for his offence against him will I lay.

[*Enter* SISAMNES.]

Couns. Behold, I see him now aggress and enter into place.

Sisam. O puissant prince and mighty king, the gods preserve
your grace!

Your grace's message came to me, your will purporting
forth;.

With grateful mind I it receiv'd, according to mine oath,

Erecting then myself with speed, before your grace's eyes,

The tenor of your princely will from you for to agnise.   80

King. Sisamnes, this the whole effect the which for you I sent:

Our mind it is to elevate you to great preferment.

My grace and gracious counsel eke hath chose you for this
cause:

In judgment you do office bear, which have the skill in laws.

We think that you accordingly by justice rule will deal,

That for offence none shall have cause of wrong you to
appeal.

Sisam. Abundant thanks unto your grace for this benignity,

To you, his counsel, in like case, with lords of clemency.

Whatso your grace to me permits, if I therein offend,

Such execution then commence, and use it to this end,   90

That all other, by that my deed, example so may take.

To admonish them to flee the same by fear it may them
make.

King. Then according to your words, if you therein offend,

I assure you even from my breast, correction shall extend.

From Persia I mean to go into the Egypt land:

Them to convince by force of arms, and win the upper hand.

While I therefore absent shall be, I do you full permit,

As governor in this my right, in that estate to sit,

For to detect, and eke correct, those that abuse my grace.

This is the total of my will.   Give answer in this case!   100

Sisam. Unworthy much, O prince, am I, and for this gift unfit;

But sith that it hath pleas'd your grace, that I in it must sit,

I do avouch unto my death, according to my skill,

With equity for to observe your grace's mind and will,

And nought from it to swerve indeed, but sincerely to stay;

Else let me taste the penalty, as I before did say.

King. Well, then, of this authority I give you full possession.

Sisam. And I will it fulfil also, as I have made profession.

King. My counsel then let us depart, a final stay to make;

To Egypt land now forth with speed my voyage I will
take.   110

Strike up your drums us to rejoice, to hear the warlike sound.
Stay you here, Sisamnes judge, and look well to your bound.
                              Exeunt King, Lord and Counsel.

Sisam. Even now the king hath me extoll'd and set me up aloft.
Now may I wear the broider'd guard and lie in down-bed soft;
Now may I purchase house and land, and have all at my will;
Now may I build a princely place, my mind for to fulfil;
Now may I abrogate the law, as I shall think it good;
If any one me now offend, I may demand his blood.
According to the proverb old, my mouth I will up-make.
Now it doth lie all in my hand to leave or else to take,   120
To deal with justice to my bound, and so to live in hope.
But oftentimes the birds be gone, while one for nest doth
     grope.
Do well or ill, I dare avouch some evil on me will speak:
No, truly yet I do not mean the king's precepts to break;
To place I mean for to return my duty to fulfil.   *Exit.*

Enter the VICE [AMBIDEXTER], *with an old capcase on his head,
an old pail about his hips for harness, a scummer and a potlid
by his side, and a rake on his shoulder.*

Amb.   Stand away, stand away, for the passion of God!
Harness'd I am, prepar'd to the field.
I would have been content at home to have bod,
But I am sent forth with my spear and shield.
     I am appointed to fight against a snail,   130
And Wilkin Wren the ancient shall bear:
I doubt not but against him to prevail,
To be a man my deeds shall [me] declare.
     If I overcome him, then a butterfly takes his part,
His weapon must be a blue-speckled hen:
But you shall see me overthrow him with a fart.
So, without conquest, he shall go home again!
     If I overcome him, I must fight with a fly,
And a black-pudding the fly's weapon must be.
At the first blow on the ground he shall lie,   140
I will be sure to thrust him through the mouth to the knee.
     To conquest these fellows the man I will play!
Ha, ha, ha! now ye will make me to smile.

[I warrant ye I will play the knave this day,]
To see if I can all men beguile.
    Ha! my name?　My name would you so fain know?
Yea, iwis, shall ye, and that with all speed:
I have forgot it, therefore I cannot show.
Ah, ah! now I have it, I have it, indeed!
    My name is Ambidexter: I signify one   150
That with both hands finely can play;
Now with King Cambises, and by and by gone,
Thus do I run this and that way.
    For while I mean with a soldier to be,
Then give I a leap to Sisamnes the judge,—
I dare avouch ye shall his destruction see!
To all kind of estates I mean for to trudge.
    Ambidexter?　Nay, he is a fellow, if ye knew all!
    Cease for a while; hereafter hear more ye shall.

Enter three ruffians, HUF, RUF, *and* SNUF, *singing.*

Huf. Gog's flesh and his wounds, these wars rejoice my heart! 160
    By his wounds, I hope to do well, for my part.
    By Gog's heart, the world shall go evil if I do not shift:
    At some old carle's budget I mean for to lift.
Ruf. By his flesh, nose, eyes, and ears,
    I will venture void of all cares.
    He is not a soldier that doth fear any doubt,
    If that he would bring his purpose about.
Snuf. Fear that fear list, it shall not be I.
    By Gog's wounds, I will make some necks stand awry.
    If I lose my share, I swear by Gog's heart,   170
    Then let another take up my part.
Huf. Yet I hope to come the richest soldier away.
Ruf. If a man ask ye, ye may hap to say nay.
Snuf. Let all men get what they can, not to leese I hope;
    Wheresoever I go, in each corner I will grope.
Amb. What and ye run into the corner of some pretty maid?
Snuf. To grope there, good fellow, I will not be afraid.

144 [*I warrant ye . . . this day,*] (C).
159 *s.d.* The song is not given. What follows is speech.
169 *necks* (C)] neck Q1, necke Q2.

Huf. Gog's wounds, what art thou that with us dost mell?
    Thou seemest to be a soldier, the truth to tell;
    Thou seemest to be harness'd, I cannot tell how.   180
    I think he came lately from riding some cow:
    Such a deform'd slave did I never see.
    Ruf, dost thou know him?   I pray thee tell me.
Ruf. No, by my troth, fellow Huf, I never see him before.
Snuf. As for me, I care not if I never see him more.
    Come, let us run his arse against the post!
Amb. Ah, ye slaves, I will be with you at host!
    Ah, ye knaves, I will teach ye how ye shall me deride!
                Here let him swinge them about.
    Out of my sight!   I can ye not abide!
    Now, goodman pouchmouth, I am a slave with you?   190
    Now have at ye afresh again even now!
    Mine arse against the post you will run?
    But I will make ye from that saying to turn.
Huf. I beseech ye heartily to be content.
Ruf. I ensure you, by mine honesty, no hurt we meant.
    Beside that, again, we do not know what ye are:
    Ye know that soldiers their stoutness will declare,
    Therefore if we have anything offended,
    Pardon our rudeness and it shall be amended.
Amb. Yea, God's pity, begin ye to entreat me?   200
    Have at ye once again! by the mass, I will beat ye.
                Fight again.
Huf. Gog's heart, let us kill him!   Suffer no longer!
                Draw their swords.
Snuf. Thou slave, we will see if thou be the stronger.
Ruf. Strike off his head at one blow!
    That we be soldiers, Gog's heart, let him know!
Amb. Oh the passion of God, I have done, by mine honesty!
    I will take your part hereafter, verily.
All. Then content, let us agree.
Amb. Shake hands with me, I shake hands with thee.
    Ye are full of courtesy, that is the best.   210
    And you take great pain, ye are a mannerly guest.
    Why, masters, do you not know me? the truth to me tell.

187 *at host* Q2 (at oste)] at the oste Q1.

All. No, trust us; not very well.

Amb. Why, I am Ambidexter, who many soldiers do love.

Huf. Gog's heart, to have thy company needs we must prove.
    We must play with both hands, with our hostess and host,
    Play with both hands, and score on the post;
    Now and then, with our captain, for many a delay,
    We will not stick with both hands to play.

Amb. The honester man ye, ye may me trust!   220

       Enter MERETRIX, *with a staff on her shoulder.*

Mer. What, is there no lads here that hath a lust
    To have a passing trull to help at their need?

Huf. Gog's heart, she is come indeed!
    What, Mistress Meretrix, by his wounds, welcome to me.

Mer. What will ye give me? I pray you, let me see.

Ruf. By his heart, she looks for gifts by and by!

Mer. What, Master Ruf! I cry you mercy.
    The last time I was with you, I got a broken head,
    And lay in the street all night for want of a bed.

Snuf. Gog's wounds, kiss me, my trull so white.   230
    In thee, I swear, is all my delight.
    If thou shouldst have had a broken head for my sake,
    I would have made his head to ache!

Mer. What, Master Ambidexter! Who look'd for you?

Amb. Mistress Meretrix, I thought not to see you here now.
    There is no remedy, at meeting I must have a kiss.

Mer. What man! I will not stick for that, by Gis!

                                   Kiss.

Amb. So now, gramercy, I pray thee be gone.

Mer. Nay, soft, my friend, I mean to have one.
    Nay, soft! I swear, and if ye were my brother,   240
    Before I let go, I will have another.

                             Kiss, kiss, kiss.

Ruf. Gog's heart, the whore would not kiss me yet.

Mer. If I be a whore, thou art a knave, then it is quit!

Huf. But hear'st thou, Meretrix? With who this night wilt
      thou lie?

Mer. With him that giveth the most money.

Huf. Gog's heart, I have no money in purse, ne yet in clout!

Mer. Then get thee hence and pack, like a lout!

Huf. Adieu, like a whore!   *Exit Huf.*

Mer.   Farewell, like a knave!

Ruf. Gog's nails, Mistress Meretrix, now he is gone,

    A match ye shall make straight with me: 250

    I will give thee sixpence to lie one night with thee.

Mer. Gog's heart, slave, dost thou think I am a sixpenny jug?

    No, 'wis, ye jack, I look a little more smug.

Snuf. I will give her eighteen pence to serve me first.

Mer. Gramercy, Snuf, thou art not the worst.

Ruf. By Gog's heart, she were better be hang'd, to forsake me

    and take thee!

Snuf. Were she so? that shall we see!

Ruf. By Gog's heart, my dagger into her I will thrust!

Snuf. Ah, ye boy, ye would do it and ye durst!

Amb. Peace, my masters; ye shall not fight.   260

    He that draws first, I will him smite.

Ruf. Gog's wounds, Master Snuf, are ye so lusty?

Snuf. Gog's sides, Master Ruf, are ye so crusty?

Ruf. You may happen to see!

Snuf. Do what thou darest to me!

> *Here draw and fight. Here she must lay on and coil
> them both; the Vice must run his way for fear;
> Snuf fling down his sword and buckler and run
> his way.*

Mer. Gog's sides, knaves! seeing to fight ye be so rough,

    Defend yourselves, for I will give ye both enough.

    I will teach ye how ye shall fall out for me!

    Yea, thou slave, Snuf! no more blows wilt thou bide?

    To take thy heels a time hast thou spied?   270

    Thou villain, seeing Snuf is gone away,

    A little better I mean thee to pay!

> *He falleth down; she falleth upon him, and beats him,
> and taketh away his weapon.*

Ruf. Alas, good Mistress Meretrix, no more!

    My legs, sides and arms with beating be sore.

248 *knave:* Because this does not rhyme, Manly conjectures "whoreson";
"whore's son" would be even better, both as retort and as rhyme.

Mer. Thou a soldier, and lose thy weapon!
    Go hence, sir boy, say a woman hath thee beaten!
Ruf. Good Mistress Meretrix, my weapon let me have;
    Take pity on me, mine honesty to save!
    If it be known this repulse I sustain,
    It will redound to my ignomy and shame.   280
Mer. If thou wilt be my man, and wait upon me,
    This sword and buckler I will give thee.
Ruf. I will do all at your commandment;
    As servant to you I will be obedient.
Mer. Then let me see how before me ye can go.
    When I speak to you, ye shall do so:
    Off with your cap at place and at board,
    "Forsooth, Mistress Meretrix," at every word.
    Tut! tut! in the camp such soldiers there be,
    One good woman would beat away two or three.   290
    Well, I am sure customers tarry at home:
    Mannerly before, and let us be gone.   *Exeunt.*

Enter AMBIDEXTER.

Amb. Oh the passion of God, be they here still or no?
    I durst not abide to see her beat them so!
    I may say to you I was in such a flight,
    Body of me, I see the hair of my head stand upright!
    When I saw her so hard upon them lay on,
    Oh the passion of God, thought I, she will be with me anon!
    I made no more ado, but avoided the thrust,
    And to my legs began for to trust;   300
    And fell a-laughing to myself, when I was once gone.
    'It is wisdom', quoth I, 'by the mass, to save one.'
    Then into this place I intended to trudge,
    Thinking to meet Sisamnes the judge.
    Behold where he cometh!   I will him meet,
    And like a gentleman I mean him to greet.

Enter SISAMNES.

Sisam. Since that the king's grace's majesty in office did me set,

---

295 *flight:* not an error for "fright" but a word now obsolete, meaning a state
  of agitation (OED 4).

What abundance of wealth to me might I get!

Now and then some vantage I achieve; much more yet may
    I take,

But that I fear unto the king that some complaint will
    make.   310

Amb. Jesu, Master Sisamnes, you are unwise!

Sisam. Why so?   I pray ye, let me agnise.

    What, Master Ambidexter, is it you?

    Now welcome to me, I make God avow!

Amb. Jesu, Master Sisamnes, with me you are well acquainted!

    By me rulers may be trimly painted.

    Ye are unwise if ye take not time while ye may:

    If ye will not now, when ye would ye shall have nay.

    What is he that of you dare make exclamation,

    Of your wrong-dealing to make explication?   320

    Can you not play with both hands, and turn with the wind?

Sisam. Believe me, your words draw deep in my mind.

    In colour wise, unto this day to bribes I have inclinèd.

    More the same for to frequent, of truth I am now minded.

    Behold, even now unto me suitors do proceed.

[*Enter* SMALL HABILITY.]

Sm. Hab. I beseech you here, good Master Judge, a poor man's
    cause to tender.

    Condemn me not in wrongful wise that never was offender!

    You know right well my right it is.   I have not for to give.

    You take away from me my due, that should my corpse
    relieve.

    The commons of you do complain, from them you devo-
    cate,   330

    With anguish great and grievous words their hearts do
    penetrate.

    The right you sell unto the wrong, your private gain to win;

    You violate the simple man, and count it for no sin.

Sisam. Hold thy tongue, thou prattling knave, and give to me
    reward,

316 *By me:* Perhaps it should be "By ye" (*i.e.*, taking you as a model).
325 Unrhymed line, probably because half a couplet is lost (rhyming on
"meed" or "greed"?), but possibly standing alone to introduce Small
Hability.

Else, in this wise, I tell thee truth, thy tale will not be heard.
Ambidexter, let us go hence, and let the knave alone.
Amb. Farewell, Small Hability, for help now get you none;
Bribes hath corrupt him good laws to pollute.　　　*Exeunt.*
Sm. Hab. Ah, naughty man that will not obey the king's con-
stitute!
With heavy heart I will return, till God redress my pain.　340
Exit.

Enter SHAME, *with a trump black.*

Shame. From among the grisly ghosts I come, from tyrant's
testy train.
Unseemly Shame, of sooth, I am, procurèd to make plain
The odious facts and shameless deeds Cambises king doth use.
All piety and virtuous life he doth it clean refuse;
Lechery and drunkenness he doth it much frequent;
The tiger's kind to imitate he hath given full consent.
He nought esteems his counsel grave, ne virtuous bringing-
up,
But daily still receives the drink of damnèd vice's cup.
He can bide no instruction, he takes so great delight
In working of iniquity for to frequent his spite.　　350
As Fame doth sound the royal trump of worthy men and trim,
So Shame doth blow with strainèd blast the trump of shame
on him.　　　　　　　　　　　　　　　　　　*Exit.*

Enter the KING, LORD, PRAXASPES, *and* SISAMNES.

King. My judge, since my departure hence, have you us'd
judgment right?
If faithful steward I ye find, the same I will requite.
Sisam. No doubt your grace shall not once hear that I have
done amiss.
Prax. I much rejoice to hear so good news as this.

Enter COMMONS' CRY *running in; speak this verse; and go
out again hastily.*

Com. Cry. Alas, alas, how are the commons oppress'd
By that vile judge, Sisamnes by name!

343 *Cambises* (Manly)] that Cambises Q.

I do not know how it should be redress'd.
To amend his life no whit he doth frame.   360
    We are undone and thrown out of door,
His damnable dealing doth us so torment.
At his hand we can find no relief nor succour.
God grant him grace for to repent!

Run away crying.

King. What doleful cries be these, my lord, that sound do in
    mine ear?
Intelligence if you can give, unto your king declare.
To me it seemeth my commons all they do lament and cry
Out of Sisamnes, judge most chief, even now standing us by.

Prax. Even so, O king, it seem'd to me, as you rehearsal made;
I doubt the judge culpable be in some respect or trade.   370

Sisam. Redoubted king, have no mistrust, no whit your mind
    dismay;
There is not one that can me charge or aught against me lay.

Enter COMMONS' COMPLAINT, *with* PROOF *and* TRIAL.

Com. Comp. Commons' Complaint I represent, with thrall of
    doleful state,
By urgent cause erected forth, my grief for to dilate.
Unto the king I will prepare my misery to tell,
To have relief of this my grief, and fetter'd feet so fell.
Redoubted prince and mighty king, myself I prostrate here!
Vouchsafe, O king, with me to bear, for this that I appear!
With humble suit I pardon crave of your most royal grace,
To give me leave my mind to break, before you in this place.

King. Commons' Complaint, keep nothing back, fear not thy
    tale to tell.   381
Whate'er he be within this land that hath not us'd thee well,
As prince's mouth shall sentence give, he shall receive the
    same.
Unfold the secrets of thy breast, for I extinguish blame.

Com. Comp. God preserve your royal grace, and send you blissful
    days,
That all your deeds might still accord, to give the gods the
    praise!
My complaint is, O mighty king, against that judge you by,

Whose careless deeds, gain to receive, hath made the
    commons cry.

He, by taking bribes and gifts, the poor he doth oppress,

Taking relief from infants young, widows and fatherless. 390

King. Untrustful traitor and corrupt judge, how likest thou
    this complaint?

Forewarning I to thee did give, of this to make restraint.

And hast thou done this devilish deed mine ire for to
    augment?

I sentence give, thou Judas judge; thou shalt thy deed
    repent.

Sisam. O puissant prince, it is not so! his complaint I deny.

Com. Comp. If it be not so, most mighty king, in place then let me
    die!

Behold that I have brought with me both Proof and Trial
    true,

To stand even here, and sentence give, what by him did
    ensue.

Proof. I, Proof, do him in this appeal: he did the commons wrong;

Unjustly he with them hath dealt, his greedy was so strong;

His heart did covet in to get, he carèd not which way. 401

The poor did leese their due and right, because they want
    to pay

Unto him for bribes, indeed,—this was his wonted use.

Whereas your grace good laws did make, he did the same
    abuse.

Trial. I, Trial, here to verify what Proof doth now unfold,

To stand against him in his wrong as now I dare be bold.

King. How likest thou this, thou caitiff vile? Canst thou the
    same deny?

Sisam. O noble king, forgive my fact! I yield to thy mercy.

King. Complaint and Proof, redress will I all this your misery.

Depart with speed, from whence you came, and straight
    command by me 410

The execution-man to come before my grace with haste.

All. For to fulfil this your request, no time we mean to waste.

                            Exeunt they three.

King. My lord, before my grace go call Otian, this judge's son,

And he shall hear and also see what his father hath done.

The father he shall suffer death, the son his room succeed,
And, if that he no better prove, so likewise shall he speed.
Prax. As your grace hath commandment given, I mean for to
fulfil.

Step aside and fetch him.

King. Accursèd judge, couldst thou consent to do this cursèd ill?
According unto thy demand, thou shalt, for this thy guilt,
Receive thy death before mine eyes, thy blood it shall be
spilt.   420

[*Enter* PRAXASPES *with* OTIAN.]

Prax. Behold, O king, Sisamnes' son before you doth appear.
King. Otian, this is my mind, therefore to me come near.
Thy father here for judgment wrong procurèd hath his death,
And thou, his son, shalt him succeed when he hath lost his
breath;
And, if that thou dost once offend, as thou seest thy father
have,
In like wise thou shalt suffer death, no mercy shall thee save.
Otian. O mighty king, vouchsafe your grace my father to remit.
Forgive his fault, his pardon I do ask of you as yet.
Alas! although my father hath your princely heart offended,
Amends for miss he will now make, and faults shall be
amended.   430
Instead of his requested life, pleaseth your grace take mine!
This offer I as tender child, so duty doth me bind.
King. Do not entreat my grace no more, for he shall die the death.
Where is the execution-man, him to bereave of breath?

Enter EXECUTION.

Exec. At hand, and if it like your grace, my duty to dispatch,
In hope that I, when deed is done, a good reward shall catch.
King. Dispatch with sword this judge's life; extinguish fear
and cares.
So done, draw thou his cursèd skin straight over both his ears.

438 *his cursèd skin:* This flaying of the covetous judge was a proverbial
example which moralists had already urged rulers to imitate: "I pray God
we may once see the sign of the skin in England" (Latimer, *Seven Sermons,*
1549).

I will see the office done, and that before mine eyes.

Exec. To do the thing my king commands I give the enterprise.

Sisam. Otian, my son, the king to death by law hath me condemn'd,   441

And you in room and office mine, his grace's will hath
plac'd;

Use justice, therefore, in this case, and yield unto no wrong,

Lest thou do purchase the like death ere ever it be long.

Otian. O father dear, these words to hear, that you must die
by force,

Bedews my cheeks with stillèd tears; the king hath no
remorse.

The grievous griefs and strainèd sighs my heart doth break
in twain,

And I deplore, most woeful child, that I should see you slain.

O false and fickle frowning dame, that turneth as the wind,

Is this the joy in father's age, thou me assign'st to find?   450

O doleful day, unhappy hour, that loving child should see

His father dear before his face thus put to death should be!

Yet, father, give me blessing thine, and let me once embrace

Thy comely corpse in folded arms, and kiss thy ancient face!

Sisam. O child, thou makes mine eyes to run, as rivers do, by
stream.

My leave I take of thee, my son; beware of this my beam!

King. Dispatch even now, thou man of death; no longer seem
to stay!

Exec. Come, Master Sisamnes, come on your way! My office I must
pay;

Forgive therefore my deed.

Sisam. I do forgive it thee, my friend; dispatch therefore with
speed!   460

Smite him in the neck with a sword to signify his death.

Prax. Behold, O king, how he doth bleed, being of life bereft!

---

441 *condemn'd:* another faulty couplet (compare 249). Perhaps substituted for
illegible "debas'd" (abased from position, OED 1).

449 *O false and fickle frowning dame:* Fortune.

456 *beam:* fault, alluding to the mote and the beam in the eye, Matthew vii. 3
(OED 3c).

458–9 Perhaps the first half of 459 is lost. "[The king's command must be ful-
fill'd]"?

King. In this wise he shall not yet be left.

    Pull his skin over his ears to make his death more vile.

    A wretch he was, a cruel thief, my commons to beguile!

Flay him with a false skin.

Otian. What child is he of nature's mould could bide the same to see,

    His father flayèd in this wise?   Oh, how it grieveth me!

King. Otian, thou seest thy father dead, and thou art in his room.

    If thou beest proud, as he hath been, even thereto shalt thou come.

Otian. O king, to me this is a glass: with grief in it I view

    Example that unto your grace I do not prove untrue.   470

Prax. Otian, convey your father hence to tomb where he shall lie.

Otian. And if it please your lordship, it shall be done by and by.

    Good execution-man, for need, help me with him away.

Exec. I will fulfil, as you to me did say.

They take him away.

King. My lord, now that my grace hath seen that finish'd is this deed,

    To question mine give tentive ear, and answer make with speed:

    Have not I done a gracious deed, to redress my commons' woe?

Prax. Yea, truly, if it please your grace, ye have indeed done so.

    But now, O king, in friendly wise, I counsel you in this,

    Certain vices for to leave that in you placed is;   480

    The vice of drunkenness, O king, which doth you sore infect,

    With other great abuses, which I wish you to detect.

King. Peace, my lord! what needeth this?   Of this I will not hear!

    To palace now I will return, and thereto make good cheer.

    God Bacchus he bestows his gifts, we have good store of wine;

    And also that the ladies be both passing brave and fine.

    But stay!   I see a lord now come, and eke a valiant knight.

    What news, my lord?   To see you here my heart it doth delight.

462 A defective line? "[Though he be dead, yet]"?
474 A defective line? "[Your gracious will]"?

Enter LORD *and* KNIGHT *to meet the* KING.

Lord. No news, O king; but of duty come, to wait upon your
    grace.
King. I thank you, my lord and loving knight; I pray you with
    me trace.   490
    My lords and knight, I pray ye tell—I will not be offended—
    Am I worthy of any crime once to be reprehended?
Prax. The Persians much do praise your grace, but one thing
    discommend,
    In that to wine subject you be, wherein you do offend.
    Sith that the might of wine's effect doth oft subdue your
    brain,
    My counsel is, to please their hearts, from it you would
    refrain.
Lord. No, no, my lord, it is not so; for this of prince they tell,
    For virtuous proof and princely facts Cyrus he doth excel.
    By that his grace by conquest great the Egyptians did
    convince,
    Of him report abroad doth pass to be a worthy prince.   500
Knight. In person of Crœsus I answer make, we may not his
    grace compare
    In whole respect for to be like Cyrus, the king's father,
    Insomuch your grace hath yet no child as Cyrus left behind,
    Even, you I mean, Cambises king, in whom I favour find.
King. Crœsus said well in saying so; but, Praxaspes, tell me why
    That to my mouth in such a sort thou should avouch a lie,
    Of drunkenness me thus to charge?   But thou with speed
    shalt see
    Whether that I a sober king or else a drunkard be.
    I know thou hast a blissful babe, wherein thou dost delight:
    Me to revenge of these thy words I will go wreak this spite:
    When I the most have tasted wine, my bow it shall be bent,
    At heart of him even then to shoot is now my whole intent;
    And if that I his heart can hit, the king no drunkard is: 513
    If heart of his I do not kill, I yield to thee in this.

497 *this of prince they tell:* not a transposition of "of this prince they tell". The
    omission of the definite article (before "prince") is typical of the play's
    diction.

Therefore, Praxaspes, fetch to me thy youngest son with speed.

There is no way, I tell thee plain, but I will do this deed.

Prax. Redoubted prince, spare my sweet child, he is mine only joy.

I trust your grace to infant's heart no such thing will employ.

If that his mother hear of this, she is so nigh her flight,

In clay her corpse will soon be shrin'd, to pass from world's delight.   520

King. No more ado!   Go fetch me him; it shall be as I say.

And if that I do speak the word, how dare ye once say nay?

Prax. I will go fetch him to your grace; but so, I trust, it shall not be!

King. For fear of my displeasure great, go fetch him unto me.

                                                    [*Exit Praxaspes.*]

Is he gone?   Now, by the gods, I will do as I say!

My lord, therefore fill me some wine, I heartily you pray,

For I must drink to make my brain somewhat intoxicate.

When that the wine is in my head, oh, trimly I can prate.

Lord. Here is the cup, with fillèd wine, thereof to take repast.

King. Give it me, to drink it off, and see no wine be waste.   530

                                                    Drink.

Once again enlarge this cup, for I must taste it still.   *Drink.*

By the gods, I think of pleasant wine I cannot take my fill!

Now drink is in, give me my bow and arrows from sir knight;

At heart of child I mean to shoot, hoping to cleave it right.

Knight. Behold, O king, where he doth come, his infant young in hand.

                [*Enter* PRAXASPES, *with the* CHILD.]

Prax. O mighty king, your grace' behest with sorrow I have scann'd,

And brought my child fro mother's knee, before you to appear,

And she thereof no whit doth know that he in place is here.

King. Set him up, my mark to be; I will shoot at his heart.

Prax. I beseech your grace not so to do! set this pretence apart!   540

Farewell, my dear and loving babe! come, kiss thy father
    dear!

A grievous sight to me it is to see thee slain even here.

Is this the gain now from the king for giving counsel good,

Before my face with such despite to spill my son's heart-
    blood?

Oh heavy day to me this is, and mother in like case!

Young Child. O father, father, wipe your face,

I see the tears run from your eye.

My mother is at home sewing of a band.

Alas! dear father, why do you cry?

King. Before me as mark now let him stand   550

I will shoot at him my mind to fulfil.

Young Child. Alas, alas! father, will you me kill?

Good Master King, do not shoot at me, my mother loves
    me best of all.   *Shoot.*

King. I have dispatch'd him, down he doth fall!

As right as a line his heart I have hit.

Nay, thou shalt see, Praxaspes, stranger news yet.

My knight, with speed his heart cut out and give it unto me.

Knight. It shall be done, O mighty king, with all celerity.

Lord. My lord Praxaspes, this had not been but your tongue
    must be walking;

To the king of correction you must needs be talking!   560

Prax. No correction, my lord; but counsel for the best.

Knight. Here is the heart, according to your grace's behest.

King. Behold, Praxaspes, thy son's own heart! Oh, how well
    the same was hit!

After this wine to do this deed I thought it very fit.

Esteem thou mayst right well thereby no drunkard is the
    king,

That in the midst of all his cups could do this valiant thing.

My lord and knight, on me attend; to palace we will go,

And leave him here to take his son when we are gone him fro.

All. With all our hearts we give consent to wait upon your grace.

[*Exeunt.*]

546–9 The simple ballad metre indicates the innocence of the speaker. Compare
Isaac in the miracle plays of Abraham's sacrifice.

Prax. A woeful man, O lord, am I, to see him in this case.   570
    My days, I deem, desires their end; this deed will help me
        hence,
    To have the blossoms of my field destroyed by violence.

Enter MOTHER.

Mother. Alas, alas! I do hear tell the king hath kill'd my son!
    If it be so, woe worth the deed, that ever it was done!
    It is even so; my lord I see, how by him he doth weep.
    What meant I, that from hands of him this child I did not
        keep?
    Alas! husband and lord, what did you mean, to fetch this
        child away?
Prax. O lady wife, I little thought for to have seen this day.
Mother. O blissful babe, O joy of womb, heart's comfort and
        delight!
    For counsel given unto the king is this thy just requite?   580
    Oh heavy day and doleful time, these mourning tunes to
        make!
    With blubber'd eyes, into mine arms from earth I will thee
        take,
    And wrap thee in mine apron white!—But, oh my heavy
        heart,
    The spiteful pangs that it sustains would make it in two
        to part,
    The death of this my son to see! O heavy mother now,
    That from thy sweet and sugar'd joy to sorrow so shouldst
        bow!
    What grief in womb did I retain before I did thee see!
    Yet at the last, when smart was gone, what joy wert thou
        to me!
    How tender was I of thy food, for to preserve thy state!
    How stillèd I thy tender heart, at times early and late!   590
    With velvet paps I gave thee suck, with issue from my breast,
    And dancèd thee upon my knee, to bring thee unto rest.
    Is this the joy of thee I reap? O king, of tiger's brood!
    O tiger's whelp, hadst thou the heart to see this child's heart-
        blood?
    Nature enforceth me, alas! in this wise to deplore,

To wring my hands,—Oh, wellaway, that I should see this
    hour!
Thy mother yet will kiss thy lips, silk-soft and pleasant
    white,
With wringing hands, lamenting for to see thee in this plight!
My lording dear, let us go home our mourning to augment.
Prax. My lady dear, with heavy heart to it I do consent,   600
Between us both the child to bear unto our lordly place.

                              Exeunt.

    Enter AMBIDEXTER.

Amb. Indeed, as ye say, I have been absent a long space.
But is not my cousin Cutpurse with you in the meantime?
To it, to it, cousin, and do your office fine!
How like you Sisamnes for using of me?
He play'd with both hands, but he sped ill-favouredly!
The king himself was godly uptrain'd:
He profess'd virtue, but I think it was feign'd.
He plays with both hands, good deeds and ill;
But it was no good deed Praxaspes' son for to kill.   610
As he for the good deed on the judge was commended,
For all his deeds else he is reprehended.
The most evil-disposed person that ever was,
All the state of his life he would not let pass:
Some good deeds he will do, though they be but few.
The like things this tyrant Cambises doth shew.
No goodness from him to none is exhibited,
But still malediction abroad is distributed;
And yet ye shall see in the rest of his race
What infamy he will work against his own grace.   620
Whist! no more words! here comes the king's brother.

  Enter LORD SMERDIS, *with* ATTENDANCE *and* DILIGENCE.

Smer. The king's brother by birth am I, issued from Cyrus' loins.
A grief to me it is to hear of this the king's repines.
I like not well of those his deeds that he doth still frequent.
I wish to God that other ways his mind he could content.
Young I am, and next to him; no moe of us there be.
I would be glad a quiet realm in this his reign to see.

Att. My lord, your good and willing heart the gods will recom-
        pense,
        In that your mind so pensive is, for those his great offence.
        My lord, his grace shall have a time to 'pair and to amend.
        Happy is he that can escape and not his grace offend.   631
Dil. If that wicked vice he could refrain, from wasting wine
        forbear,
        A moderate life he would frequent, amending this his square.
Amb. My lord, and if your honour it shall please,
        I can inform you what is best for your ease.
        Let him alone, of his deeds do not talk,
        Then by his side ye may quietly walk;
        After his death you shall be king,
        Then may you reform each kind of thing;
        In the meantime live quietly, do not with him deal.   640
        So shall it redound much to your weal.
Smer. Thou sayest true, my friend; that is the best;
        I know not whether he love me, or do me detest.
Att. Lean from his company all that you may.
        I, faithful Attendance, will your honour obey.
        If against your honour he take any ire,
        His grace is as like to kindle his fire
        To your honour's destruction as otherwise.
Dil. Therefore, my lord, take good advise,
        And I, Diligence, your case will so tender   650
        That to his grace your honour shall be none offender.
Smer. I thank you both, entire friends; with my honour still
        remain.
Amb. Behold where the king doth come with his train!

           Enter KING *and a* LORD.

King. O lording dear and brother mine, I joy your state to see,
        Surmising much what is the cause you absent thus from me.
Smer. Pleaseth your grace, no absence I, but ready to fulfil,
        At all assays, my prince and king, in that your grace me will.
        What I can do in true defence to you, my prince, aright,
        In readiness I always am to offer forth my might.

653 *s.d. a Lord* Q2] 1 Lord Q1. But Diligence (who is on stage) doubles with 1
Lord.

King. And I the like to you again do here avouch the same.   660

All. For this your good agreement here, now praisèd be God's name!

Amb. But hear ye, noble prince; hark in your ear:
It is best to do as I did declare.

King. My lord and brother Smerdis, now this is my mind and will:
That you to court of mine return, and thereto tarry still,
Till my return within short space, your honour for to greet.

Smer. At your behest so will I do till time again we meet.
My leave I take from you, O king; even now I do depart.

        Exeunt Smerdis, Attendance, and Diligence.

King. Farewell, lord and brother mine! farewell with all my heart!
My lord, my brother Smerdis is of youth and manly might,   670
And in his sweet and pleasant face my heart doth take delight.

Lord. Yea, noble prince, if that your grace before his honour die,
He will succeed, a virtuous king, and rule with equity.

King. As you have said, my lord, he is chief heir next my grace;
And, if I die to-morrow, next he shall succeed my place.

Amb. And if it please your grace, O king, I heard him say:
For your death unto the gods day and night he did pray;
He would live so virtuously and get him such a praise
That Fame by trump his due deserts in honour should upraise.
He said your grace deservèd had the cursing of all men,   680
That ye should never after him get any praise again.

King. Did he speak thus of my grace, in such despiteful wise?
Or else dost thou presume to fill my princely ears with lies?

Lord. I cannot think it in my heart that he would report so.

King. How sayest thou? speak the truth: was it so or no?

Amb. I think so, if it please your grace, but I cannot tell.

King. Thou play'st with both hands, now I perceive well!

---

665 *thereto* (C) (*i.e.*, therewithal)] there to Q. At 484, "thereto" is divided in
    Q1 and corrected in Q2.
679 *in honour* Q2]   ,his honour Q1.
684 *report so:* From the awkward metre I conjecture that Preston wrote "report
    you so", eliding "he would" to "he'd".

But, for to put all doubts aside and to make him leese his
    hope,
He shall die by dint of sword or else by choking rope.
Shall he succeed when I am gone, to have more praise
    than I?   690
Were he father as brother mine, I swear that he shall die.
To palace mine I will therefore, his death for to pursue.

Exit [with Lord].

Amb. Are ye gone?   Straightway I will follow you.
    How like ye now, my masters?   Doth not this gear cotton?
    The proverb old is verified: soon ripe, and soon rotten!
    He will not be quiet till his brother be kill'd.
    His delight is wholly to have his blood spill'd.
    Marry, sir, I told him a notable lie;
    If it were to do again, man, I durst do it, I!
    Marry, when I had done, to it I durst not stand;   700
    Thereby you may perceive I use to play with each hand.
    But how now, cousin Cutpurse, with whom play you?
    Take heed, for his hand is groping even now!
    Cousin, take heed, if you do secretly grope.
    If ye be taken, cousin, ye must look through a rope.

Exit.

Enter LORD SMERDIS *alone.*

Smer. I am wandering alone, here and there to walk.
    The Court is so unquiet, in it I take no joy.
    Solitary to myself now I may talk.
    If I could rule, I wist what to say.

Enter CRUELTY *and* MURDER *with bloody hands.*

Cruel. My coequal partner, Murder, come away;   710
    From me long thou mayest not stay.
Murd. Yes, from thee I may stay, but not thou from me:
    Therefore I have a prerogative above thee.
Cruel. But in this case we must together abide.
    Come, come!   Lord Smerdis I have spied:
    Lay hands on him with all festination,
    That on him we may work our indignation!
Smer. How now, my friends? what have you to do with me?
Murd. King Cambises hath sent us unto thee,

Commanding us straitly, without mercy or favour,   720
Upon thee to bestow our behaviour,
With cruelty to murder you and make you away.

Strike him in divers places.

Smer. Yet pardon me, I heartily you pray!
Consider, the king is a tyrant tyrannious,
And all his doings be damnable and pernicious:
Favour me therefore; I did him never offend.

A little bladder of vinegar pricked.

Cruel. No favour at all; your life is at an end.
Even now I strike, his body to wound.
Behold, now his blood springs out on the ground!
Murd. Now he is dead, let us present him to the king.   730
Cruel. Lay to your hand, away him to bring.   *Exeunt.*

Enter AMBIDEXTER.

Amb. Oh the passion of God, yonder is a heavy court:
Some weeps, some wails, and some make great sport.
Lord Smerdis by Cruelty and Murder is slain;
But, Jesus! for want of him how some do complain!
If I should have had a thousand pound, I could not forbear
     weeping.
Now Jesus have his blessed soul in keeping!
Ah good lord! to think on him, how it doth me grieve!
I cannot forbear weeping, ye may me believe.   *Weep.*
Oh my heart! how my pulses do beat,   740
With sorrowful lamentations I am in such a heat!
Ah, my heart, how for him it doth sorrow!
Nay, I have done, in faith, now, and God give you good
     morrow!
Ha! ha!   Weep?   Nay, laugh, with both hands to play!
The king through his cruelty hath made him away.
But hath not he wrought a most wicked deed,
Because king after him he should not proceed,
His own natural brother, and having no more,
To procure his death by violence sore?
In spite, because his brother should never be king,   750

722 *s.d.* This, and the *s.d.* four lines later, are anticipatory, referring to
    Cruelty's line, 728.

His heart being wicked consented to this thing.
Now hath he no more brothers nor kindred alive.
If the king use this gear still, he cannot long thrive.

Enter HOB *and* LOB.

Hob. God's hat, neighbour, come away! it's time to market to go!
Lob. God's vast, naybor, zay ye zo?
The clock hath stricken vive, ich think by Lakin.
Bum vay, vrom sleep cham not very well waken.
But, naybor Hob, naybor Hob, what have ye to zell?
Hob. Bum troth, naybor Lob, to you I chill tell:
Chave two goslings and a chine of good pork,   760
There is no vatter between this and York.
Chave a pot of strawberries and a calf's head,
A zennight zince to-morrow it hath been dead.
Lob. Chave a score of eggs and of butter a pound;
Yesterday a nest of goodly young rabbits I vound.
Chave vorty things mo, of more and of less;
My brain is not very good them to express.
But, God's hat, naybor, wotst what?
Hob. No, not well, naybor; what's that?
Lob. Bum vay, naybor, master king is a zhrode lad!   770
Zo God help me, and holidam, I think the vool be mad!
Zome zay he deal cruelly: his brother he did kill,
And also a goodly young lad's heart-blood he did spill.
Hob. Vorbod of God, naybor! has he play'd zuch a voolish deed?
Amb. Goodman Hob and goodman Lob, God be your speed!
As you two towards market do walk,
Of the king's cruelty I did hear you talk;
I ensure you he is a king most vile and pernicious;
His doings and life are odious and vicious.
Lob. It were a good deed zomebody would break his head.   780
Hob. Bum vay, naybor Lob, I chould he were dead!
Amb. So would I, Lob and Hob, with all my heart!
[*Aside.*] Now with both hands will ye see me play my part.
Ah, ye whoreson traitorly knaves,

754 In the conventional rustic speech beginning here, z stands for s, and v for f.
  "Ich" means "I", so "I chill" is "I will" ("Ich will"), "chave" is "I
  have", and "cham" is "I am". "Bum vay" is "by my faith". "Zhrode"
  is "shrewd".

Hob and Lob, out upon you, slaves!

Lob. And thou call'st me knave, thou art another!
My name is Lob, and Hob my next naybor.

Amb. Hob and Lob! ah, ye country patches!
Ah, ye fools, ye have made wrong matches!
Ye have spoken treason against the king's grace: 790
For it I will accuse ye before his face.
Then for the same ye shall be martyr'd;
At the least ye shall be hang'd, drawn and quarter'd.

Hob. O gentleman, ye shall have two pear-pies, and tell not
of me!

Lob. By God, a vat goose chill give thee:
I think no hurt, by my vather's soul I zwear!

Hob. Chave liv'd well all my life-time, my naybors among;
And now chould be loth to come to zuch wrong.
To be hang'd and quarter'd the grief would be great!

Lob. A foul evil on thee, Hob!   Who bid thee on it treat?   800
Vor it was thou that first did him name.

Hob. Thou liest like a varlet and thou zay'st the zame!
It was zuch a voolish Lob as thou.

Lob. Speak many words, and, by cod's nails I vow
Upon thy pate my staff I will lay!

Amb. [*aside.*] By the mass, I will cause them to make a fray.—
Yea, Lob, thou sayest true: all came through him.

Lob. Bum vay, thou Hob, a little would make me ye trim!
Give thee a zwap on thy nose till thy heart ache!

Hob. If thou darest, do it!   Else, man, cry creak!   810
I trust, before thou hurt me,
With my staff chill make a Lob of thee!

> *Here let them fight with their staves, not come near*
> *[one] another by three or four yards; the Vice set*
> *them on as hard as he can; one of their wives come*
> *out, and all to-beat the Vice; he run away.*

Enter MARIAN MAY-BE-GOOD, HOB'S *wife, running in with a*
broom, and part them.

Marian. Oh the body of me, husband Hob, what mean you to fight?
For the passion of God, no more blows smite!
Neighbours and friends so long, and now to fall out?

What! in your age to seem so stout?

If I had not parted ye, one had kill'd another.

Lob. I had not car'd, I swear by God's Mother!

Marian. Shake hands again at the request of me;

As ye have been friends, so friends still be.   820

Hob. Bum troth, cham content and zay'st word, naybor Lob.

Lob. I am content; agreed, naybor Hob!

> *Shake hands and laugh heartily one at another.*

Marian. So, get you to market; no longer stay.

And with yonder knave let me make a fray.

Hob. Content, wife Marian, chill do as thou dost say;

But buss me, ich pray thee, at going away!

> *Exeunt Hob, Lob.*

Marian. Thou whoreson knave, and prickear'd boy, why didst
thou let them fight?

If one had kill'd another here, couldst thou their deaths
requite?

It bears a sign by this thy deed a cowardly knave thou art,

Else wouldst thou draw that weapon thine, like a man them
to part.   830

Amb. What, Marian May-be-good, are you come prattling?

Ye may hap to get a box on the ear with your tattling.

If they had kill'd one another, I had not car'd a pease.

> *Here let her swinge him in her broom; she gets him down,
> and he her down, thus one on top of another make
> pastime.*

Marian. Ah, villain, myself on thee I must ease!

Give me a box on the ear? that will I try.

Who shall be master, thou shalt see by and by!

Amb. Oh, no more, no more, I beseech you heartily!

Even now I yield, and give you the mastery.

> *Run his way out while she is down.*

Marian. Ah, thou knave, dost thou throw me down and run
thy way?

If he were here again, oh, how I would him pay!   840

I will after him; and, if I can him meet,

With these my nails his face I will greet.   [*Exit.*]

---

832 *tattling* (C)] talking Q. Necessary to the rhyme, and easily misread in manu-
script.

Enter VENUS *leading out her son,* CUPID, *blind: he must have a bow and two shafts, one headed with gold and th' other headed with lead.*

Venus. Come forth, my son, unto my words attentive ears resign.
What I pretend, see you frequent, to force this game of mine.
The king a kinswoman hath, adorn'd with beauty store;
And I wish that Diana's gifts they twain shall keep no more,
But use my silver sugar'd game their joys for to augment.
When I do speak, to wound his heart, Cupid my son, consent,
And shoot at him the shaft of love, that bears the head of gold,
To wound his heart in lovers' wise, his grief for to unfold.   850
Though kin she be unto his grace, that nature me expel,
Against the course thereof he may in my game please me well.
Wherefore, my son, do not forget; forthwith pursue the deed!

Cupid. Mother, I mean for to obey as you have whole decreed.
But you must tell me, mother dear, when I shall arrow draw,
Else your request to be attain'd will not be worth a straw.
I am blind and cannot see, but still do shoot by guess.
The poets well, in places store, of my might do express.

Venus. Cupid, my son, when time shall serve that thou shalt do this deed,
Then warning I to thee will give; but see thou shoot with speed.   860

Enter a LORD, *a* LADY, *and a* WAITING-MAID.

Lord. Lady dear, to king akin, forthwith let us proceed
To trace abroad the beauty fields, as erst we had decreed.
The blowing buds, whose savoury scents our sense will much delight;
The sweet smell of musk white-rose, to please the appetite;
The chirping birds, whose pleasant tunes therein shall hear record,

865 *shall hear record:* elliptical for "we shall hear them record".

That our great joy we shall it find in field to walk abroad,
On lute and cittern there to play a heavenly harmony,
Our ears shall hear, heart to content, our sports to beautify.

Lady. Unto your words, most comely lord, myself submit
    do I;
To trace with you in field so green I mean not to deny.   870
                        Here trace up and down playing.

Maid. And, I, your waiting-maid, at hand with diligence will be,
    For to fulfil with heart and hand, when you shall command
    me.

                Enter KING, LORD, *and* KNIGHT.

King. Come on, my lord and knight; abroad our mirth let us
    employ.
Since he is dead, this heart of mine in corpse I feel it joy.
Should brother mine have reignèd king when I had yielded
    breath?
A thousand brothers I rather had to put them all to death.
But, oh, behold, where I do see a lord and lady fair!
For beauty she most worthy is to sit in prince's chair.

Venus. Shoot forth, my son; now is the time that thou must
    wound his heart.

Cupid. Content you, mother; I will do my part.   880
                Shoot there, and go out Venus and Cupid.

King. Of truth, my lord, in eye of mine all ladies she doth excel.
Can none report what dame she is, and to my grace it tell?

Lord. Redoubted prince, pleaseth your grace, to you she is akin,
Cousin-german nigh of birth, by mother's side come in.

Knight. And that her waiting-maiden is, attending her upon.
He is a lord of prince's court, and will be there anon.
They sport themselves in pleasant field, to former usèd
    use.

King. My lord and knight, of truth I speak: my heart it cannot
    choose
But with my lady I must speak and so express my mind.
My lord and ladies, walking there, if you will favour find,   890
Present yourselves unto my grace, and by my side come
    stand.

First Lord. We will fulfil, most mighty king, as your grace doth
   command.

King. Lady dear, intelligence my grace hath got of late,
   You issued out of mother's stock and kin unto my state.
   According to rule of birth you are cousin-german mine.
   Yet do I wish that farther off this kindred I could find,
   For Cupid he, that eyeless boy, my heart hath so enflam'd
   With beauty you me to content the like cannot be nam'd;
   For, since I enter'd in this place and on you fix'd mine eyes,
   Most burning fits about my heart in ample wise did rise. 900
   The heat of them such force doth yield, my corpse they
     scorch, alas!
   And burns the same with wasting heat, as Titan doth the
     grass.
   And, sith this heat is kindled so, and fresh in heart of me,
   There is no way but of the same the quencher you must be.
   My meaning is that beauty yours my heart with love doth
     wound;
   To give me love, mind to content, my heart hath you out-
     found,
   And you are she must be my wife, else shall I end my days.
   Consent to this, and be my queen, to wear the crown with
     praise!

Lady. If it please your grace, O mighty king, you shall not this
   request.
   It is a thing that nature's course doth utterly detest, 910
   And high it would the gods displease,—of all that is the
     worst.
   To grant your grace to marry so, it is not that I durst.
   Yet humble thanks I render now unto you, mighty king,
   That you vouchsafe to great estate so gladly would me bring.
   Were it not it were offence, I would it not deny,
   But such great honour to achieve my heart I would apply.
   Therefore, O king, with humble heart in this I pardon crave.
   My answer is: in this request your mind ye may not have.

King. May I not? nay, then, I will, by all the gods I vow!
   And I will marry thee as wife,—this is mine answer now. 920

896 *farther off* (C)] farther of Q. He regrets the nearness of their blood relationship.

Who dare say nay what I pretend, who dare the same withstand,

Shall lose his head and have report as traitor through my land.

There is no nay; I will you have, and you my queen shall be.

Lady. Then, mighty king, I crave your grace to hear the words of me:

Your counsel take of lordings' wit, the laws aright peruse.

If I with safe may grant this deed, I will it not refuse.

King. No, no! what I have said to you, I mean to have it so.

For counsel theirs I mean not, I, in this respect to go.

But to my palace let us go, the marriage to prepare;

For to avoid my will in this, I can it not forbear.   930

Lady. O God, forgive me, if I do amiss!

The king by compulsion enforceth me this.

Maid. Unto the gods for your estate I will not cease to pray,

That you may be a happy queen and see most joyful day.

King. Come on, my lords, with gladsome hearts let us rejoice with glee!

Your music show to joy this deed at the request of me!

Both. For to obey your grace's words our honours do agree.

                                                                Exeunt.

Enter AMBIDEXTER.

Amb. Oh the passion of me! marry, as ye say, yonder is a royal court.

There is triumphing and sport upon sport,

Such loyal lords, with such lordly exercise,   940

Frequenting such pastime as they can devise,

Running at tilt, jousting, with running at the ring,

Masking and mumming, with each kind of thing,

Such dancing, such singing, with musical harmony,

Believe me, I was loth to absent their company.

But will you believe?   Jesu, what haste they made till they were married!

Not for a million of pounds one day longer they would have tarried!

Oh! there was a banquet royal and superexcellent;

Thousands and thousands at that banquet was spent.

I muse of nothing but how they can be married so soon.   950
I care not if I be married before to-morrow at noon,
If marriage be a thing that so may be had.
How say you, maid? to marry me will ye be glad?
Out of doubt, I believe it is some excellent treasure,
Else to the same belongs abundant pleasure.
Yet with mine ears I have heard some say:
" That ever I was married, now cursèd be the day!"
Those be they that with curst wives be match'd,
That husband for hawk's-meat of them is up-snatch'd,
Head broke with a bedstaff, face all to-bescratch'd;—   960
"Knave!" "slave!" and "villain!", a coil'd coat now and then,
When the wife hath given it, she will say, " Alas, good man!"
Such were better unmarried, my masters, I trow,
Than all their life after to be match'd with a shrow.

Enter PREPARATION.

Prep. With speed I am sent all things to prepare,
My message to do as the king did declare.
His grace doth mean a banquet to make,
Meaning in this place repast for to take.
Well, the cloth shall be laid, and all things in readiness,
To court to return, when done is my business.   970
Amb. A proper man and also a fit
For the king's estate to prepare a banquet!
Prep. What, Ambidexter?   Thou art not unknown!
A mischief on all good faces, so that I curse not mine own!
Now, in the knave's name, shake hands with me.
Amb. Well said, goodman pouchmouth; your reverence I see.
I will teach ye, if your manners no better be!
Ah, ye slave, the king doth me a gentleman allow;
Therefore I look that to me ye should bow.   *Fight.*
Prep. Good Master Ambidexter, pardon my behaviour;   980
For this your deeds you are a knave for your labour!
Amb. Why, ye stale counterly villain, nothing but knave?
                                                        Fight.

959 *hawk's-meat:* food for hawks. Figurative language, meaning that such il
  tempered women snap up husbands as eagerly as a hawk seizes its prey.
982 *counterly:* fit for the Counter, a London prison.

Prep. I am sorry your mastership offended I have;
          Shake hands, that between us agreement may be.
          I was over-shot with myself, I do see.
          Let me have your help this furniture to provide.
          The king from this place will not long abide.
                              Set the fruit on the board.
Amb. Content: it is the thing that I would wish;
          I myself will go fetch one dish.
                    *Let the Vice fetch a dish of nuts, and let them fall in the
                    bringing of them in.*
Prep. Cleanly, Master Ambidexter; for fair on the ground they
          lie.   990
Amb. I will have them up again by and by.
Prep. To see all in readiness I will put you in trust;
          There is no nay, to the court needs I must.
                              Exit Preparation.
Amb. Have ye no doubt but all shall be well.—
          Marry, sir, as you say, this gear doth excel!
          All things is in a readiness, when they come hither,
          The king's grace and the queen both together.
          I beseech ye, my masters, tell me, is it not best
          That I be so bold as to bid a guest?
          He is as honest a man as ever spurr'd cow,—   1000
          My cousin Cutpurse, I mean; I beseech ye, judge you.
          Believe me, cousin, if to be the king's guest ye could be taken,
          I trust that offer would not be forsaken.
          But, cousin, because to that office ye are not like to come,
          Frequent your exercises, a horn on your thumb,
          A quick eye, a sharp knife, at hand a receiver;
          But then take heed, cousin, ye be a cleanly conveyer.
          Content yourself, cousin; for this banquet you are unfit,
          When such as I at the same am not worthy to sit.

                    Enter KING, QUEEN, *and his train.*

King. My queen and lords, to take repast, let us attempt the
          same;   1010
          Here is the place; delay no time, but to our purpose frame.

1009 *s.d.* Q2, expanding the *Enter* of Q1 (which lacks space for more).

Queen. With willing hearts your whole behest we mind for to
obey.

All. And we, the rest of prince's train, will do as you do say.

Sit at the banquet.

King. Methink mine ears doth wish the sound of music's
harmony;

Here, for to play before my grace, in place I would them spy.

Play at the banquet.

Amb. They be at hand, sir, with stick and fiddle;

They can play a new dance, called Hey-diddle-diddle.

King. My queen, perpend; what I pronounce, I will not violate,

But one thing which my heart makes glad I mind to
explicate:

You know in court uptrainèd is a lion very young;   1020

Of one litter two whelps beside, as yet not very strong;

I did request one whelp to see and this young lion fight;

But lion did the whelp convince, by strength of force and
might.

His brother whelp, perceiving that the lion was too good,

And he by force was like to see the other whelp his blood,

With force to lion he did run, his brother for to help;

A wonder great it was to see that friendship in a whelp!

So then the whelps between them both the lion did convince,

Which thing to see before mine eyes did glad the heart of
prince.   *At this tale told, let the Queen weep.*

Queen. These words to hear makes stilling tears issue from
crystal eyes.   1030

King. What dost thou mean, my spouse, to weep for loss of
any prise?

Queen. No, no, O king, but as you see friendship in brothers
whelp,

When one was like to have repulse, the other yielded help.

And was this favour show'd in dogs, to shame of royal king?

Alack, I wish these ears of mine had not once heard this
thing!

Even so should you, O mighty king, to brother been a stay,

And not, without offence to you, in such wise him to slay.

In all assays it was your part his cause to have defended,

And whosoever had him misus'd, to have them reprehended.

But faithful love was more in dog than it was in your
grace.   1040

King. O cursèd caitiff vicious and vile, I hate thee in this place!

This banquet is at an end; take all these things away.

Before my face thou shalt repent the words that thou dost
say.

O wretch most vile, didst thou the cause of brother mine so
tender,

The loss of him should grieve thy heart, he being none
offender?

It did me good his death to have, so will it to have thine;

What friendship he had at my hands, the same even thou
shalt find.

I give consent, and make a vow, that thou shalt die the
death;

By Cruel's sword and Murder fell even thou shalt lose thy
breath.

Ambidexter, see with speed to Cruelty ye go;   1050

Cause him hither to approach, Murder with him also.

Amb. I ready am for to fulfil,

If that it be your grace's will.

King. Then nought oblight my message given; absent thyself
away.

Amb. Then in this place I will no longer stay.—

If that I durst, I would mourn your case;

But, alas! I dare not, for fear of his grace.

Exit Ambidexter.

King. Thou cursed jill, by all the gods I take an oath and swear,

That flesh of thine these hands of mine in pieces small could
tear;

But thou shalt die by dint of sword: there is no friend
ne fee   1060

Shall find remorse at prince's hand, to have the life of thee.

Queen. O mighty king and husband mine, vouchsafe to hear
me speak,

And licence give to spouse of thine her patient mind to
break!

1049 *thy breath* Q2] the breath Q1.

For tender love unto your grace my words I did so frame;
For pure love doth heart of king me violate and blame.
And to your grace is this offence, that I should purchase
    death?
Then cursèd time that I was queen, to shorten this my
    breath!
Your grace doth know by marriage true I am your wife
    and spouse,
And one to save another's health at trothplight made our
    vows;
Therefore, O king, let loving queen at thy hand find remorse,
Let pity be a mean to quench that cruel raging force,   1071
And pardon, plight from prince's mouth, yield grace unto
    your queen,
That amity with faithful zeal may ever be us between!
King. Ah, caitiff vile, to pity thee my heart it is not bent,
Ne yet to pardon your offence it is not mine intent.
First Lord. Our mighty prince, with humble suit of your grace
    this I crave,
That this request it may take place, your favour for to
    have.
Let mercy yet abundantly the life of queen preserve,
Sith she in most obedient wise your grace's will doth serve.
As yet your grace but while with her hath had cohabitation,
And sure this is no desert why to yield her indignation.   1081
Therefore, O king, her life prolong, to joy her days in bliss!
Second Lord. Your grace shall win immortal fame in granting
    unto this.
She is a queen whose goodly hue excels the royal rose,
For beauty bright Dame Nature she a large gift did dispose.
For comeliness who may compare?   Of all she bears the bell.
This should give cause to move your grace to love her very
    well.
Her silver breast in those your arms, to sing the songs of
    love;
Fine qualities most excellent to be in her you prove;
A precious pearl of price to prince, a jewel passing all.   1090
Therefore, O king, to beg remorse on both my knees I fall;
To grant her grace to have her life, with heart I do desire.

King. You villains twain, with raging force ye set my heart
    on fire!
    If I consent that she shall die, how dare ye crave her life?
    You two to ask this at my hand doth much enlarge my
        strife.
    Were it not for shame, you two should die, that for her life
        do sue!
    But favour mine from you is gone, my lords, I tell you true.
    I sent for Cruelty of late; if he would come away,
    I would commit her to his hands his cruel part to play.
    Even now I see where he doth come; it doth my heart delight.

Enter CRUELTY *and* MURDER.

Cruel. Come, Murder, come; let us go forth with might;   1101
    Once again the king's commandment we must fulfil.
Murd. I am contented to do it with a good will.
King. Murder and Cruelty, for both of you I sent,
    With all festination your offices to frequent.
    Lay hold on the queen; take her to your power,
    And make her away within this hour!
    Spare for no fear, I do you full permit.
    So I from this place do mean for to flit.
Both. With courageous hearts, O king, we will obey.   1110
King. Then come, my lords, let us depart away.
Both the Lords. With heavy hearts we will do all your grace doth
        say.   *Exeunt King and Lords.*
Cruel. Come, lady and queen, now are you in our handling;
    In faith, with you we will use no dandling.
Murd. With all expedition I, Murder, will take place;
    Though thou be a queen, ye be under my grace.
Queen. With patience I will you both obey.
Cruel. No more words, but go with us away!
Queen. Yet, before I die, some psalm to God let me sing.
Both. We be content to permit you that thing.   1120
Queen. Farewell, you ladies of the court, with all your masking
        hue!
    I do forsake these broider'd guards and all the fashions new,
    The court and all the courtly train wherein I had delight;
    I banish'd am from happy sport, and all by spiteful spite;

Yet with a joyful heart to God a psalm I mean to sing,
Forgiving all [men] and the king of each kind of thing.

Sing and exeunt.

Enter AMBIDEXTER *weeping.*

Amb. Ah, ah, ah, ah! I cannot choose but weep for the queen!
    Nothing but mourning now at the court there is seen.
    Oh, oh, my heart, my heart!   Oh, my bum will break!
    Very grief so torments me that scarce I can speak.   1130
    Who could but weep for the loss of such a lady?
    That I cannot do, I swear by mine honesty.
    But, Lord! so the ladies mourn, crying " Alack!"
    Nothing is worn now but only black:
    I believe all [the] cloth in Watling Street to make gowns
        would not serve,—
    If I make a lie, the devil let me starve!
    All ladies mourn, both young and old;
    There is not one that weareth a point's worth of gold.
    There is a sort for fear for the king do pray
    That would have him dead, by the mass, I dare say.   1140
    What a king was he that hath us'd such tyranny!
    He was akin to Bishop Bonner, I think verily!
    For both their delights was to shed blood,
    But never intended to do any good.
    Cambises put a judge to death,—that was a good deed,—
    But to kill the young child was worse to proceed;
    To murder his brother and then his own wife,
    So help me God and holidam, it is pity of his life!
    Hear ye?   I will lay twenty thousand pound
    That the king himself doth die by some wound.   1150
    He hath shed so much blood that his will be shed;
    If it come so to pass, in faith, then he is sped.

Enter the KING, *without a gown, a sword thrust up into his side,*
bleeding.

King. Out! alas! what shall I do? my life is finishèd!

1136 *me* (C)] ye Q.
1141 *Bishop Bonner:* Bishop of London during Mary's reign. Many Protestants
    were executed in his diocese, and he is one of the villains of Foxe's *Acts and*
    Monuments of the English Martyrs (1563).

Wounded I am by sudden chance, my blood is minishèd.
Gog's heart, what means might I make, my life to preserve?
Is there nought to be my help? nor is there nought to serve?
Out upon the court and lords that there remain!
To help my grief in this my case will none of them take pain?
Who but I in such a wise his death's wound could have got?
As I on horseback up did leap, my sword from scabbard
    shot,   1159
And ran me thus into the side, as you right well may see:
A marvell's chance unfortunate that in this wise should be!
I feel myself a-dying now, of life bereft am I,
And death hath caught me with his dart, for want of blood
    I spy.
Thus gasping here on ground I lie; for nothing I do care;
A just reward for my misdeeds my death doth plain declare.
                    Here let him quake and stir.

Amb. How now, noble king? pluck up your heart!
    What, will you die, and from us depart?
    Speak to me and you be alive!
    He cannot speak, but behold, how with death he doth
        strive.   1170
    Alas, good king! alas, he is gone!
    The devil take me if for him I make any moan.
    I did prognosticate of his end, by the mass;
    Like as I did say, so is it come to pass!
    I will be gone; if I should be found here,
    That I should kill him it would appear.
    For fear with his death they do me charge,
    Farewell, my masters, I will go take barge;
    I mean to be packing; now is the tide;
    Farewell, my masters, I will no longer abide!   1180
                              Exit Ambidexter.

            Enter three LORDS.

First Lord. Behold, my lords, it is even so as he to us did tell:
    His grace is dead, upon the ground, by dint of sword most fell.
Second Lord. As he in saddle would have leap'd, his sword from
        sheath did go,
    Goring him up into the side,—his life was ended so.

Third Lord. His blood so fast did issue out that nought could
    him prolong;

    Yet, before he yielded up the ghost, his heart was very
    strong.

First Lord. A just reward for his misdeeds the gods above hath
    wrought,

    For certainly the life he led was to be counted nought.

Second Lord. Yet a princely burial he shall have, according his
    estate;

    And more of him here at this time we have not to dilate.

Third Lord. My lords, let us take him up, to carry him away.   1191

Both. Content we are with one accord to do as you do say.

                                          Exeunt all.

EPILOGUS

[*Enter* EPILOGUE.]

Right gentle audience, here have you perus'd
The tragical history of this wicked king.
According to our duty, we have not refus'd,
But to our best intent express'd everything.
We trust none is offended for this our doing;
    Our author craves likewise, if he have squar'd amiss,
    By gentle admonition to know where the fault is.

His good will shall not be neglected to amend the same.
Praying all to bear, therefore, with his simple deed
Until the time serve a better he may frame,   10
Thus yielding you thanks, to end we decreed
That you so gently have suffer'd us to proceed,
    In such patient wise as to hear and see,
    We can but thank ye therefore, we can do no more, we!

1187 *the gods* (C)] the God Q. I emend in spite of the singular verb, for plural
    noun with singular verb is common 16th century usage. At 386, 679 and
    911 Q incorrectly has "the God" for "the gods". When the God of the
    Christian religion is meant (66, 340, 364, 385, 625, 661, 931, 1119, 1125, as
    well as in all the blasphemous oaths) the article is never used. Both the
    words "God" and "Gods" are normally given a capital initial in both Qq
    (except 76 in Q1).

As duty binds us, for our noble Queen let us pray,
And for her honourable council, the truth that they may use,
To practise justice and defend her grace each day;
To maintain God's word they may not refuse,
To correct all those that would her grace and grace's laws abuse;
    Beseeching God over us she may reign long,   21
    To be guided by truth and defended from wrong.

    Amen, quoth Thomas Preston.

The Spanish Tragedy

[Dramatis Personae

Ghost of Andrea, a Spanish nobleman, } *Chorus.*
Revenge.

KING OF SPAIN.
CYPRIAN DUKE OF CASTILE, *his brother.*
LORENZO, *the Duke's son.*
BEL-IMPERIA, *Lorenzo's sister.*

VICEROY OF PORTUGAL.
BALTHAZAR, *his son.*
DON PEDRO, *the Viceroy's brother.*

HIERONIMO, *Marshal of Spain.*
ISABELLA, *his wife.*
HORATIO, *their son.*

Spanish General.
Deputy.
DON BAZULTO, *an old man.*
Three Citizens.

Portuguese Ambassador.
ALEXANDRO, } *Portuguese Noblemen.*
VILLUPPO,
Two Portuguese.

PEDRINGANO, *Bel-imperia's servant.*
CHRISTOPHIL, *Bel-imperia's custodian.*
Lorenzo's Page.
SERBERINE, *Balthazar's servant.*
Isabella's Maid.
Messenger.
Hangman.
Three Kings and three Knights in the first Dumb-show.
Hymen and two torch-bearers in the second.

BAZARDO, *a Painter.*
PEDRO and JAQUES, *Hieronimo's servants.*

Army. Noblemen. Halberdiers. Officers. Three Watchmen. Drummer.
   Trumpeters. Servants, etc.]

The Spanish Tragedy

ACT I

[SCENE I]

Enter the Ghost of Andrea, *and with him* Revenge.

Ghost. When this eternal substance of my soul
    Did live imprison'd in my wanton flesh,
    Each in their function serving other's need,
    I was a courtier in the Spanish court.
    My name was Don Andrea; my descent,
    Though not ignoble, yet inferior far
    To gracious fortunes of my tender youth:
    For there in prime and pride of all my years,
    By duteous service and deserving love,
    In secret I possess'd a worthy dame,   10
    Which hight sweet Bel-imperia by name.
    But, in the harvest of my summer joys,
    Death's winter nipp'd the blossoms of my bliss,
    Forcing divorce betwixt my love and me.
    For in the late conflict with Portingale
    My valour drew me into danger's mouth,
    Till life to death made passage through my wounds.
    When I was slain, my soul descended straight
    To pass the flowing stream of Acheron;
    But churlish Charon, only boatman there,   20
    Said that, my rites of burial not perform'd,
    I might not sit amongst his passengers.
    Ere Sol had slept three nights in Thetis' lap,
    And slak'd his smoking chariot in her flood,
    By Don Horatio, our knight marshal's son,
    My funerals and obsequies were done.
    Then was the ferryman of hell content
    To pass me over to the slimy strand,
    That leads to fell Avernus' ugly waves.

There, pleasing Cerberus with honey'd speech,   30
I pass'd the perils of the foremost porch.
Not far from hence, amidst ten thousand souls,
Sat Minos, Aeacus, and Rhadamanth;
To whom no sooner 'gan I make approach,
To crave a passport for my wand'ring ghost,
But Minos, in graven leaves of lottery,
Drew forth the manner of my life and death.
" This knight," quoth he, " both liv'd and died in love,
And for his love tried fortune of the wars,
And by war's fortune lost both love and life."   40
" Why then," said Aeacus, " convey him hence,
To walk with lovers in our fields of love,
And spend the course of everlasting time
Under green myrtle-trees and cypress shades."
" No, no," said Rhadamanth, " it were not well
With loving souls to place a martialist:
He died in war, and must to martial fields,
Where wounded Hector lives in lasting pain,
And Achilles' Myrmidons do scour the plain."
Then Minos, mildest censor of the three,   50
Made this device to end the difference:
" Send him," quoth he, " to our infernal king,
To doom him as best seems his majesty."
To this effect my passport straight was drawn.
In keeping on my way to Pluto's court,
Through dreadful shades of ever-glooming night,
I saw more sights than thousand tongues can tell,
Or pens can write, or mortal hearts can think.
Three ways there were: that on the right-hand side
Was ready way unto the 'foresaid fields,   60
Where lovers live and bloody martialists,
But either sort contain'd within his bounds.
The left-hand path, declining fearfully,
Was ready downfall to the deepest hell,
Where bloody Furies shakes their whips of steel,
And poor Ixion turns an endless wheel;
Where usurers are chok'd with melting gold,
And wantons are embrac'd with ugly snakes,

And murderers groan with never-killing wounds,
And perjur'd wights scalded in boiling lead,   70
And all foul sins with torments overwhelm'd.
'Twixt these two ways I trod the middle path,
Which brought me to the fair Elysian green,
In midst whereof there stands a stately tower,
The walls of brass, the gates of adamant.
Here finding Pluto with his Proserpine,
I show'd my passport, humbled on my knee;
Whereat fair Proserpine began to smile,
And begg'd that only she might give my doom:
Pluto was pleas'd, and seal'd it with a kiss.   80
Forthwith, Revenge, she rounded thee in th' ear,
And bade thee lead me through the gates of horn,
Where dreams have passage in the silent night.
No sooner had she spoke, but we were here—
I wot not how—in twinkling of an eye.
Revenge. Then know, Andrea, that thou art arriv'd
Where thou shalt see the author of thy death,
Don Balthazar, the prince of Portingale,
Depriv'd of life by Bel-imperia.
Here sit we down to see the mystery,   90
And serve for Chorus in this tragedy.

[SCENE II]

Enter SPANISH KING, General, CASTILE, *and* HIERONIMO.

King. Now say, lord General, how fares our camp?
Gen. All well, my sovereign liege, except some few
That are deceas'd by fortune of the war.
King. But what portends thy cheerful countenance,
And posting to our presence thus in haste?
Speak, man, hath fortune given us victory?
Gen. Victory, my liege, and that with little loss.

90 *Here sit we down:* probably on stools on the platform rather than above. The
upper stage will be required in two highly dramatic scenes (II. ii and IV. iv)
as well as in the short III. ix. It is usual for plays to begin on the platform,
especially when the opening speech is so long and important.

King. Our Portingales will pay us tribute then?

Gen. Tribute and wonted homage therewithal.

King. Then bless'd be heaven and guider of the heavens,   10
    From whose fair influence such justice flows.

Cast. O multum dilecte Deo, tibi militat aether,
    Et conjuratae curvato poplite gentes
    Succumbunt; recti soror est victoria juris.

King. Thanks to my loving brother of Castile.
    But, General, unfold in brief discourse
    Your form of battle and your war's success,
    That, adding all the pleasure of thy news
    Unto the height of former happiness,
    With deeper wage and greater dignity   20
    We may reward thy blissful chivalry.

Gen. Where Spain and Portingale do jointly knit
    Their frontiers, leaning on each other's bound,
    There met our armies in their proud array:
    Both furnish'd well, both full of hope and fear,
    Both menacing alike with daring shows,
    Both vaunting sundry colours of device,
    Both cheerly sounding trumpets, drums, and fifes,
    Both raising dreadful clamours to the sky,
    That valleys, hills, and rivers made rebound,   30
    And heaven itself was frighted with the sound.
    Our battles both were pitch'd in squadron form,
    Each corner strongly fenc'd with wings of shot;
    But ere we join'd and came to push of pike,
    I brought a squadron of our readiest shot
    From out our rearward, to begin the fight:
    They brought another wing to encounter us.
    Meanwhile our ordnance play'd on either side,
    And captains strove to have their valours tried.
    Don Pedro, their chief horsemen's colonel,   40
    Did with his cornet bravely make attempt
    To break the order of our battle ranks:

12–14 "O well-belov'd of God, th' heavens fight for thee,/And spell-bound
    peoples fall on bended knee;/For victory is sister of true right." (Metrical
    translation here and later from McIlwraith's edition of *Five Elizabethan
    Tragedies*, Oxford University Press, World's Classics Series, 1938.)

But Don Rogero, worthy man of war,
March'd forth against him with our musketeers,
And stopp'd the malice of his fell approach.
While they maintain hot skirmish to and fro,
Both battles join, and fall to handy blows,
Their violent shot resembling th' ocean's rage,
When, roaring loud, and with a swelling tide,
It beats upon the rampiers of huge rocks,   50
And gapes to swallow neighbour-bounding lands.
Now while Bellona rageth here and there,
Thick storms of bullets rain like winter's hail,
And shiver'd lances dark the troubled air.
           Pede pes et cuspide cuspis;
Arma sonant armis, vir petiturque viro.
On every side drop captains to the ground,
And soldiers, some ill-maim'd, some slain outright:
Here falls a body sunder'd from his head,
There legs and arms lie bleeding on the grass,   60
Mingled with weapons and unbowell'd steeds,
That scattering overspread the purple plain.
In all this turmoil, three long hours and more,
The victory to neither part inclin'd,
Till Don Andrea, with his brave lanciers,
In their main battle made so great a breach,
That, half dismay'd, the multitude retir'd:
But Balthazar, the Portingales' young prince,
Brought rescue, and encourag'd them to stay.
Here-hence the fight was eagerly renew'd,   70
And in that conflict was Andrea slain:
Brave man at arms, but weak to Balthazar.
Yet while the prince, insulting over him,
Breath'd out proud vaunts, sounding to our reproach,
Friendship and hardy valour, join'd in one,
Prick'd forth Horatio, our knight marshal's son,
To challenge forth that prince in single fight.
Not long between these twain the fight endur'd,
But straight the prince was beaten from his horse,

55–6 "Foot against foot, lance against lance is thrust,/Arms clash on arms, man
is attacked by man." (McIlwraith.)

And forc'd to yield him prisoner to his foe.   80
When he was taken, all the rest they fled,
And our carbines pursu'd them to the death,
Till, Phœbus waning to the western deep,
Our trumpeters were charg'd to sound retreat.
King. Thanks, good lord General, for these good news;
And for some argument of more to come,
Take this and wear it for thy sovereign's sake.
                              Give him his chain.
But tell me now, hast thou confirm'd a peace?
Gen. No peace, my liege, but peace conditional,
That if with homage tribute be well paid,   90
The fury of your forces will be stay'd:
And to this peace their viceroy hath subscrib'd,
                              Give the King a paper.
And made a solemn vow that, during life,
His tribute shall be truly paid to Spain.
King. These words, these deeds, become thy person well.
But now, Knight Marshal, frolic with thy king,
For 'tis thy son that wins this battle's prize.
Hier. Long may he live to serve my sovereign liege,
And soon decay unless he serve my liege.
King. Nor thou, nor he, shall die without reward.   100
                              A tucket afar off.
What means the warning of this trumpet's sound?
Gen. This tells me that your grace's men of war,
Such as war's fortune hath reserv'd from death,
Come marching on towards your royal seat,
To show themselves before your majesty,
For so I gave in charge at my depart.
Whereby by demonstration shall appear,
That all, except three hundred or few more,
Are safe return'd, and by their foes enrich'd.

The Army enters; BALTHAZAR *between* LORENZO *and* HORATIO,
captive.

King. A gladsome sight!   I long to see them here.   110
                              They enter and pass by.
Was that the warlike prince of Portingale,

That by our nephew was in triumph led?
Gen. It was, my liege, the prince of Portingale.
King. But what was he that on the other side
      Held him by th' arm, as partner of the prize?
Hier. That was my son, my gracious sovereign;
      Of whom though from his tender infancy
      My loving thoughts did never hope but well,
      He never pleas'd his father's eyes till now,
      Nor fill'd my heart with over-cloying joys.   120
King. Go, let them march once more about these walls,
      That, staying them, we may confer and talk
      With our brave prisoner and his double guard.
      Hieronimo, it greatly pleaseth us
      That in our victory thou have a share,
      By virtue of thy worthy son's exploit.   *Enter again.*
      Bring hither the young prince of Portingale:
      The rest march on; but ere they be dismiss'd,
      We will bestow on every soldier
      Two ducats and on every leader ten,   130
      That they may know our largess welcomes them.
            Exeunt all [the Army] but Balthazar, Lorenzo, and Horatio.
      Welcome, Don Balthazar! welcome, nephew!
      And thou, Horatio, thou art welcome too.
      Young prince, although thy father's hard misdeeds,
      In keeping back the tribute that he owes,
      Deserve but evil measure at our hands,
      Yet shalt thou know that Spain is honourable.
Bal. The trespass that my father made in peace
      Is now controll'd by fortune of the wars;
      And cards once dealt, it boots not ask why so.   140
      His men are slain, a weakening to his realm,
      His colours seiz'd, a blot unto his name,
      His son distress'd, a corsive to his heart:
      These punishments may clear his late offence.
King. Ay, Balthazar, if he observe this truce,
      Our peace will grow the stronger for these wars.
      Meanwhile live thou, though not in liberty,
      Yet free from bearing any servile yoke;
      For in our hearing thy deserts were great,

And in our sight thyself art gracious.   150
Bal. And I shall study to deserve this grace.
King. But tell me—for their holding makes me doubt—
　　To which of these twain art thou prisoner?
Lor. To me, my liege.
Hor.　　　　　　　　　To me, my sovereign.
Lor. This hand first took his courser by the reins.
Hor. But first my lance did put him from his horse.
Lor. I seiz'd his weapon, and enjoy'd it first.
Hor. But first I forc'd him lay his weapons down.
King. Let go his arm, upon our privilege.

　　　　　　　　　　　　　　　　　　Let him go.

　　Say, worthy prince, to whether did'st thou yield?   160
Bal. To him in courtesy, to this perforce:
　　He spake me fair, this other gave me strokes;
　　He promis'd life, this other threaten'd death;
　　He won my love, this other conquer'd me;
　　And, truth to say, I yield myself to both.
Hier. But that I know your grace for just and wise,
　　And might seem partial in this difference,
　　Enforc'd by nature and by law of arms
　　My tongue should plead for young Horatio's right.
　　He hunted well that was a lion's death,   170
　　Not he that in a garment wore his skin;
　　So hares may pull dead lions by the beard.
King. Content thee, Marshal, thou shalt have no wrong,
　　And, for thy sake, thy son shall want no right.
　　Will both abide the censure of my doom?
Lor. I crave no better than your grace awards.
Hor. Nor I, although I sit beside my right.
King. Then, by my judgment, thus your strife shall end:
　　You both deserve and both shall have reward.
　　Nephew, thou took'st his weapon and his horse: 180
　　His weapons and his horse are thy reward.
　　Horatio, thou did'st force him first to yield:
　　His ransom therefore is thy valour's fee;
　　Appoint the sum, as you shall both agree.
　　But, nephew, thou shalt have the prince in guard,
　　For thine estate best fitteth such a guest:

      Horatio's house were small for all his train.
      Yet, in regard thy substance passeth his,
      And that just guerdon may befall desert,
      To him we yield the armour of the prince.   190
      How likes Don Balthazar of this device?
Bal. Right well, my liege, if this provison were,
      That Don Horatio bear us company,
      Whom I admire and love for chivalry.
King. Horatio, leave him not that loves thee so.—
      Now let us hence to see our soldiers paid,
      And feast our prisoner as our friendly guest.   *Exeunt.*

[SCENE III]

Enter VICEROY, ALEXANDRO, VILLUPPO [, *and* Attendants].

Vic. Is our ambassador despatch'd for Spain?
Alex. Two days, my liege, are pass'd since his depart.
Vic. And tribute-payment gone along with him?
Alex. Ay, my good lord.
Vic. Then rest we here awhile in our unrest,
      And feed our sorrows with some inward sighs,
      For deepest cares break never into tears.
      But wherefore sit I in a regal throne?
      This better fits a wretch's endless moan.

                              Falls to the ground.

      Yet this is higher than my fortunes reach,   10
      And therefore better than my state deserves.
      Ay, ay, this earth, image of melancholy,
      Seeks him whom fates adjudge to misery:
      Here let me lie; now am I at the lowest.
          Qui jacet in terra, non habet unde cadat.
          In me consumpsit vires fortuna nocendo:
          Nil superest ut jam possit obesse magis.
      Yes, Fortune may bereave me of my crown:
      Here, take it now;—let Fortune do her worst,
      She will not rob me of this sable weed: 20
      O no, she envies none but pleasant things.

15–17 "He who is prostrate hath no where to fall./Fortune hath spent her force
for ill on me:/ Greater disaster cannot be in store."

Such is the folly of despiteful chance!
Fortune is blind, and sees not my deserts;
So is she deaf, and hears not my laments;
And could she hear, yet is she wilful mad,
And therefore will not pity my distress.
Suppose that she could pity me, what then?
What help can be expected at her hands
Whose foot is standing on a rolling stone,
And mind more mutable than fickle winds?   30
Why wail I then, where's hope of no redress?
O yes, complaining makes my grief seem less.
My late ambition hath distain'd my faith,
My breach of faith occasion'd bloody wars,
Those bloody wars have spent my treasure,
And with my treasure my people's blood,
And with their blood, my joy and best belov'd,
My best belov'd, my sweet and only son.
O, wherefore went I not to war myself?
The cause was mine; I might have died for both: 40
My years were mellow, his but young and green;
My death were natural, but his was forc'd.
Alex. No doubt, my liege, but still the prince survives.
Vic. Survives! ay, where?
Alex. In Spain, a prisoner by mischance of war.
Vic. Then they have slain him for his father's fault.
Alex. That were a breach to common law of arms.
Vic. They reck no laws that meditate revenge.
Alex. His ransom's worth will stay from foul revenge.
Vic. No, if he liv'd, the news would soon be here.   50
Alex. Nay, evil news fly faster still than good.
Vic. Tell me no more of news, for he is dead.
Vil. My sovereign, pardon the author of ill news,
     And I'll bewray the fortune of thy son.
Vic. Speak on, I'll guerdon thee whate'er it be:
     Mine ear is ready to receive ill news,
     My heart grown hard 'gainst mischief's battery.
     Stand up, I say, and tell thy tale at large.
Vil. Then hear that truth which these mine eyes have seen:
     When both the armies were in battle join'd,   60

Don Balthazar, amidst the thickest troops,
To win renown did wondrous feats of arms:
Amongst the rest I saw him hand to hand
In single fight with their lord general;
Till Alexandro, that here counterfeits
Under the colour of a duteous friend,
Discharg'd his pistol at the prince's back,
As though he would have slain their general:
But therewithal Don Balthazar fell down;
And when he fell, then we began to fly: 70
But had he liv'd, the day had sure been ours.
Alex. O wicked forgery!   O traitorous miscreant!
Vic. Hold thou thy peace!   But now, Villuppo, say,
   Where then became the carcase of my son?
Vil. I saw them drag it to the Spanish tents.
Vic. Ay, ay, my nightly dreams have told me this.—
   Thou false, unkind, unthankful, traitorous beast,
   Wherein had Balthazar offended thee
   That thou shouldst thus betray him to our foes?
   Was't Spanish gold that bleared so thine eyes   80
   That thou couldst see no part of our deserts?
   Perchance, because thou art Terceira's lord,
   Thou hadst some hope to wear this diadem,
   If first my son and then myself were slain;
   But thy ambitious thought shall break thy neck.
   Ay, this was it that made thee spill his blood:
                    Take the crown and put it on again.
   But I'll now wear it till thy blood be spilt.
Alex. Vouchsafe, dread sovereign, to hear me speak.
Vic. Away with him; his sight is second hell.
   Keep him till we determine of his death: 90
                    [*Exit Alexandro, guarded.*]
   If Balthazar be dead, he shall not live.
   Villuppo, follow us for thy reward.   *Exit Viceroy.*
Vil. Thus have I with an envious, forgèd tale
   Deceiv'd the king, betray'd mine enemy,
   And hope for guerdon of my villany.   *Exit.*

93–5 Villuppo's name suggests his character: Italian *inviluppo*, entanglement;
   avviluppare, to grasp, enfold.

[SCENE IV]

Enter HORATIO *and* BEL-IMPERIA

Bel. Signior Horatio, this is the place and hour
    Wherein I must entreat thee to relate
    The circumstance of Don Andrea's death,
    Who, living, was my garland's sweetest flower,
    And in his death hath buried my delights.
Hor. For love of him and service to yourself,
    I nill refuse this heavy doleful charge;
    Yet tears and sighs, I fear, will hinder me.
    When both our armies were enjoin'd in fight,
    Your worthy chevalier amidst the thick'st,   10
    For glorious cause still aiming at the fairest,
    Was at the last by young Don Balthazar
    Encounter'd hand to hand: their fight was long,
    Their hearts were great, their clamours menacing,
    Their strength alike, their strokes both dangerous.
    But wrathful Nemesis, that wicked power,
    Envying at Andrea's praise and worth,
    Cut short his life, to end his praise and worth.
    She, she herself, disguis'd in armour's mask—
    As Pallas was before proud Pergamus—   20
    Brought in a fresh supply of halberdiers,
    Which paunch'd his horse, and ding'd him to the ground.
    Then young Don Balthazar with ruthless rage,
    Taking advantage of his foe's distress,
    Did finish what his halberdiers begun,
    And left not, till Andrea's life was done.
    Then, though too late, incens'd with just remorse,
    I with my band set forth against the prince,
    And brought him prisoner from his halberdiers.
Bel. Would thou hadst slain him that so slew my love!   30
    But then was Don Andrea's carcase lost?
Hor. No, that was it for which I chiefly strove,

11 *For glorious cause . . . fairest:* "Attempting worthiest deeds for his glorious
cause (Bel-imperia's favour)."
20 *Pergamus:* Troy (*Aeneid* II. 615–16).

Nor stepp'd I back till I recover'd him:
I took him up, and wound him in mine arms,
And wielding him unto my private tent,
There laid him down, and dew'd him with my tears,
And sigh'd and sorrow'd as became a friend.
But neither friendly sorrow, sighs, nor tears
Could win pale death from his usurpèd right.
Yet this I did, and less I could not do: 40
I saw him honour'd with due funeral.
This scarf I pluck'd from off his lifeless arm,
And wear it in remembrance of my friend.

Bel. I know the scarf: would he had kept it still;
For had he liv'd, he would have kept it still,
And worn it for his Bel-imperia's sake:
For 'twas my favour at his last depart.
But now wear thou it both for him and me;
For after him thou hast deserv'd it best.
But for thy kindness in his life and death,   50
Be sure, while Bel-imperia's life endures,
She will be Don Horatio's thankful friend.

Hor. And, madam, Don Horatio will not slack
Humbly to serve fair Bel-imperia.
But now, if your good liking stand thereto,
I'll crave your pardon to go seek the prince;
For so the duke, your father, gave me charge.   *Exit.*

Bel. Ay, go, Horatio, leave me here alone;
For solitude best fits my cheerless mood.
Yet what avails to wail Andrea's death,   60
From whence Horatio proves my second love?
Had he not lov'd Andrea as he did,
He could not sit in Bel-imperia's thoughts.
But how can love find harbour in my breast,
Till I revenge the death of my belov'd?
Yes, second love shall further my revenge.
I'll love Horatio, my Andrea's friend,
The more to spite the prince that wrought his end;
And where Don Balthazar, that slew my love,
Himself now pleads for favour at my hands,   70
He shall, in rigour of my just disdain,

Reap long repentance for his murderous deed.
For what was 't else but murderous cowardice,
So many to oppress one valiant knight,
Without respect of honour in the fight?
And here he comes that murder'd my delight.

Enter LORENZO *and* BALTHAZAR.

Lor. Sister, what means this melancholy walk?
Bel. That for a while I wish no company.
Lor. But here the prince is come to visit you.
Bel. That argues that he lives in liberty.   80
Bal. No, madam, but in pleasing servitude.
Bel. Your prison then, belike, is your conceit.
Bal. Ay, by conceit my freedom is enthrall'd.
Bel. Then with conceit enlarge yourself again.
Bal. What if conceit have laid my heart to gage?
Bel. Pay that you borrow'd, and recover it.
Bal. I die, if it return from whence it lies.
Bel. A heartless man, and live?   A miracle!
Bal. Ay, lady, love can work such miracles.
Lor. Tush, tush, my lord! let go these ambages,   90
     And in plain terms acquaint her with your love.
Bel. What boots complaint, when there's no remedy?
Bal. Yes, to your gracious self must I complain,
     In whose fair answer lies my remedy,
     On whose perfection all my thoughts attend,
     In whose aspect mine eyes find beauty's bower,
     In whose translucent breast my heart is lodg'd.
Bel. Alas, my lord, these are but words of course,
     And but device to drive me from this place.

                She, in going in, lets fall her glove, which
                    Horatio, coming out, takes up.

Hor. Madam, your glove.   100
Bel. Thanks, good Horatio; take it for thy pains.
Bal. Signior Horatio stoop'd in happy time.
Hor. I reap'd more grace than I deserv'd or hop'd.
Lor. My lord, be not dismay'd for what is past:

96 *In whose* (C)] On whose Q. Repeated from 95.

        You know that women oft are humorous;
        These clouds will overblow with little wind:
        Let me alone, I'll scatter them myself.
        Meanwhile, let us devise to spend the time
        In some delightful sports and revelling.
Hor. The king, my lords, is coming hither straight,   110
        To feast the Portingale ambassador;
        Things were in readiness before I came.
Bal. Then here it fits us to attend the king,
        To welcome hither our ambassador,
        And learn my father and my country's health.

Enter the Banquet, Trumpets, the KING, *and* Ambassador.

King. See, lord Ambassador, how Spain entreats
        Their prisoner Balthazar, thy viceroy's son:
        We pleasure more in kindness than in wars.
Amb. Sad is our king, and Portingale laments,
        Supposing that Don Balthazar is slain.   120
Bal. [*aside.*] So am I slain, by beauty's tyranny.——
        You see, my lord, how Balthazar is slain:
        I frolic with the Duke of Castile's son,
        Wrapp'd every hour in pleasures of the court,
        And grac'd with favour of his majesty.
King. Put off your greetings till our feast be done;
        Now come and sit with us, and taste our cheer.
                                Sit to the banquet.

        Sit down, young prince, you are our second guest;
        Brother, sit down; and, nephew, take your place.
        Signior Horatio, wait thou upon our cup;   130
        For well thou hast deservèd to be honour'd.
        Now, lordings, fall to; Spain is Portugal,
        And Portugal is Spain: we both are friends;
        Tribute is paid, and we enjoy our right.
        But where is old Hieronimo, our marshal?
        He promis'd us, in honour of our guest,
        To grace our banquet with some pompous jest.

Enter HIERONIMO *with a* Drum, *three* Knights, *each* [*hangs up*] *his*

137 [*hangs up*] (C). *See* 140, 151.

scutcheon; then he fetches three Kings, *they take their crowns and them captive.*

Hieronimo, this masque contents mine eye,
Although I sound not well the mystery.
Hier. The first arm'd knight, that hung his scutcheon up,   140
                    He takes the scutcheon and gives it to the King.
Was English Robert, Earl of Gloucester,
Who, when King Stephen bore sway in Albion,
Arriv'd with five and twenty thousand men
In Portingale and by success of war
Enforc'd the king, then but a Saracen,
To bear the yoke of the English monarchy.
King. My lord of Portingale, by this you see
That which may comfort both your king and you,
And make your late discomfort seem the less.
But say, Hieronimo, what was the next?   150
Hier. The second knight, that hung his scutcheon up,
                            He doth as he did before.
Was Edmund, Earl of Kent in Albion,
When English Richard wore the diadem.
He came likewise, and razèd Lisbon walls,
And took the King of Portingale in fight;
For which and other such-like service done
He after was created Duke of York.
King. This is another special argument
That Portingale may deign to bear our yoke,
When it by little England hath been yok'd.   160
But now, Hieronimo, what was the last?
Hier. The third and last, not least in our account,
                            Doing as before.
Was, as the rest, a valiant Englishman,
Brave John of Gaunt, the Duke of Lancaster,
As by his scutcheon plainly may appear.
He with a puissant army came to Spain,
And took our King of Castile prisoner.

161 *was* (C)] were Q. Compare 150, and both replies.

Amb. This is an argument for our viceroy
     That Spain may not insult for her success,
     Since English warriors likewise conquer'd Spain,   170
     And made them bow their knees to Albion.
King. Hieronimo, I drink to thee for this device,
     Which hath pleas'd both the ambassador and me:
     Pledge me, Hieronimo, if thou love thy king.

                               Takes the cup of Horatio.

     My lord, I fear we sit but over-long,
     Unless our dainties were more delicate;
     But welcome are you to the best we have.
     Now let us in, that you may be despatch'd:
     I think our council is already set.   *Exeunt omnes.*

[SCENE V]

Ghost of Andrea, Revenge.

Andrea. Come we for this from depth of underground,
     To see him feast that gave me my death's wound?
     These pleasant sights are sorrow to my soul:
     Nothing but league, and love, and banqueting?
Revenge. Be still, Andrea; ere we go from hence,
     I'll turn their friendship into fell despite,
     Their love to mortal hate, their day to night,
     Their hope into despair, their peace to war,
     Their joys to pain, their bliss to misery.

174 *thy* (J. Schick, ed. *The Spanish Tragedy*, 1898)] the Q. Compare I. ii. 96.

ACT II

[SCENE I]

Enter LORENZO *and* BALTHAZAR.

Lor. My lord, though Bel-imperia seem thus coy,
Let reason hold you in your wonted joy:
In time the savage bull sustains the yoke,
In time all haggard hawks will stoop to lure,
In time small wedges cleave the hardest oak,
In time the flint is pierc'd with softest shower,
And she in time will fall from her disdain,
And rue the suff'rance of your friendly pain.

Bal. No, she is wilder, and more hard withal,
Than beast, or bird, or tree, or stony wall.   10
But wherefore blot I Bel-imperia's name?
It is my fault, not she, that merits blame.
My feature is not to content her sight,
My words are rude, and work her no delight.
The lines I send her are but harsh and ill,
Such as do drop from Pan and Marsyas' quill.
My presents are not of sufficient cost,
And being worthless, all my labour's lost.
Yet might she love me for my valiancy:
Ay, but that's slander'd by captivity.   20
Yet might she love me to content her sire:
Ay, but her reason masters his desire.
Yet might she love me as her brother's friend:
Ay, but her hopes aim at some other end.
Yet might she love me to uprear her state:
Ay, but perhaps she hopes some nobler mate.
Yet might she love me as her beauty's thrall:

3–6, 9–10 Adapted from a sonnet in Watson's *Hecatompathia* (1582).

Ay, but I fear she cannot love at all.

Lor. My lord, for my sake leave these ecstasies,
   And doubt not but we'll find some remedy.   30
   Some cause there is that lets you not be lov'd;
   First that must needs be known, and then remov'd.
   What if my sister love some other knight?

Bal. My summer's day will turn to winter's night.

Lor. I have already found a stratagem,
   To sound the bottom of this doubtful theme.
   My lord, for once you shall be rul'd by me;
   Hinder me not, whate'er you hear or see.
   By force or fair means will I cast about
   To find the truth of all this question out.   40
   Ho, Pedringano!

Ped. Signior!

Lor. Vien qui presto.

Enter PEDRINGANO.

Ped. Hath your lordship any service to command me?

Lor. Ay, Pedringano, service of import;
   And, not to spend the time in trifling words,
   Thus stands the case: it is not long, thou know'st,
   Since I did shield thee from my father's wrath,
   For thy conveyance in Andrea's love,
   For which thou wert adjudg'd to punishment: 50
   I stood betwixt thee and thy punishment,
   And since, thou know'st how I have favour'd thee.
   Now to these favours will I add reward,
   Not with fair words, but store of golden coin,
   And lands and living join'd with dignities,
   If thou but satisfy my just demand:
   Tell truth, and have me for thy lasting friend.

Ped. Whate'er it be your lordship shall demand,
   My bounden duty bids me tell the truth,
   If case it lie in me to tell the truth.   60

Lor. Then, Pedringano, this is my demand:
   Whom loves my sister Bel-imperia?

43 *Vien qui presto:* Come here quickly.

    For she reposeth all her trust in thee.
    Speak, man, and gain both friendship and reward:
    I mean, whom loves she in Andrea's place?

Ped. Alas, my lord, since Don Andrea's death
    I have no credit with her as before;
    And therefore know not if she love or no.

Lor. Nay, if thou dally, then I am thy foe,   [*Draw his sword.*]
    And fear shall force what friendship cannot win: 70
    Thy death shall bury what thy life conceals;
    Thou diest for more esteeming her than me.

Ped. O stay, my lord!

Lor. Yet speak the truth, and I will guerdon thee,
    And shield thee from whatever can ensue,
    And will conceal whate'er proceeds from thee.
    But if thou dally once again, thou diest.

Ped. If madam Bel-imperia be in love——

Lor. What, villain! ifs and ands?   [*Offer to kill him.*]

Ped. O stay, my lord, she loves Horatio.   80

                       Balthazar starts back.

Lor. What, Don Horatio, our knight marshal's son?

Ped. Even him, my lord.

Lor. Now say but how thou know'st he is her love,
    And thou shalt find me kind and liberal:
    Stand up, I say, and fearless tell the truth.

Ped. She sent him letters, which myself perus'd,
    Full-fraught with lines and arguments of love,
    Preferring him before Prince Balthazar.

Lor. Swear on this cross that what thou say'st is true,
    And that thou wilt conceal what thou hast told.   90

Ped. I swear to both, by him that made us all.

Lor. In hope thine oath is true, here's thy reward:
    But if I prove thee perjur'd and unjust,
    This very sword, whereon thou took'st thine oath,
    Shall be the worker of thy tragedy.

Ped. What I have said is true, and shall, for me,
    Be still conceal'd from Bel-imperia.

69, 79 *s.d.* Q4.
83 *thou know'st* (R. Dodsley, *Old Plays*, 1744.)] knowst thou Q (with interrogation mark at end of line).

     Besides, your honour's liberality
     Deserves my duteous service, even till death.
Lor. Let this be all that thou shalt do for me: 100
     Be watchful when and where these lovers meet,
     And give me notice in some secret sort.
Ped. I will, my lord.
Lor. Then shalt thou find that I am liberal.
     Thou know'st that I can more advance thy state
     Than she; be therefore wise, and fail me not.
     Go and attend her, as thy custom is,
     Lest absence make her think thou dost amiss.

                          Exit Pedringano.

     Why so: *tam armis quam ingenio:*
     Where words prevail not, violence prevails;   110
     But gold doth more than either of them both.
     How likes Prince Balthazar this stratagem?
Bal. Both well and ill; it makes me glad and sad:
     Glad, that I know the hinderer of my love;
     Sad, that I fear she hates me whom I love.
     Glad, that I know on whom to be reveng'd;
     Sad, that she'll fly me, if I take revenge.
     Yet must I take revenge, or die myself,
     For love resisted grows impatient.
     I think Horatio be my destin'd plague: 120
     First in his hand he brandishèd a sword,
     And with that sword he fiercely wagèd war,
     And in that war he gave me dangerous wounds,
     And by those wounds he forcèd me to yield,
     And by my yielding I became his slave.
     Now in his mouth he carries pleasing words,
     Which pleasing words do harbour sweet conceits,
     Which sweet conceits are lim'd with sly deceits,
     Which sly deceits smooth Bel-imperia's ears,
     And through her ears dive down into her heart,   130
     And in her heart set him where I should stand.
     Thus hath he ta'en my body by his force,
     And now by sleight would captivate my soul:

107 *tam armis quam ingenio:* by force as well as cunning.

But in his fall I'll tempt the destinies,
And either lose my life, or win my love.
Lor. Let's go, my lord; your staying stays revenge.
Do you but follow me, and gain your love:
Her favour must be won by his remove.   *Exeunt.*

[SCENE II]

Enter HORATIO *and* BEL-IMPERIA.

Hor. Now, madam, since by favour of your love
Our hidden smoke is turn'd to open flame,
And that with looks and words we feed our thoughts
(Two chief contents, where more cannot be had),
Thus in the midst of love's fair blandishments,
Why show you sign of inward languishments?
> *Pedringano showeth all to the Prince and*
> *Lorenzo, placing them in secret* [above].
Bel. My heart, sweet friend, is like a ship at sea:
She wisheth port, where, riding all at ease,
She may repair what stormy times have worn,
And leaning on the shore, may sing with joy   10
That pleasure follows pain, and bliss annoy.
Possession of thy love is th' only port
Wherein my heart, with fears and hopes long toss'd,
Each hour doth wish and long to make resort,
There to repair the joys that it hath lost,
And, sitting safe, to sing in Cupid's quire
That sweetest bliss is crown of love's desire.
> *Balthazar above.*
Bal. O sleep, mine eyes, see not my love profan'd;
Be deaf, my ears, hear not my discontent;
Die, heart: another joys what thou deserv'st.   20
Lor. Watch still, mine eyes, to see this love disjoin'd;
Hear still, mine ears, to hear them both lament;
Live, heart, to joy at fond Horatio's fall.

17 *s.d.* Supplementary, not contradictory, to l. 6 *s.d.*

Bel. Why stands Horatio speechless all this while?
Hor. The less I speak, the more I meditate.
Bel. But whereon dost thou chiefly meditate?
Hor. On dangers past, and pleasures to ensue.
Bal. On pleasures past, and dangers to ensue.
Bel. What dangers and what pleasures dost thou mean?
Hor. Dangers of war, and pleasures of our love.   30
Lor. Dangers of death, but pleasures none at all.
Bel. Let dangers go, thy war shall be with me:
    But such a war as breaks no bond of peace.
    Speak thou fair words, I'll cross them with fair words;
    Send thou sweet looks, I'll meet them with sweet looks;
    Write loving lines, I'll answer loving lines;
    Give me a kiss, I'll countercheck thy kiss:
    Be this our warring peace, or peaceful war.
Hor. But, gracious madam, then appoint the field,
    Where trial of this war shall first be made.   40
Bal. Ambitious villain, how his boldness grows!
Bel. Then be thy father's pleasant bower the field,
    Where first we vow'd a mutual amity;
    The court were dangerous, that place is safe.
    Our hour shall be when Vesper 'gins to rise,
    That summons home distressful travellers:
    There none shall hear us but the harmless birds;
    Happily the gentle nightingale
    Shall carol us asleep ere we be ware,
    And, singing with the prickle at her breast,   50
    Tell our delight and mirthful dalliance.
    Till then each hour will seem a year and more.
Hor. But, honey sweet, and honourable love,
    Return we now into your father's sight:
    Dangerous suspicion waits on our delight.
Lor. Ay, danger mixed with jealous despite
    Shall send thy soul into eternal night.   *Exeunt.*

[SCENE III]

Enter KING OF SPAIN, Portingale Ambassador,
DON CYPRIAN, *etc.*

King. Brother of Castile, to the prince's love
     What says your daughter Bel-imperia?
Cyp. Although she coy it, as becomes her kind,
     And yet dissemble that she loves the prince,
     I doubt not, I, but she will stoop in time.
     And were she froward, which she will not be,
     Yet herein shall she follow my advice,
     Which is to love him or forgo my love.
King. Then, lord Ambassador of Portingale,
     Advise thy king to make this marriage up,   10
     For strengthening of our late-confirmèd league;
     I know no better means to make us friends.
     Her dowry shall be large and liberal:
     Besides that she is daughter and half-heir
     Unto our brother here, Don Cyprian,
     And shall enjoy the moiety of his land,
     I'll grace her marriage with an uncle's gift,
     And this it is in case the match go forward,
     The tribute which you pay shall be releas'd,
     And if by Balthazar she have a son,   20
     He shall enjoy the kingdom after us.
Amb. I'll make the motion to my sovereign liege,
     And work it, if my counsel may prevail.
King. Do so, my lord, and if he give consent,
     I hope his presence here will honour us,
     In celebration of the nuptial day;
     And let himself determine of the time.
Amb. Will't please your grace command me ought beside?
King. Commend me to the king, and so farewell.
     But where's Prince Balthazar to take his leave?   30
Amb. That is perform'd already, my good lord.
King. Amongst the rest of what you have in charge,
     The prince's ransom must not be forgot:
     That's none of mine, but his that took him prisoner;

And well his forwardness deserves reward:
It was Horatio, our knight marshal's son.
Amb. Between us there's a price already pitch'd,
And shall be sent with all convenient speed.
King. Then once again farewell, my lord.
Amb. Farewell, my lord of Castile, and the rest. *Exit.*
King. Now, brother, you must take some little pains 41
To win fair Bel-imperia from her will:
Young virgins must be rulèd by their friends.
The prince is amiable, and loves her well;
If she neglect him and forgo his love,
She both will wrong her own estate and ours.
Therefore, whiles I do entertain the prince
With greatest pleasure that our court affords,
Endeavour you to win your daughter's thought:
If she give back, all this will come to naught. *Exeunt.*

[SCENE IV]

Enter HORATIO, BEL-IMPERIA, *and* PEDRINGANO.

Hor. Now that the night begins with sable wings
To overcloud the brightness of the sun,
And that in darkness pleasures may be done,
Come, Bel-imperia, let us to the bower,
And there in safety pass a pleasant hour.
Bel. I follow thee, my love, and will not back,
Although my fainting heart controls my soul.
Hor. Why, make you doubt of Pedringano's faith?
Bel. No, he is as trusty as my second self.—
Go, Pedringano, watch without the gate, 10
And let us know if any make approach.
Ped. [*aside.*] Instead of watching, I'll deserve more gold
By fetching Don Lorenzo to this match. *Exit Pedringano.*
Hor. What means my love?
Bel. I know not what myself;
And yet my heart foretells me some mischance.
Hor. Sweet, say not so; fair fortune is our friend,

And heavens have shut up day to pleasure us.
The stars, thou see'st, hold back their twinkling shine,
And Luna hides herself to pleasure us.
Bel. Thou hast prevail'd; I'll conquer my misdoubt,   20
And in thy love and counsel drown my fear.
I fear no more; love now is all my thoughts.
Why sit we not? for pleasure asketh ease.
Hor. The more thou sitt'st within these leafy bowers,
The more will Flora deck it with her flowers.
Bel. Ay, but if Flora spy Horatio here,
Her jealous eye will think I sit too near.
Hor. Hark, madam, how the birds record by night,
For joy that Bel-imperia sits in sight.
Bel. No, Cupid counterfeits the nightingale,   30
To frame sweet music to Horatio's tale.
Hor. If Cupid sing, then Venus is not far:
Ay, thou art Venus, or some fairer star.
Bel. If I be Venus, thou must needs be Mars;
And where Mars reigneth, there must needs be wars.
Hor. Then thus begin our wars: put forth thy hand,
That it may combat with my ruder hand.
Bel. Set forth thy foot to try the push of mine.
Hor. But first my looks shall combat against thine.
Bel. Then ward thyself: I dart this kiss at thee.   40
Hor. Thus I retort the dart thou threw'st at me.
Bel. Nay then, to gain the glory of the field,
My twining arms shall yoke and make thee yield.
Hor. Nay then, my arms are large and strong withal:
Thus elms by vines are compass'd, till they fall.
Bel. O, let me go; for in my troubled eyes
Now may'st thou read that life in passion dies.
Hor. O, stay a while, and I will die with thee;
So shalt thou yield, and yet have conquer'd me.
Bel. Who's there?   Pedringano! we are betray'd!   50

50 *Who's there? Pedringano!* (Schick)] *Whose there Pedringano?* Q. Editors
agree that this is not a question addressed to Pedringano. Whether Bel-
imperia calls out for him before the murderers enter, or exclaims in dismay
at seeing him in their company, is not clear. The next *s.d.* suggests that all
of them, not just Pedringano, are "disguised", and in the title-page woodcut of 1615 (*see* note to 53 *s.d.*) Lorenzo has a black mask over his whole

Enter LORENZO, BALTHAZAR, SERBERINE, PEDRINGANO,
disguised.

Lor. My lord, away with her, take her aside.—
      O, sir, forbear: your valour is already tried.
      Quickly despatch, my masters.

                              They hang him in the arbour.

Hor. What, will you murder me?
Lor. Ay, thus, and thus: these are the fruits of love.

                                    They stab him.

Bel. O, save his life, and let me die for him!
      O, save him, brother, save him, Balthazar:
      I lov'd Horatio, but he lov'd not me.
Bal. But Balthazar loves Bel-imperia.
Lor. Although his life were still ambitious-proud,   60
      Yet is he at the highest now he is dead.
Bel. Murder! murder! Help, Hieronimo, help!
Lor. Come, stop her mouth, away with her.

                        Exeunt [leaving Horatio's body].

Enter HIERONIMO *in his shirt, etc.*

Hier. What outcries pluck me from my naked bed,
      And chill my throbbing heart with trembling fear,
      Which never danger yet could daunt before?
      Who calls Hieronimo? speak, here I am.
      I did not slumber, therefore 'twas no dream.
      No, no, it was some woman cried for help,
      And there within this garden did she cry,   70
      And in this garden must I rescue her.—

---

      face (he is identifiable by the words "Stop her mouth", 63, emerging from
      his lips in a scroll). Bel-imperia certainly recognizes Lorenzo and Bal-
      thazar (57).
53 *s.d.* The arbour is depicted in the title-page woodcut of the murder (first in
      Q7, 1615: often reproduced) as a trellis-work arch about seven feet high
      and three feet wide, with what seem to be artificial leaves stuck to its outer
      sides. It does not look wide enough to contain the lovers' seat (23–9) on
      which they embrace passionately; perhaps this was nearer the front of the
      platform.
63 *s.d.* The woodcut of 1615 shows him in shirt, breeches, hose and slippers; on
      his head he wears a small hat (nightcap?); he carries a torch in his left
      hand and a sword (183 *s.d.*) in his right.

But stay, what murd'rous spectacle is this?
A man hang'd up and all the murderers gone!
And in my bower, to lay the guilt on me!
This place was made for pleasure, not for death.

He cuts him down.

Those garments that he wears I oft have seen.—
Alas, it is Horatio, my sweet son!
On no, but he that whilom was my son!
O, was it thou that call'dst me from my bed?
O speak, if any spark of life remain: 80
I am thy father; who hath slain my son?
What savage monster, not of human kind,
Hath here been glutted with thy harmless blood,
And left thy bloody corpse dishonour'd here,
For me, amidst these dark and deathful shades,
To drown thee with an ocean of my tears?
O heavens, why made you night to cover sin?
By day this deed of darkness had not been.
O earth, why didst thou not in time devour
The vild profaner of this sacred bower?   90
O poor Horatio, what hadst thou misdone,
To leese thy life, ere life was new begun?
O wicked butcher, whatsoe'er thou wert,
How could thou strangle virtue and desert?
Ay me most wretched, that have lost my joy,
In leesing my Horatio, my sweet boy!

Enter ISABELLA.

Isab. My husband's absence makes my heart throb.—
     Hieronimo!
Hier. Here, Isabella, help me to lament;
     For sighs are stopp'd, and all my tears are spent.   100
Isab. What world of grief—My son Horatio!
     O, where's the author of this endless woe?
Hier. To know the author were some ease of grief;
     For in revenge my heart would find relief.
Isab. Then is he gone? and is my son gone too?
     O, gush out, tears, fountains and floods of tears;
     Blow, sighs, and raise an everlasting storm;

For outrage fits our cursèd wretchedness.
[*Ay me, Hieronimo, sweet husband, speak!*
Hier. *He supp'd with us to-night, frolic and merry,*   110
And said he would go visit Balthazar
At the duke's palace: there the prince doth lodge.
He had no custom to stay out so late:
He may be in his chamber; some go see.
Roderigo, ho!

Enter PEDRO and JAQUES.

Isab. *Ay me, he raves! sweet Hieronimo!*
Hier. *True, all Spain takes note of it.*
Besides, he is so generally belov'd;
His majesty the other day did grace him
With waiting on his cup: these be favours,   120
Which do assure me he cannot be short-liv'd.
Isab. *Sweet Hieronimo!*
Hier. *I wonder how this fellow got his clothes!—*
Sirrah, sirrah, I'll know the truth of all:
Jaques, run to the Duke of Castile's presently,
And bid my son Horatio to come home:
I and his mother have had strange dreams to-night.
Do ye hear me, sir?
Jaques.   *Ay, sir.*
Hier.   *Well, sir, be gone.*
Pedro, come hither; know'st thou who this is?
Ped. *Too well, sir.*
Hier.   *Too well! who, who is it?   Peace, Isabella!*   130
Nay, blush not, man.
Ped.   *It is my lord Horatio.*
Hier. *Ha, ha! St. James, but this doth make me laugh,*
That there are more deluded than myself.
Ped. *Deluded?*
Hier.   *Ay:*
I would have sworn myself, within this hour,
That this had been my son Horatio,

121 *me he* Q5 (1603)] *me* Q4. Some editors read "he": this gives a "much
stronger" line (Edwards); on the other hand, the verse of this "addition"
contains other lines as rhythmically free as that printed here.

     His garments are so like.
     Ha! are they not great persuasions?
Isab. *O, would to God it were not so!*
Hier. *Were not, Isabella? dost thou dream it is?*   140
     Can thy soft bosom entertain a thought,
     That such a black deed of mischief should be done
     On one so pure and spotless as our son?
     Away, I am ashamèd.
Isab.   *Dear Hieronimo,*
     Cast a more serious eye upon my grief:
     Weak apprehension gives but weak relief.
Hier. *It was a man, sure, that was hang'd up here;*
     A youth, as I remember: I cut him down.
     If it should prove my son now after all—
     Say you? say you?—Light! lend me a taper;   150
     Let me look again.—O God!
     Confusion, mischief, torment, death and hell,
     Drop all your stings at once in my cold bosom,
     That now is stiff with horror: kill me quickly!
     Be gracious to me, thou infective night,
     And drop this deed of murder down on me;
     Gird in my waste of grief with thy large darkness,
     And let me not survive to see the light
     May put me in the mind I had a son.
Isab. *O sweet Horatio! O my dearest son!*   160
Hier. *How strangely had I lost my way to grief!*]
     Sweet, lovely rose, ill-pluck'd before thy time,
     Fair, worthy son, not conquer'd, but betray'd,
     I'll kiss thee now, for words with tears are stay'd.
Isab. And I'll close up the glasses of his sight,
     For once these eyes were only my delight.
Hier. See'st thou this handkercher besmear'd with blood?
     It shall not from me, till I take revenge.
     See'st thou those wounds that yet are bleeding fresh?
     I'll not entomb them, till I have reveng'd.   170
     Then will I joy amidst my discontent;

---

167 *this handkercher:* perhaps Andrea's scarf given to Horatio by Bel-imperia
(Mulryne), but more probably a handkerchief with which Hieronimo has
tried to stanch Horatio's blood.

Till then my sorrow never shall be spent.

Isab. The heavens are just; murder cannot be hid:
Time is the author both of truth and right,
And time will bring this treachery to light.

Hier. Meanwhile, good Isabella, cease thy plaints,
Or, at the least, dissemble them awhile:
So shall we sooner find the practice out,
And learn by whom all this was brought about.
Come, Isabel, now let us take him up,   *They take him up.*
And bear him in from out this cursèd place.   181
I'll say his dirge; singing fits not this case.

O aliquis mihi quas pulchrum ver educat herbas
                    Hieronimo sets his breast unto his sword.
Misceat, et nostro detur medicina dolori;
Aut, si qui faciunt animis oblivia, succos
Praebeat; ipse metam magnum quaecunque per orbem
Gramina Sol pulchras effert in luminis oras;
Ipse bibam quicquid meditatur saga veneni,
Quicquid et herbarum vi caeca nenia nectit:
Omnia perpetiar, lethum quoque, dum semel omnis   190
Noster in extincto moriatur pectore sensus.—

180 *s.d.* Inconsistent with the action that accompanies Hieronimo's Latin
    speech, 183 *s.d.* and 186 *s.d.* Edwards discusses this problem.
183–96 *O aliquis etc:*
                    "Compound for me all herbs that the fair spring
                    Breeds forth, to serve as salve unto my pain;
                    Or bring me blossoms of oblivion.
                    Myself will garner all fell seeds the sun
                    Draws to the shores of light, and I will drink
                    All venoms any sorceress can devise,
                    And all the fatal poisons herbs provide;
                    I will essay all these, until at once
                    All senses perish in my dying breast.—
                    So then shall I ne'er see thy face, dear son,
                    And shall eternal darkness cover thee?
                    With thee I'll die: thus would I pass the bourne.—
                    No, no! I will not yield my life so soon,
                    Lest so thy death should lack its due revenge."
                    (McIlwraith).

Ergo tuos oculos nunquam, mea vita, videbo,
Et tua perpetuus sepelivit lumina somnus?
Emoriar tecum: sic, sic juvat ire sub umbras.—
At tamen absistam properato cedere letho,
Ne mortem vindicta tuam tam nulla sequatur.

       Here he throws it from him and bears the body away.

[SCENE V]

Ghost of Andrea, Revenge.

Andrea. Brought'st thou me hither to increase my pain?
    I look'd that Balthazar should have been slain:
    But 'tis my friend Horatio that is slain,
    And they abuse fair Bel-imperia,
    On whom I doted more than all the world,
    Because she lov'd me more than all the world.
Revenge. Thou talk'st of harvest when the corn is green:
    The end is crown of every work well done;
    The sickle comes not till the corn be ripe.
    Be still, and ere I lead thee from this place,   10
    I'll show thee Balthazar in heavy case.

ACT III

[SCENE I]

Enter VICEROY OF PORTINGALE, Nobles, VILLUPPO.

Vic. Infortunate condition of kings,
    Seated amidst so many helpless doubts!
    First we are plac'd upon extremest height,
    And oft supplanted with exceeding heat,
    But ever subject to the wheel of chance;
    And at our highest never joy we so,
    As we both doubt and dread our overthrow.
    So striveth not the waves with sundry winds,
    As fortune toileth in the affairs of kings,
    That would be fear'd, yet fear to be belov'd,   10
    Sith fear or love to kings is flattery.
    For instance, lordings, look upon your king,
    By hate deprivèd of his dearest son,
    The only hope of our successive line.
Nob. I had not thought that Alexandro's heart
    Had been envenom'd with such extreme hate;
    But now I see that words have several works,
    And there's no credit in the countenance.
Vil. No: for, my lord, had you beheld the train
    That feignèd love had colour'd in his looks,   20
    When he in camp consorted Balthazar,
    Far more inconstant had you thought the sun,
    That hourly coasts the centre of the earth,
    Than Alexandro's purpose to the prince.
Vic. No more, Villuppo, thou has said enough,
    And with thy words thou slay'st our wounded thoughts.
    Nor shall I longer dally with the world,
    Procrastinating Alexandro's death:
    Go some of you, and fetch the traitor forth,
    That, as he is condemnèd, he may die.   30

Enter ALEXANDRO, *with a* Nobleman *and* Halberts.

Nob. In such extremes will nought but patience serve.
Alex. But in extremes what patience shall I use?
    Nor discontents it me to leave the world,
    With whom there nothing can prevail but wrong.
Nob. Yet hope the best.
Alex.   'Tis heaven is my hope:
    As for the earth, it is too much infect
    To yield me hope of any of her mould.
Vic. Why linger ye? bring forth that daring fiend,
    And let him die for his accursèd deed.
Alex. Not that I fear the extremity of death   40
    (For nobles cannot stoop to servile fear)
    Do I, O king, thus discontented live.
    But this, O this, torments my labouring soul,
    That thus I die suspected of a sin,
    Whereof, as heav'ns have known my secret thoughts,
    So am I free from this suggestion.
Vic. No more, I say! to the tortures! when?
    Bind him, and burn his body in those flames,
            They bind him to the stake.
    That shall prefigure those unquenchèd fires
    Of Phlegethon, preparèd for his soul.   50
Alex. My guiltless death will be aveng'd on thee,
    On thee, Villuppo, that hath malic'd thus,
    Or for thy meed hast falsely me accus'd.
Vil. Nay, Alexandro, if thou menace me,
    I'll lend a hand to send thee to the lake,
    Where those thy words shall perish with thy works:
    Injurious traitor! monstrous homicide!

Enter Ambassador [*and* Attendants]

Amb. Stay, hold a while;
    And here—with pardon of his majesty—
    Lay hands upon Villuppo.
Vic.   Ambassador,   60
    What news hath urg'd this sudden enterance?
Amb. Know, sovereign lord, that Balthazar doth live.

Vic. What say'st thou? liveth Balthazar our son?
Amb. Your highness' son, Lord Balthazar, doth live;
　　　And, well entreated in the court of Spain,
　　　Humbly commends him to your majesty.
　　　These eyes beheld; and these my followers,
　　　With these, the letters of the king's commends,
　　　　　　　　　　　　　　　　　Gives him letters.
　　　Are happy witnesses of his highness' health.
　　　　　　　　The King looks on the letters, and proceeds.
Vic. " Thy son doth live, your tribute is receiv'd;　　　70
　　　The peace is made, and we are satisfied.
　　　The rest resolve upon as things propos'd
　　　For both our honours and thy benefit."
Amb. These are his highness' farther articles.
　　　　　　　　　　　　　　He gives him more letters.
Vic. Accursèd wretch, to intimate these ills
　　　Against the life and reputation
　　　Of noble Alexandro! Come, my lord,　　　*[Unbind him.]*
　　　Let him unbind thee, that is bound to death,
　　　To make a quital for thy discontent.　　　*They unbind him.*
Alex. Dread lord, in kindness you could do no less,　　　80
　　　Upon report of such a damnèd fact;
　　　But thus we see our innocence hath sav'd
　　　The hopeless life which thou, Villuppo, sought
　　　By thy suggestions to have massacred.
Vic. Say, false Villuppo, wherefore didst thou thus
　　　Falsely betray Lord Alexandro's life?
　　　Him whom thou know'st that no unkindness else,
　　　But ev'n the slaughter of our dearest son,
　　　Could once have mov'd us to have misconceiv'd.
Alex. Say, treacherous Villuppo, tell the king:　　　90
　　　Wherein hath Alexandro us'd thee ill?

77 *Come, my lord,* Unbind him. (C)] Come my Lord vnbinde him Q. I take the
　last two words as a *s.d.* applying to the Viceroy. He begins to unbind
　Alexandro with his own hands, promising him lifelong amends for having
　mistrusted him, 78–9. Alexandro graciously accepts the apology, 80–1.
　Meanwhile the attendants assist in unbinding him, 79 *s.d.* Some editors
　take 78–9 to mean that Villuppo is condemned to death and must first
　unbind Alexandro; but the Viceroy does not think of Villuppo till 85–9,
　nor condemn him till 97–101.

Vil. Rent with remembrance of so foul a deed,
          My guilty soul submits me to thy doom:
          For not for Alexandro's injuries,
          But for reward and hope to be preferr'd,
          Thus have I shamelessly hazarded his life.
Vic. Which, villain, shall be ransom'd with thy death,
          And not so mean a torment as we here
          Devis'd for him who, thou said'st, slew our son,
          But with the bitterest torments and extremes   100
          That may be yet invented for thine end.
                              Alexandro seems to entreat.
          Entreat me not! go, take the traitor hence:
                              Exit Villuppo [*guarded*].
          And, Alexandro, let us honour thee
          With public notice of thy loyalty.—
          To end those things articulated here
          By our great lord, the mighty King of Spain,
          We with our council will deliberate.
          Come, Alexandro, keep us company.   *Exeunt.*

[SCENE II]

Enter HIERONIMO.

Hier. O eyes! no eyes, but fountains fraught with tears;
          O life! no life, but lively form of death;
          O world! no world, but mass of public wrongs,
          Confus'd and fill'd with murder and misdeeds!
          O sacred heavens! if this unhallow'd deed,
          If this inhuman and barbarous attempt,
          If this incomparable murder thus
          Of [son of] mine, but now no more my son,
          Shall unreveal'd and unrevengèd pass,

6 *inhuman and barbarous:* The Q spelling "inhumane" resists Cairncross's otherwise attractive reading "inhuman barbarous", which assumes that "and"
  was wrongly introduced by the influence of the last two letters of "inhuman".
8 [*son of*] (C). Completes the metre and the antithesis.

How should we term your dealings to be just,   10
If you unjustly deal with those that in your justice trust?
The night, sad secretary to my moans,
With direful visions wakes my vexèd soul,
And with the wounds of my distressful son
Solicits me for notice of his death.
The ugly fiends do sally forth of hell,
And frame my steps to unfrequented paths,
And fear my heart with fierce inflamèd thoughts.
The cloudy day my discontents records,
Early begins to register my dreams,   20
And drive me forth to seek the murderer.
Eyes, life, world, heav'ns, hell, night, and day,
See, search, shew, send some man, some mean, that may—
                                        A letter falleth.

What's here? a letter? tush! it is not so!—
A letter written to Hieronimo!   *Red ink.*
" For want of ink, receive this bloody writ:
Me hath my hapless brother hid from thee;
Revenge thyself on Balthazar and him,
For these were they that murderèd thy son.
Hieronimo, revenge Horatio's death,   30
And better fare than Bel-imperia doth."
What means this unexpected miracle?
My son slain by Lorenzo and the prince!
What cause had they Horatio to malign?
Or what might move thee, Bel-imperia,
To accuse thy brother, had he been the mean?
Hieronimo, beware!—thou art betray'd,
And to entrap thy life this train is laid.
Advise thee therefore, be not credulous:
This is devisèd to endanger thee,   40
That thou, by this, Lorenzo shouldst accuse,
And he, for thy dishonour done, should draw
Thy life in question and thy name in hate.
Dear was the life of my belovèd son,
And of his death behoves me be reveng'd:
Then hazard not thine own, Hieronimo,
But live t' effect thy resolution.

I therefore will by circumstances try,
What I can gather to confirm this writ;
And, heark'ning near the Duke of Castile's house,   50
Close, if I can, with Bel-imperia,
To listen more, but nothing to bewray.

Enter PEDRINGANO.

Now, Pedringano!

Ped.   Now, Hieronimo!

Hier. Where's thy lady?

Ped.   I know not; here's my lord.

Enter LORENZO.

Lor. How now, who's this? Hieronimo?

Hier.   My lord!

Ped. He asketh for my lady Bel-imperia.

Lor. What to do, Hieronimo?   The duke, my father, hath,
Upon some disgrace, awhile remov'd her hence;
But if it be ought I may inform her of,
Tell me, Hieronimo, and I'll let her know it.   60

Hier. Nay, nay, my lord, I thank you; it shall not need.
I had a suit unto her, but too late,
And her disgrace makes me unfortunate.

Lor. Why so, Hieronimo? use me.

Hier. Oh no, my lord; I dare not; it must not be;
I humbly thank your lordship.

Lor.   Why then, farewell.

Hier. My grief no heart, my thoughts no tongue can tell.   *Exit.*

Line 64 and first part of 65 (O no . . . lordship) are replaced, in all the Qq. from
    1602 onwards, by the following lines:
        Hier. *Who? you, my lord?*
            I reserve your favour for a greater honour;
            This is a very toy, my lord, a toy.
        Lor. *All's one, Hieronimo, acquaint me with it.*
        Hier. *I' faith, my lord, it is an idle thing;*
            I must confess I ha' been too slack, too tardy,
            Too remiss unto your honour.
        Lor.   *How now, Hieronimo?*
        Hier. *In troth, my lord, it is a thing of nothing:*
            The murder of a son, or so——
            A thing of nothing, my lord!

Lor. Come hither, Pedringano, see'st thou this?

Ped. My lord, I see it, and suspect it too.

Lor. This is that damnèd villain Serberine,   70
  That hath, I fear, reveal'd Horatio's death.

Ped. My lord, he could not, 'twas so lately done;
  And since he hath not left my company.

Lor. Admit he have not, his condition's such,
  As fear or flattering words may make him false.
  I know his humour, and therewith repent
  That e'er I us'd him in this enterprise.
  But, Pedringano, to prevent the worst,
  And 'cause I know thee secret as my soul,
  Here, for thy further satisfaction, take thou this,   80
          Gives him more gold.
  And hearken to me—thus it is devis'd:
  This night thou must (and, prithee, so resolve)
  Meet Serberine at Saint Luigi's Park—
  Thou know'st 'tis here hard by behind the house—
  There take thy stand, and see thou strike him sure:
  For die he must, if we do mean to live.

Ped. But how shall Serberine be there, my lord?

Lor. Let me alone; I'll send to him to meet
  The prince and me, where thou must do this deed.

Ped. It shall be done, my lord, it shall be done;   90
  And I'll go arm myself to meet him there.

Lor. When things shall alter, as I hope they will,
  Then shalt thou mount for this; thou know'st my mind.
          Exit Pedringano.

  Chi l'è? Jeron!

      Enter Page.

Page.   My lord?

Lor.   Go, sirrah, to Serberine,
  And bid him forthwith meet the prince and me
  At Saint Luigi's Park, behind the house;
  This evening, boy!

Page.   I go, my lord.

94 *Chi l'è? Jeron!* (C)] *Che le Ieron.* Q. "Who's there? [*i.e.*, Attend me !] Jeron!
[the page's name]."

Lor. But, sirrah, let the hour be eight o'clock:
    Bid him not fail.
Page.   I fly, my lord.   *Exit.*
Lor. Now to confirm the complot thou hast cast   100
    Of all these practices, I'll spread the watch,
    Upon precise commandment from the king,
    Strongly to guard the place where Pedringano
    This night shall murder hapless Serberine.
    Thus must we work that will avoid distrust;
    Thus must we practise to prevent mishap,
    And thus one ill another must expulse.
    This sly enquiry of Hieronimo
    For Bel-imperia breeds suspicion,
    And this suspicion bodes a further ill.   110
    As for myself, I know my secret fault,
    And so do they; but I have dealt for them:
    They that for coin their souls endangerèd,
    To save my life, for coin shall venture theirs;
    And better 'tis that base companions die,
    Than by their life to hazard our good haps.
    Nor shall they live, for me to fear their faith:
    I'll trust myself, myself shall be my friend;
    For die they shall, slaves are ordain'd to no other end.
                         Exit.

[SCENE III]

Enter PEDRINGANO, *with a pistol.*

Ped. Now, Pedringano, bid thy pistol hold,
    And hold on, Fortune! once more favour me;
    Give but success to mine attempting spirit,
    And let me shift for taking of mine aim.
    Here is the gold: this is the gold propos'd;

115 *'tis* (C)] its Q. "It's" is unidiomatic in the line: "it is" must turn to "'tis",
    even though "'tis" is not found till Q3 (1599). I think "fits" a more
    likely reading than "it's".
119 *For die they shall:* Cairncross regards these words as an extra-metrical inter-
    polation from III. iv. 37; he reads "ordainèd". But they seem necessary
    to clarify the sense after 118.

It is no dream that I adventure for,
But Pedringano is possess'd thereof.
And he that would not strain his conscience
For him that thus his liberal purse hath stretch'd,
Unworthy such a favour, may he fail,　　　　　　10
And, wishing, want, when such as I prevail.
As for the fear of apprehension,
I know, if need should be, my noble lord
Will stand between me and ensuing harms;
Besides, this place is free from all suspect:
Here therefore will I stay and take my stand.

Enter the Watch.

1. I wonder much to what intent it is
   That we are thus expressly charg'd to watch.
2. 'Tis by commandment in the king's own name.
3. But we were never wont to watch and ward　　20
   So near the duke, his brother's house before.
2. Content yourself, stand close, there's somewhat in't.

Enter SERBERINE.

Ser. Here, Serberine, attend and stay thy pace;
　　For here did Don Lorenzo's page appoint
　　That thou by his command shouldst meet with him.
　　How fit a place, if one were so dispos'd,
　　Methinks this corner is to close with one.
Ped. Here comes the bird that I must seize upon:
　　Now, Pedringano, or never, play the man!
Ser. I wonder that his lordship stays so long,　　30
　　Or wherefore should he send for me so late?
Ped. For this, Serberine!—and thou shalt ha't.　　*Shoots the dag.*
　　So, there he lies; my promise is perform'd.

The Watch.

1. Hark, gentlemen, this is a pistol shot.
2. And here's one slain;—stay the murderer.
Ped. Now by the sorrows of the souls in hell,
　　　　　　　　　　　　He strives with the Watch.
　　Who first lays hand on me, I'll be his priest.

   3. Sirrah, confess, and therein play the priest,
       Why has thou thus unkindly kill'd the man?
Ped. Why? because he walk'd abroad so late.   40
   3. Come, sir, you had been better kept your bed,
       Than have committed this misdeed so late.
   2. Come, to the marshal's with the murderer!
   1. On to Hieronimo's! help me here
       To bring the murder'd body with us too.
Ped. Hieronimo? carry me before whom you will:
       Whate'er he be, I'll answer him and you;
       And do your worst, for I defy you all.   *Exeunt.*

[SCENE IV]

Enter LORENZO *and* BALTHAZAR.

Bal. How now, my lord, what makes you rise so soon?
Lor. Fear of preventing our mishaps too late.
Bal. What mischief is it that we not mistrust?
Lor. Our greatest ills we least mistrust, my lord,
       And inexpected harms do hurt us most.
Bal. Why, tell me, Don Lorenzo, tell me, man,
       If ought concerns our honour and your own.
Lor. Nor you, nor me, my lord, but both in one:
       For I suspect, and the presumption's great,
       That by those base confederates in our fault   10
       Touching the death of Don Horatio,
       We are betray'd to old Hieronimo.
Bal. Betray'd, Lorenzo? tush! it cannot be.
Lor. A guilty conscience, urgèd with the thought
       Of former evils, easily cannot err:
       I am persuaded, and dissuade me not,
       That all's revealèd to Hieronimo.
       And therefore know that I have cast it thus:—

[*Enter* Page.]

       But here's the page.   How now?   what news with thee?
Page. My lord, Serberine is slain.   20
Bal. Who? Serberine, my man?

Page. Your highness' man, my lord.
Lor. Speak, page, who murder'd him?
Page. He that is apprehended for the fact.
Lor. Who?
Page. Pedringano.
Bal. Is Serberine slain, that lov'd his lord so well?
      Injurious villain, murderer of his friend!
Lor. Hath Pedringano murder'd Serberine?
      My lord, let me entreat you to take the pains   30
      To exasperate and hasten his revenge
      With your complaints unto my lord the king.
      This their dissension breeds a greater doubt.
Bal. Assure thee, Don Lorenzo, he shall die,
      Or else his highness hardly shall deny.
      Meanwhile I'll haste the marshal-sessions:
      For die he shall for this his damnèd deed.   *Exit Balthazar.*
Lor. Why so, this fits our former policy,
      And thus experience bids the wise to deal.
      I lay the plot: he prosecutes the point;   40
      I set the trap: he breaks the worthless twigs,
      And sees not what wherewith the bird was lim'd.
      Thus hopeful men, that mean to hold their own,
      Must look like fowlers to their dearest friends.
      He runs to kill whom I have holp to catch,
      And no man knows it was my reaching fatch.
      'Tis hard to trust unto a multitude,
      Or any one, in mine opinion,
      When men themselves their secrets will reveal.

                Enter a Messenger *with a letter.*

      Boy!   50
Page.   My lord?
Lor. What's he?
Mes.   I have a letter to your lordship.
Lor. From whence?
Mes.   From Pedringano that's imprison'd.
Lor. So, he is in prison then?
Mes.   Ay, my good lord.
Lor. What would he with us?—He writes us here,

To stand good lord, and help him in distress.—
Tell him I have his letters, know his mind,
And what we may, let him assure him of.
Fellow, begone: my boy shall follow thee.

Exit Messenger.

This works like wax; yet once more try thy wits.   60
Boy, go, convey this purse to Pedringano;
Thou know'st the prison, closely give it him,
And be advis'd that none be there about:
Bid him be merry still, but secret;
And though the marshal-sessions be to-day,
Bid him not doubt of his delivery.
Tell him his pardon is already sign'd,
And thereon bid him boldly be resolv'd:
For, were he ready to be turnèd off—
As 'tis my will the uttermost be tried—   70
Thou with his pardon shalt attend him still.
Show him this box, tell him his pardon's in't;
But open't not, and if thou lov'st thy life;
But let him wisely keep his hopes unknown:
He shall not want while Don Lorenzo lives.
Away!

Page.   I go, my lord, I run.

Lor. But, sirrah, see that this be cleanly done.   *Exit Page.*
Now stands our fortune on a tickle point,
And now or never ends Lorenzo's doubts.
One only thing is uneffected yet,   80
And that's to see the executioner.
But to what end?   I list not trust the air
With utterance of our pretence therein,
For fear the privy whisp'ring of the wind
Convey our words amongst unfriendly ears,
That lie too open to advantages.
E quel che voglio io, nessun lo sa;
Intendo io: quel mi basterà.   *Exit.*

87–8 "What my intent is, that no man doth know;/ 'Tis in my mind, and it is
better so." (McIlwraith).

[SCENE V]

Enter Boy, *with the box.*

Boy. My master hath forbidden me to look in this box; and, by
my troth, 'tis likely, if he had not warned me, I should not
have had so much idle time; for we men's-kind, in our
minority, are like women in their uncertainty: that they
are most forbidden, they will soonest attempt: so I now.
——By my bare honesty, here's nothing but the bare
empty box: were it not sin against secrecy, I would say it
were a piece of gentlemanlike knavery. I must go to
Pedringano, and tell him his pardon is in this box; nay, I
would have sworn it, had I not seen the contrary.—I cannot
choose but smile to think how the villain will flout the
gallows, scorn the audience, and descant on the hangman,
and all presuming of his pardon from hence. Will't not be
an odd jest for me to stand and grace every jest he makes,
pointing my finger at this box, as who would say: " Mock
on, here's thy warrant." Is't not a scurvy jest that a man
should jest himself to death? Alas! poor Pedringano, I
am in a sort sorry for thee; but if I should be hanged with
thee, I cannot weep.   *Exit.*

[SCENE VI]

Enter HIERONIMO *and the* Deputy

Hier. Thus must we toil in other men's extremes,
        That know not how to remedy our own;
        And do them justice, when unjustly we,
        For all our wrongs, can compass no redress.
        But shall I never live to see the day,
        That I may come, by justice of the heavens,
        To know the cause that may my cares allay?
        This toils my body, this consumeth age,
        That only I to all men just must be,
        And neither gods nor men be just to me.   10
Dep. Worthy Hieronimo, your office asks

        A care to punish such as do transgress.

Hier. So is't my duty to regard his death

        Who, when he liv'd, deserv'd my dearest blood.

        But come, for that we came for: let's begin;

        For here lies that which bids me to be gone.

Enter Officers, Boy, *and* PEDRINGANO, *with a letter in his hand,*
bound.

Dep. Bring forth the prisoner, for the court is set.

Ped. Gramercy, boy, but it was time to come;

        For I had written to my lord anew

        A nearer matter that concerneth him,   20

        For fear his lordship had forgotten me.

        But sith he hath remember'd me so well—

        Come, come, come on, when shall we to this gear?

Hier. Stand forth, thou monster, murderer of men,

        And here, for satisfaction of the world,

        Confess thy folly, and repent thy fault;

        For there's thy place of execution.

Ped. This is short work: well, to your marshalship

        First I confess—nor fear I death therefore—

        I am the man, 'twas I slew Serberine.   30

        But, sir, then you think this shall be the place

        Where we shall satisfy you for this gear?

Dep. Ay, Pedringano.

Ped.   Now I think not so.

Hier. Peace, impudent, for thou shalt find it so:

        For blood with blood shall, while I sit as judge,

        Be satisfièd, and the law discharg'd.

        And though myself cannot receive the like,

        Yet will I see that others have their right.

        Despatch: the fault's approvèd and confess'd,

        And by our law he is condemn'd to die.   40

Hangm. Come on, sir, are you ready?

Ped. To do what, my fine, officious knave?

Hangm. To go to this gear.

Ped. O sir, you are too forward: thou wouldst fain furnish me

---

16 *here:* in his heart.

with a halter, to disfurnish me of my habit. So I should
go out of this gear, my raiment, into that gear, the rope.
But, hangman, now I spy your knavery, I'll not change
without boot, that's flat.

Hangm. Come, sir.

Ped. So, then, I must up?   50

Hangm. No remedy.

Ped. Yes, but there shall be for my coming down.

Hangm. Indeed, here's a remedy for that.

Ped. How? be turned off?

Hangm. Ay, truly; come, are you ready? I pray, sir, despatch;
the day goes away.

Ped. What, do you hang by the hour? if you do, I may chance
to break your old custom.

Hangm. Faith, you have reason; for I am like to break your
young neck.   60

Ped. Dost thou mock me, hangman? pray God, I be not preserved to break your knave's pate for this.

Hangm. Alas, sir! you are a foot too low to reach it, and I hope
you will never grow so high while I am in the office.

Ped. Sirrah, dost see yonder boy with the box in his hand?

Hangm. What, he that points to it with his finger?

Ped. Ay, that companion.

Hangm. I know him not; but what of him?

Ped. Dost thou think to live till his old doublet will make thee
a new truss?   70

Hangm. Ay, and many a fair year after, to truss up many a
honester man than either thou or he.

Ped. What hath he in his box, as thou thinkest?

Hangm. Faith, I cannot tell, nor I care not greatly; methinks
you should rather hearken to your soul's health.

Ped. Why, sirrah hangman, I take it that that is good for the
body is likewise good for the soul: and it may be, in that
box is balm for both.

Hangm. Well, thou art even the merriest piece of man's flesh
that e'er groaned at my office door!   80

Ped. Is your roguery become an office with a knave's name?

45 *my habit:* The hanged man's clothes went to the hangman.

Hangm. Ay, and that shall all they witness that see you seal it
    with a thief's name.

Ped. I prithee, request this good company to pray with me.

Hangm. Ay, marry, sir, this is a good motion: my masters, you
    see here's a good fellow—

Ped. Nay, nay, now I remember me, let them alone till some
    other time; for now I have no great need.

Hier. I have not seen a wretch so impudent.

    O monstrous times, where murder's set so light,   90
    And where the soul, that should be shrin'd in heaven,
    Solely delights in interdicted things,
    Still wand'ring in the thorny passages,
    That intercepts itself of happiness.
    Murder!   O bloody monster!   God forbid
    A fault so foul should 'scape unpunishèd.
    Despatch, and see this execution done!—
    This makes me to remember thee, my son.

                               Exit Hieronomo.

Ped. Nay, soft, no haste.

Dep. Why, wherefore stay you?   Have you hope of life?   100

Ped. Why, ay!

Hangm. As how?

Ped. Why, rascal, by my pardon from the king.

Hangm. Stand you on that?   then you shall off with this.

                                 He turns him off.

Dep. So, executioner;—convey him hence;
    But let his body be unburièd:
    Let not the earth be chokèd or infect
    With that which heaven contemns, and men neglect.

                                   Exeunt.

[SCENE VII]

Enter HIERONIMO.

Hier. Where shall I run to breathe abroad my woes,
    My woes, whose weight hath wearièd the earth?
    Or mine exclaims, that have surcharg'd the air

86 *fellow*—(C)] fellow. Q. The Hangman begins to exhort the crowd, but
    Pedringano cuts him short.

With ceaseless plaints for my deceasèd son?
The blust'ring winds, conspiring with my words,
At my lament have mov'd the leafless trees,
Disrob'd the meadows of their flower'd green,
Made mountains marsh with spring-tides of my tears,
And broken through the brazen gates of hell.
Yet still tormented is my tortur'd soul   10
With broken sighs and restless passions,
That wingèd mount; and, hovering in the air,
Beat at the windows of the brightest heavens,
Soliciting for justice and revenge:
But they are plac'd in those empyreal heights,
Where, countermur'd with walls of diamond,
I find the place impregnable; and they
Resist my woes, and give my words no way.

Enter Hangman *with a letter.*

Hangm. O lord, sir! God bless you, sir! the man, sir, Petergade,
     sir, he that was so full of merry conceits—   20
Hier. Well, what of him?
Hangm. O lord, sir, he went the wrong way; the fellow had a
     fair commission to the contrary. Sir, here is his passport;
     I pray you, sir, we have done him wrong.
Hier. I warrant thee, give it me.
Hangm. You will stand between the gallows and me?
Hier. Ay, ay.
Hangm. I thank your lord worship.   *Exit Hangman.*
Hier. And yet, though somewhat nearer me concerns,
     I will, to ease the grief that I sustain,   30
     Take truce with sorrow while I read on this.
     " My lord, I writ, as mine extremes requir'd,
     That you would labour my delivery:
     If you neglect, my life is desperate,
     And in my death I shall reveal the troth.
     You know, my lord, I slew him for your sake,
     And as confederate with the prince and you,
     Won by rewards and hopeful promises,

32 *writ* (Manly)] write Q.
37 *as* (Edwards)] was Q.

I holp to murder Don Horatio too."—
Holp he to murder mine Horatio?   40
And actors in th' accursèd tragedy
Wast thou, Lorenzo, Balthazar and thou,
Of whom my son, my son deserv'd so well?
What have I heard, what have mine eyes beheld?
O sacred heavens, may it come to pass
That such a monstrous and detested deed,
So closely smother'd, and so long conceal'd,
Shall thus by this be vengèd or reveal'd?
Now see I what I durst not then suspect,
That Bel-imperia's letter was not feign'd,   50
Nor feignèd she, though falsely they have wrong'd
Both her, myself, Horatio, and themselves.
Now may I make compare 'twixt hers and this,
Of every accident; I ne'er could find
Till now, and now I feelingly perceive
They did what heaven unpunish'd would not leave.
O false Lorenzo! are these thy flatt'ring looks?
Is this the honour that thou didst my son?
And Balthazar—bane to thy soul and me!—
Was this the ransom he reserv'd thee for?   60
Woe to the cause of these constrainèd wars!
Woe to thy baseness and captivity,
Woe to thy birth, thy body and thy soul,
Thy cursèd father, and thy conquer'd self!
And bann'd with bitter execrations be
The day and place where he did pity thee!
But wherefore waste I mine unfruitful words,
When naught but blood will satisfy my woes?
I will go plain me to my lord the king,
And cry aloud for justice through the court,   70
Wearing the flints with these my wither'd feet,
And either purchase justice by entreats,
Or tire them all with my revenging threats.   *Exit.*

59 *bane to thy soul and me:* a difficult phrase. Since the "he" of 60 must be
Horatio (compare 65–6), I am inclined to emend "thy soul" to "my
son". As it stands, it seems to mean that the murder ("this", 60) was
baneful to Hieronimo's happiness and Balthazar's soul.

[SCENE VIII]

Enter ISABELLA *and her* Maid.

Isab. So that, you say, this herb will purge the eye,
    And this, the head?—
    Ah, but none of them will purge the heart!
    No, there's no medicine left for my disease,
    Nor any physic to recure the dead.   *She runs lunatic.*
    Horatio!   O, where's Horatio?
Maid. Good madam, affright not thus yourself
    With outrage for your son Horatio:
    He sleeps in quiet in the Elysian fields.
Isab. Why, did I not give you gowns and goodly things,   10
    Bought you a whistle and a whipstalk too,
    To be revengèd on their villanies?
Maid. Madam, these humours do torment my soul.
Isab. My soul—poor soul! thou talks of things
    Thou know'st not what: my soul hath silver wings,
    That mounts me up unto the highest heavens;
    To heav'n: ay, there sits my Horatio,
    Back'd with a troop of fiery Cherubins,
    Dancing about his newly healèd wounds,
    Singing sweet hymns and chanting heavenly notes: 20
    Rare harmony to greet his innocence,
    That died, ay died, a mirror in our days.
    But say, where shall I find the men, the murderers,
    That slew Horatio?   Whither shall I run
    To find them out that murderèd my son?   *Exeunt.*

[SCENE IX]

BEL-IMPERIA *at a window.*

Bel. What means this outrage that is offer'd me?
    Why am I thus sequester'd from the court?
    No notice!   Shall I not know the cause
    Of these my secret and suspicious ills?

Accursèd brother, unkind murderer,
Why bends thou thus thy mind to martyr me?
Hieronimo, why writ I of thy wrongs,
Or why art thou so slack in thy revenge?
Andrea, O Andrea! that thou saw'st
Me for thy friend Horatio handled thus,   10
And him for me thus causeless murderèd!—
Well, force perforce, I must constrain myself
To patience, and apply me to the time,
Till heav'n, as I have hop'd, shall set me free.

Enter CHRISTOPHIL.

Chris. Come, madam Bel-imperia, this may not be.   *Exeunt.*

[SCENE X]

Enter LORENZO, BALTHAZAR, *and the* Page.

Lor. Boy, talk no further; thus far things go well.
     Thou art assurèd that thou saw'st him dead?
Page. Or else, my lord, I live not.
Lor.   That's enough.
     As for his resolution in his end,
     Leave that to him with whom he sojourns now.
     Here, take my ring and give it Christophil,
     And bid him let my sister be enlarg'd,
     And bring her hither straight.—   *Exit Page.*
     This that I did was for a policy,
     To smooth and keep the murder secret,   10
     Which, as a nine-days' wonder, being o'erblown,
     My gentle sister will I now enlarge.
Bal. And time, Lorenzo: for my lord the duke,
     You heard, enquirèd for her yester-night.
Lor. Why, and my lord, I hope you heard me say
     Sufficient reason why she kept away;
     But that's all one.   My lord, you love her?
Bal.   Ay.
Lor. Then in your love beware; deal cunningly:
     Salve all suspicions, only soothe me up;

And if she hap to stand on terms with us,   20
As for her sweetheart and concealment so,
Jest with her gently: under feignèd jest
Are things conceal'd that else would breed unrest.—
But here she comes.

Enter BEL-IMPERIA.

Now, sister!

Bel.   Sister?—No!
Thou art no brother, but an enemy;
Else wouldst thou not have us'd thy sister so:
First, to affright me with thy weapons drawn,
And with extremes abuse my company;
And then to hurry me, like whirlwind's rage,
Amidst a crew of thy confederates,   30
And clap me up, where none might come at me,
Nor I at any to reveal my wrongs.
What madding fury did possess thy wits?
Or wherein is't that I offended thee?

Lor. Advise you better, Bel-imperia,
For I have done you no disparagement;
Unless, by more discretion than deserv'd,
I sought to save your honour and mine own.

Bel. Mine honour? why, Lorenzo, wherein is't
That I neglect my reputation so,   40
As you, or any, need to rescue it?

Lor. His highness and my father were resolv'd
To come confer with old Hieronimo,
Concerning certain matters of estate,
That by the viceroy was determinèd.

Bel. And wherein was mine honour touch'd in that?

Bal. Have patience, Bel-imperia; hear the rest.

Lor. Me (next in sight) as messenger they sent,
To give him notice that they were so nigh:
Now when I came, consorted with the prince,   50
And unexpected, in an arbour there,
Found Bel-imperia with Horatio—

28 *And with extremes abuse my company:* "And use fatal violence to my companion" (Boas).

Bel. How then?

Lor. Why, then, remembering that old disgrace,
    Which you for Don Andrea had endur'd,
    And now were likely longer to sustain,
    By being found so meanly accompanied,
    Though rather—for I knew no readier mean—
    To thrust Horatio forth my father's way.

Bal. And carry you obscurely somewhere else,   60
    Lest that his highness should have found you there.

Bel. Ev'n so, my lord?   And you are witness
    That this is true which he entreateth of?
    You, gentle brother, forg'd this for my sake,
    And you, my lord, were made his instrument?
    A work of worth, worthy the noting too!
    But what's the cause that you conceal'd me since?

Lor. Your melancholy, sister, since the news
    Of your first favourite Don Andrea's death,
    My father's old wrath hath exasperate.   70

Bal. And better was't for you, being in disgrace,
    To absent yourself, and give his fury place.

Bel. But why had I no notice of his ire?

Lor. That were to add more fuel to your fire,
    Who burnt like Ætna for Andrea's loss.

Bel. Hath not my father then enquir'd for me?

Lor. Sister, he hath, and thus excus'd I thee.

                        He whispereth in her ear.

    But, Bel-imperia, see the gentle prince;
    Look on thy love, behold young Balthazar,
    Whose passions by thy presence are increas'd;   80
    And in whose melancholy thou may'st see
    Thy hate, his love; thy flight, his following thee.

Bel. Brother, you are become an orator—
    I know not, I, by what experience—
    Too politic for me, past all compare,
    Since last I saw you; but content yourself:
    The prince is meditating higher things.

Bal. 'Tis of thy beauty then that conquers kings;
    Of those thy tresses, Ariadne's twines,
    Wherewith my liberty thou hast surpris'd;   90

      Of that thine ivory front, my sorrow's map,
      Wherein I see no haven to rest my hope.
Bel. To love and fear, and both at once, my lord,
      In my conceit, are things of more import
      Than women's wits are to be busied with.
Bal. 'Tis I that love.
Bel.   Whom?
Bal.   Bel-imperia.
Bel. But I that fear.
Bal.   Whom?
Bel.   Bel-imperia.
Lor. Fear [you] yourself?
Bel.   Ay, brother.
Lor.   How?
Bel.   As those
      That, what they love, are loath and fear to lose.
Bal. Then, fair, let Balthazar your keeper be.   100
Bel. No, Balthazar doth fear as well as we:
      Et tremulo metui pavidum junxere timorem,
      Et vanum stolidae proditionis opus.
Lor. Nay, and you argue things so cunningly,
      We'll go continue this discourse at court.
Bal. Led by the loadstar of her heavenly looks,
      Wends poor, oppressèd Balthazar,
      As o'er the mountains walks the wanderer,
      Incertain to effect his pilgrimage.   *Exeunt.*

[SCENE XI]

Enter two Portingales, *and* HIERONIMO *meets them.*

   1. By your leave, sir.
Hier. ['*Tis neither as you think, nor as you think,*
      Nor as you think; you're wide all:
      These slippers are not mine, they were my son Horatio's.

98 *[you]* (C).
102–3 "They join'd to trembling fright a quivering fear,/ A futile act of blockish
    self-betrayal." (MacIlwraith).
107 A defective line. Perhaps "Wends poor love-oppressèd Balthazar", pro-
    nouncing "poor" as a disyllable.

My son! and what's a son?   A thing begot
Within a pair of minutes, thereabout;
A lump bred up in darkness, and doth serve
To ballace these light creatures we call women;
And, at nine moneths' end, creeps forth to light.
What is there yet in a son,   10
To make a father dote, rave, or run mad?
Being born, it pouts, cries, and breeds teeth.
What is there yet in a son?   He must be fed,
Be taught to go, and speak.   Ay, or yet?
Why might not a man love a calf as well?
Or melt in passion o'er a frisking kid,
As for a son?   Methinks, a young bacon,
Or a fine little smooth horse colt,
Should move a man as much as doth a son:
For one of these, in very little time,   20
Will grow to some good use; whereas a son,
The more he grows in stature and in years,
The more unsquar'd, unbevell'd, he appears,
Reckons his parents among the rank of fools,
Strikes care upon their heads with his mad riots;
Makes them look old, before they meet with age.
This is a son!—And what a loss were this,
Consider'd truly?——O, but my Horatio
Grew out of reach of these insatiate humours:
He lov'd his loving parents;   30
He was my comfort, and his mother's joy,
The very arm that did hold up our house:
Our hopes were storèd up in him,
None but a damnèd murderer could hate him.
He had not seen the back of nineteen year,
When his strong arm unhors'd the proud Prince Balthazar,
And his great mind,
Too full of honour, took him up to mercy—
That valiant, but ignoble Portingale!
Well, heaven is heaven still!   40
And there is Nemesis, and Furies,

38 *up to* (C)] vs to Q.

And things call'd whips,
And they sometimes do meet with murderers:
They do not always 'scape, that's some comfort.
Ay, ay, ay; and then time steals on,
And steals, and steals, till violence leaps forth
Like thunder wrapp'd in a ball of fire,
And so doth bring confusion to them all.]
Good leave have you: nay, I pray you go,
For I'll leave you, if you can leave me so.

2. Pray you, which is the next way to my lord the duke's?
Hier. The next way from me.

1.   To his house, we mean.   51
Hier. O, hard by: 'tis yon house that you see.

2. You could not tell us if his son were there?
Hier. Who, my Lord Lorenzo?

1.   Ay, sir.

He goeth in at one door and comes out at another.
Hier.   O, forbear!

For other talk for us far fitter were.
But if you be importunate to know
The way to him, and where to find him out,
Then list to me, and I'll resolve your doubt.
There is a path upon your left-hand side,
That leadeth from a guilty conscience   60
Unto a forest of distrust and fear,
A darksome place, and dangerous to pass:
There shall you meet with melancholy thoughts,
Whose baleful humours if you but uphold,
It will conduct you to despair and death;
Whose rocky cliffs when you have once beheld,
Within a hugy dale of lasting night,
That, kindl'd with the world's iniquities,
Doth cast up filthy and detested fumes,
Not far from thence, where murderers have built   70

54 *s.d.* It is unthinkable that this pointless action interrupts a line of verse. The
  s.d. surely anticipates Hieronimo's exit. He is to begin Scene xii at a
  different door to show that this is a different occasion. A similar effect is
  needed when xiii follows the additional xiiA.
54–5 *O, forbear! . . . fitter were:* He implies (as his subsequent imagery confirms)
  that Lorenzo is the devil.

A habitation for their cursèd souls,
There, in a brazen cauldron, fix'd by Jove
In his fell wrath upon a sulphur flame,
Yourselves shall find Lorenzo bathing him
In boiling lead and blood of innocents.

1. Ha, ha, ha!

Hier. Ha, ha, ha!

Why, ha, ha, ha!   Farewell, good ha, ha, ha!   *Exit.*

2. Doubtless this man is passing lunatic,
Or imperfection of his age doth make him dote.   80
Come, let's away to seek my lord the duke.   *Exeunt.*

[SCENE XII]

Enter HIERONIMO, *with a poniard in one hand and
a rope in the other.*

Hier. Now, sir, perhaps I come and see the king;
The king sees me, and fain would hear my suit:
Why, is not this a strange and seld-seen thing,
That standers-by with toys should strike me mute?
Go to, I see their shifts, and say no more.
Hieronimo, 'tis time for thee to trudge:
Down by the dale that flows with purple gore,
Standeth a fiery tower; there sits a judge
Upon a seat of steel and molten brass,
And 'twixt his teeth he holds a fire-brand,   10
That leads unto the lake where hell doth stand.
Away, Hieronimo! to him be gone:
He'll do thee justice for Horatio's death.
Turn down this path, thou shalt be with him straight,
Or this, and then thou need'st not take thy breath:
This way or that way!——Soft and fair, not so:
For if I hang or kill myself, let's know
Who will revenge Horatio's murder then?

1 *s.d.* The rope and dagger are the traditional means of suicide in 16th century
literature (*e.g.*, Spenser's *Faerie Queene*, I. ix. 29) : they are Hieronimo's two
"paths" or "ways", 14–16. At 19 *s.d.* he rejects them, and at 20 *s.d.* he
conceals them. "This way" (20) is literal, meaning the way to the King.

No, no! fie, no! pardon me, I'll none of that.
> *He flings away the dagger and halter.*
This way I'll take, and this way comes the king: 20
> *He takes them up again.*
And here I'll have a fling at him, that's flat;
And, Balthazar, I'll be with thee to bring,
And thee, Lorenzo! Here's the king—nay, stay;
And here, ay here—there goes the hare away.

Enter KING, Ambassador, CASTILE, *and* LORENZO.

King. Now show, ambassador, what our viceroy saith:
  Hath he receiv'd the articles we sent?
Hier. Justice, O, justice to Hieronimo!
Lor. Back! see'st thou not the king is busy?
Hier. O, is he so?
King. Who is he that interrupts our business?   30
Hier. Not I.   Hieronimo, beware! go by, go by!
Amb. Renownèd King, he hath receiv'd and read
  Thy kingly proffers, and thy promis'd league;
  And, as a man extremely over-joy'd
  To hear his son so princely entertain'd,
  Whose death he had so solemnly bewail'd,
  This for thy further satisfaction
  And kingly love, he kindly lets thee know:
  First, for the marriage of his princely son
  With Bel-imperia, thy belovèd niece,   40
  The news are more delightful to his soul,
  Than myrrh or incense to the offended heavens.
  In person, therefore, will he come himself,
  To see the marriage rites solemnisèd,
  And, in the presence of the court of Spain,
  To knit a sure inexplicable band
  Of kingly love and everlasting league
  Betwixt the crowns of Spain and Portingale.
  There will he give his crown to Balthazar,
  And make a queen of Bel-imperia.   50
King. Brother, how like you this our viceroy's love?

46 *inexplicable* Q2 (1594)] inexecrable Q1. Indissoluble.

Cast. No doubt, my lord, it is an argument
     Of honourable care to keep his friend,
     And wondrous zeal to Balthazar his son;
     Nor am I least indebted to his grace,
     That bends his liking to my daughter thus.
Amb. Now last, dread lord, here hath his highness sent
     (Although he send not that his son return)
     His ransom due to Don Horatio.
Hier. Horatio! who calls Horatio?   60
King. And well remember'd: thank his majesty.
     Here, see it given to Horatio.
Hier. Justice, O, justice, justice, gentle king!
King. Who is that?   Hieronimo?
Hier. Justice, O, justice!   O my son, my son!
     My son, whom naught can ransom or redeem!
Lor. Hieronimo, you are not well-advis'd.
Hier. Away, Lorenzo, hinder me no more;
     For thou hast made me bankrupt of my bliss.
     Give me my son! you shall not ransom him!   70
     Away! I'll rip the bowels of the earth,
                       He diggeth with his dagger.
    And ferry over to th' Elysian plains,
    And bring my son to show his deadly wounds.
    Stand from about me!
    I'll make a pickaxe of my poniard,
    And here surrender up my marshalship;
    For I'll go marshal up the fiends in hell,
    To be avengèd on you all for this.
King. What means this outrage?
    Will none of you restrain his fury?   80
Hier. Nay, soft and fair! you shall not need to strive:
    Needs must he go that the devils drive.
                           Exit.

King. What accident hath happ'd Hieronimo?
    I have not seen him to demean him so.
Lor. My gracious lord, he is with extreme pride,
    Conceiv'd of young Horatio his son,
    And covetous of having to himself
    The ransom of the young prince Balthazar,

Distract, and in a manner lunatic.

King. Believe me, nephew, we are sorry for't: 90
    This is the love that fathers bear their sons.
    But, gentle brother, go give to him this gold,
    The prince's ransom; let him have his due.
    For what he hath, Horatio shall not want;
    Haply Hieronimo hath need thereof.

Lor. But if he be thus helplessly distract,
    'Tis requisite his office be resign'd,
    And given to one of more discretion.

King. We shall increase his melancholy so.
    'Tis best that we see further in it first, 100
    Till when ourself will execute the place.
    And, brother, now bring in the ambassador,
    That he may be a witness of the match
    'Twixt Balthazar and Bel-imperia,
    And that we may prefix a certain time,
    Wherein the marriage shall be solemnis'd,
    That we may have thy lord, the viceroy, here.

Amb. Therein your highness highly shall content
    His majesty, that longs to hear from hence.

King. On, then, and hear you, lord ambassador——   *Exeunt.*

[SCENE XIIA]

Enter JAQUES and PEDRO.

Jaq. I wonder, Pedro, why our master thus
    At midnight sends us with our torches light,
    When man, and bird, and beast, are all at rest,
    Save those that watch for rape and bloody murder?

Ped. O Jaques, know thou that our master's mind
    Is much distraught, since his Horatio died,
    And—now his agèd years should sleep in rest,
    His heart in quiet—like a desperate mon,

---

101 *execute the place* (C; conj. J. P. Collier, ed. *Dodsley's Old Plays,* 1825.)]
exempt the place Q (misreading "execute" as "exemte"?). Fulfil the office
(OED 4a).

Grows lunatic and childish for his son.
Sometimes, as he doth at his table sit,   10
He speaks as if Horatio stood by him;
Then starting in a rage, falls on the earth,
Cries out " Horatio, where is my Horatio? "
So that with extreme grief and cutting sorrow
There is not left in him one inch of man:
See, where he comes.

Enter HIERONIMO.

Hier. *I pry through every crevice of each wall,*
  Look on each tree, and search through every brake,
  Beat at the bushes, stamp our grandam earth,
  Dive in the water, and stare up to heaven: 20
  Yet cannot I behold my son Horatio.—
  How now, who's there? spirits, spirits?
Ped. *We are your servants that attend you, sir.*
Hier. *What make you with your torches in the dark?*
Ped. *You bid us light them, and attend you here.*
Hier. *No, no, you are deceiv'd! not I;—you are deceiv'd!*
  Was I so mad to bid you light your torches now?
  Light me your torches at the mid of noon,
  Whenas the sun-god rides in all his glory;
  Light me your torches then.
Ped.   *Then we burn daylight.*   30
Hier. *Let it be burnt;   Night is a murd'rous slut,*
  That would not have her treasons to be seen;
  And yonder pale-fac'd Hecate there, the moon,
  Doth give consent to that is done in darkness,
  And all those stars that gaze upon her face,
  Are aglets on her sleeve, pins on her train;
  And those that should be powerful and divine,
  Do sleep in darkness, when they most should shine.
Ped. *Provoke them not, fair sir, with tempting words:*
  The heav'ns are gracious, and your miseries   40
  And sorrow makes you speak you know not what.
Hier. *Villain, thou liest, and thou doest nought*
  But tell me I am mad: thou liest, I am not mad!
  I know thee to be Pedro, and he Jaques.

I'll prove it to thee; and were I mad, how could I?
Where was she that same night when my Horatio was murder'd?
She should have shone: search thou the book.
Had the moon shone,
In my boy's face there was a kind of grace,
That I know—nay, I do know—had the murderer seen him,   50
His weapon would have fall'n and cut the earth,
Had he been fram'd of naught but blood and death.
Alack! when mischief doth it knows not what,
What shall we say to mischief?

Enter ISABELLA.

Isab. *Dear Hieronimo, come in a-doors;*
      O, seek not means so to increase thy sorrow.
Hier. *Indeed, Isabella, we do nothing here;*
      I do not cry: ask Pedro, and ask Jaques;
      Not I indeed; we are very merry, very merry.
Isab. *How? be merry here, be merry here?*   60
      Is not this place, and this the very tree,
      Where my Horatio died, where he was murder'd?
Hier. *Was—do not say what: let her weep it out.*
      This was the tree; I set it of a kernel:
      And when our hot Spain could not let it grow,
      But that the infant and the human sap
      Began to wither, duly twice a morning
      Would I be sprinkling it with fountain-water.
      At last it grew and grew, and bore and bore,
      Till at the length   70
      It grew a gallows, and did bear our son:
      It bore thy fruit and mine—O wicked, wicked plant!
One knocks within at the door.
      See who knock there.
Ped.   *It is a painter, sir.*
Hier. *Bid him come in, and paint some comfort,*
      For surely there's none lives but painted comfort.
      Let him come in!—One knows not what may chance:
      God's will that I should set this tree!—but even so
      Masters ungrateful servants rear from nought,
      And then they hate them that did bring them up.

Enter the Painter.

Paint. *God bless you, sir.*
Hier.   *Wherefore? why, thou scornful villain?*   80
        How, where, or by what means should I be bless'd?
Isab. *What wouldst thou have, good fellow?*
Paint.   *Justice, madam.*
Hier. *O ambitious beggar!*
        Wouldst thou have that that lives not in the world?
        Why, all the undelv'd mines cannot buy
        An ounce of justice, 'tis a jewel so inestimable.
        I tell thee,
        God hath engross'd all justice in his hands,
        And there is none but what comes from him.
Paint. *O, then I see*   90
        That God must right me for my murder'd son.
Hier. *How, was thy son murder'd?*
Paint. *Ay, sir; no man did hold a son so dear.*
Hier. *What, not as thine? that's a lie,*
        As massy as the earth: I had a son,
        Whose least unvalu'd hair did weigh
        A thousand of thy sons: and he was murder'd.
Paint. *Alas, sir, I had no more but he.*
Hier. *Nor I, nor I: but this same one of mine*
        Was worth a legion.   But all is one.   100
        Pedro, Jaques, go in a-doors; Isabella, go,
        And this good fellow here and I
        Will range this hideous orchard up and down,
        Like to two lions reavèd of their young.
        Go in a-doors, I say.
                        Exeunt.   The Painter and he sits down.
                Come, let's talk wisely now.
        Was thy son murder'd?
Paint.   *Ay, sir.*
Hier.   *So was mine.*
        How dost take it? art thou sometimes mad?
        Is there no tricks that comes before thine eyes?
Paint. *O Lord, yes, sir.*

Hier. Art a painter? canst paint me a tear, or a wound, a groan,
or a sigh? canst paint me such a tree as this?   111

Paint. Sir, I am sure you have heard of my painting: my name's
Bazardo.

Hier. Bazardo! afore God, an excellent fellow. Look you, sir,
do you see, I'd have you paint me in my gallery, in your
oil-colours matted, and draw me five years younger than I
am—do ye see, sir, let five years go; let them go—like
the Marshal of Spain, my wife Isabella standing by me, with
a speaking look to my son Horatio, which should intend to
this or some such-like purpose: " God bless thee, my sweet
son;" and my hand leaning upon his head, thus, sir; do you
see?—may it be done?   122

Paint. Very well, sir.

Hier. Nay, I pray, mark me, sir: then, sir, would I have you
paint me this tree, this very tree. Canst paint a doleful cry?

Paint. Seemingly, sir.

Hier. Nay, it should cry; but all is one. Well, sir, paint me a
youth run through and through with villains' swords, hanging
upon this tree. Canst thou draw a murderer?

Paint. I'll warrant you, sir; I have the pattern of the most
notorious villains that ever lived in all Spain.   131

Hier. O, let them be worse, worse: stretch thine art, and let their
beards be of Judas his own colour; and let their eye-brows
jutty over: in any case observe that. Then, sir, after some
violent noise, bring me forth in my shirt, and my gown under
mine arm, with my torch in my hand, and my sword reared up
thus:—and with these words:

          "What noise is this? who calls Hieronimo?"

May it be done?

Paint. Yea, sir.   140

Hier. Well, sir; then bring me forth, bring me through alley and
alley, still with a distracted countenance going along, and let
my hair heave up my night-cap. Let the clouds scowl, make
the moon dark, the stars extinct, the winds blowing, the bells
tolling, the owl shrieking, the toads croaking, the minutes
jarring, and the clock striking twelve. And then at last, sir,
starting, behold a man hanging, and tottering, and tottering, as

*you know the wind will wave a man, and I with a trice to cut him
down. And looking upon him by the advantage of my torch, find
it to be my son Horatio.   There you may show a passion, there
you may show a passion!   Draw me like old Priam of Troy,
crying: " The house is afire, the house is afire, as the torch
over my head! "   Make me curse, make me rave, make me cry,
make me mad, make me well again, make me curse hell,
invocate heaven, and in the end leave me in a trance—and so
forth.*   156

Paint. *And is this the end?*

Hier. *O no, there is no end: the end is death and madness!   As
I am never better than when I am mad, then methinks I am
a brave fellow, then I do wonders: but reason abuseth me,
and there's the torment, there's the hell.   At the last, sir, bring
me to one of the murderers; were he as strong as Hector,
thus would I tear and drag him up and down.*

> He beats the Painter in, then comes out again, with a
> book in his hand.

[SCENE XIII]

Enter HIERONIMO, *with a book in his hand.*

Vindicta mihi!
Ay, heaven will be reveng'd of every ill;
Nor will they suffer murder unrepaid.
Then stay, Hieronimo, attend their will:
For mortal men may not appoint their time!—
" *Per scelus semper tutum est sceleribus iter.*"
Strike and strike home, where wrong is offer'd thee;

---

158 *there is no end:* the end is not there. (Stress the adverb.) Hieronimo is pictur-
    ing the story as a kind of triptych: before the murder; the murder;
    revenge for the murder (161–2, "At the last, sir, bring me to one of the
    murderers").
1 *s.d. a book:* Seneca's tragedies, from which he reads out 6 ("Through crime is
    ever the safe way for crime") and 12–13 (translated in 14–17), and quotes
    35 ("It is an idle remedy for ills"). (McIlwraith.)
Vindicta mihi! "Vengeance is mine; I will repay, saith the Lord." (Romans xii.
    19.)

For evils unto ills conductors be,
And death's the worst of resolution.
For he that thinks with patience to contend   10
To quiet life, his life shall easily end.—
" *Fata si miseros juvant, habes salutem;*
Fata si vitam negant, habes sepulchrum: "
If destiny thy miseries do ease,
Then hast thou health, and happy shalt thou be;
If destiny deny thee life, Hieronimo,
Yet shalt thou be assurèd of a tomb:
If neither, yet let this thy comfort be:
Heaven covereth him that hath no burial.
And to conclude, I will revenge his death!   20
But how? not as the vulgar wits of men,
With open, but inevitable ills,
As by a secret, yet a certain mean,
Which under kindship will be cloakèd best.
Wise men will take their opportunity
Closely and safely, fitting things to time.
But in extremes advantage hath no time;
And therefore all times fit not for revenge.
Thus therefore will I rest me in unrest,
Dissembling quiet in unquietness,   30
Not seeming that I know their villanies,
That my simplicity may make them think
That ignorantly I will let all slip;
For ignorance, I wot, and well they know,
Remedium malorum iners est.
Nor ought avails it me to menace them,
Who, as a wintry storm upon a plain,
Will bear me down with their nobility.
No, no, Hieronimo, thou must enjoin
Thine eyes to observation, and thy tongue   40
To milder speeches than thy spirit affords,
Thy heart to patience, and thy hands to rest,
Thy cap to courtesy, and thy knee to bow,

---

22 *inevitable:* The intended sense seems to be its opposite, "evitable" (in 16th
century use; see OED): open reprisals can be avoided, secret ones are
certain to succeed.

Till to revenge thou know, when, where and how.
                                        A noise within.
How now, what noise? what coil is that you keep?

Enter a Servant.

Serv. Here are a sort of poor petitioners,
      That are importunate, and it shall please you, sir,
      That you should plead their cases to the king.
Hier. That I should plead their several actions?
      Why, let them enter, and let me see them.   50

Enter three Citizens *and an* Old Man.

  1. So I tell you this: for learning and for law,
     There is not any advocate in Spain
     That can prevail, or will take half the pain
     That he will, in pursuit of equity.
Hier. Come near, you men, that thus importune me.—
      [*Aside.*] Now must I bear a face of gravity;
      For thus I us'd, before my marshalship,
      To plead in causes as corregidor.—
      Come on, sirs, what's the matter?
  2.   Sir, an action.
Hier. Of battery?
  2.   Mine of debt.
Hier.   Give place.   60
  2. No, sir, mine is an action of the case.
  3. Mine an *ejectione firmae* by a lease.
Hier. Content you, sirs; are you determinèd
      That I should plead your several actions?
  1. Ay, sir, and here's my declaration.
  2. And here is my bond.
  3.   And here is my lease.
                                   They give him papers.

Hier. But wherefore stands yon silly man so mute,
      With mournful eyes and hands to heav'n uprear'd?
      Come hither, father, let me know thy cause.
Senex. O worthy sir, my cause, but slightly known,   70

May move the hearts of warlike Myrmidons,
And melt the Corsic rocks with ruthful tears.

Hier. Say, father, tell me what's thy suit?

Senex. No, sir, could my woes
  Give way unto my most distressful words,
  Then could I not in paper, as you see,
  With ink bewray what blood began in me.

Hier. What's here?   " The humble supplication
  Of Don Bazulto for his murder'd son."

Senex. Ay, sir.

Hier.   No, sir, it was my murder'd son: 80
  O my son, my son, O my son Horatio!
  But mine, or thine, Bazulto, be content.
  Here, take my handkercher, and wipe thine eyes,
  Whiles wretched I in thy mishaps may see
  The lively portrait of my dying self.

                              He draweth out a bloody napkin.

  O no, not this; Horatio, this was thine;
  And when I dy'd it in thy dearest blood,
  This was a token 'twixt thy soul and me,
  That of thy death revengèd I should be.
  But here, take this, and this—what, my purse?—   90
  Ay, this, and that, and all of them are thine;
  For all as one are our extremities.

1. O, see the kindness of Hieronimo!

2. This gentleness shows him a gentleman.

Hier. See, see, O see thy shame, Hieronimo;
  See here a loving father to his son!
  Behold the sorrows and the sad laments,
  That he delivereth for his son's decease!
  If love's effects so strives in lesser things,
  If love enforce such moods in meaner wits,   100
  If love express such power in poor estates:
  Hieronimo, whenas a raging sea,

---

71 *Myrmidons:* Achilles's followers.

72 *Corsic rocks:* rocks of Corsica (Senecan image).

90 Q punctuates " this, what my purse? " Perhaps it should be " this—what not?
my purse?", which would restore metre and make good sense.

Toss'd with the wind and tide, o'erturneth them,
The upper billows course of waves do keep,
Whilst lesser waters labour in the deep:
Then sham'st thou not, Hieronimo, to neglect
The sweet revenge of thy Horatio?
Though on this earth justice will not be found,
I'll down to hell, and in this passion
Knock at the dismal gates of Pluto's court,   110
Getting by force, as once Alcides did,
A troop of Furies and tormenting hags
To torture Don Lorenzo and the rest.
Yet lest the triple-headed porter should
Deny my passage to the slimy strand,
The Thracian poet thou shalt counterfeit:
Come on, old father, be my Orpheus,
And if thou canst no notes upon the harp,
Then sound the burden of thy sore heart's grief,
Till we do gain that Proserpine may grant   120
Revenge on them that murderèd my son.
Then will I rent and tear them, thus and thus,
Shiv'ring their limbs in pieces with my teeth.

                                        Tear the papers.
1. O sir, my declaration!   *Exit Hieronimo, and they after.*
2.   Save my bond!

                    Enter HIERONIMO.

3. Alas, my lease! it cost me ten pound,
   And you, my lord, have torn the same.
Hier. That cannot be, I gave it never a wound;
   Show me one drop of blood fall from the same:

103 *o'erturneth them* (C)] ore turnest then Q.
104 *do keep* (C)] to keep Q. Hieronimo reflects that in a storm the stronger
   waves keep their course, and that he should therefore (being of higher
   rank) excel the old man's passion and dedication.
124 *s.d.,* 125 *s.d.* Placed thus in Q, but they are anticipatory: he has only one
   exit (at 130, followed by the Citizens) and one entry (a few moments later,
   to Bazulto). The direction at 130 gives a supplementary account of the stage
   business.
125 After this line, Q repeats "2. Saue my bond.", probably in the compositor's
   confusion over the placing of the stage directions (see previous note). I
   omit.

How is it possible I should slay it then?
Tush, no; run after, catch me if you can.   130
Exeunt all but the Old Man.   Bazulto remains till Hieronimo
enters again, who, staring him in the face, speaks.

Hier. And art thou come, Horatio, from the depth,
To ask for justice in this upper earth,
To tell thy father thou art unreveng'd,
To wring more tears from Isabella's eyes,
Whose lights are dimm'd with over-long laments?
Go back, my son, complain to Aeacus,
For here's no justice; gentle boy, be gone,
For justice is exilèd from the earth:
Hieronimo will bear thee company.
Thy mother cries on righteous Rhadamanth   140
For just revenge against the murderers.

Senex. Alas, my lord, whence springs this troubled speech?

Hier. But let me look on my Horatio.
Sweet boy, how art thou chang'd in death's black shade!
Had Proserpine no pity on thy youth,
But suffer'd thy fair crimson-colour'd spring
With wither'd winter to be blasted thus?
Horatio, thou art older than thy father:
Ah, ruthless fate, that favour thus transforms!

Baz. Ah, my good lord, I am not your young son.   150

Hier. What, not my son? thou then a Fury art,
Sent from the empty kingdom of black night
To summon me to make appearance
Before grim Minos and just Rhadamanth,
To plague Hieronimo that is remiss,
And seeks not vengeance for Horatio's death.

Baz. I am a grievèd man, and not a ghost,
That came for justice for my murder'd son.

Hier. Ay, now I know thee, now thou nam'st thy son:
Thou art the lively image of my grief;   160
Within thy face, my sorrows I may see.
Thy eyes are gumm'd with tears, thy cheeks are wan,
Thy forehead troubled, and thy mutt'ring lips
Murmur sad words abruptly broken off
By force of windy sighs thy spirit breathes,

And all this sorrow riseth for thy son:
And selfsame sorrow feel I for my son.
Come in, old man, thou shalt to Isabel;
Lean on my arm: I thee, thou me, shalt stay,
And thou, and I, and she will sing a song,   170
Three parts in one, but all of discords fram'd:
Talk not of cords, but let us now be gone,
For with a cord Horatio was slain.   *Exeunt.*

[SCENE XIV]

Enter KING OF SPAIN, *the* DUKE, VICEROY, *and* LORENZO,
BALTHAZAR, DON PEDRO, *and* BEL-IMPERIA.

King. Go, brother, 'tis the Duke of Castile's cause;
    Salute the Viceroy in our name.
Cast.   I go.
Vic. Go forth, Don Pedro, for thy nephew's sake,
    And greet the Duke of Castile.
Ped.   It shall be so.
King. And now to meet these Portuguese:
    For as we now are, so sometimes were these,
    Kings and commanders of the western Indies.
    Welcome, brave Viceroy, to the court of Spain,
    And welcome all his honourable train!
    'Tis not unknown to us for why you come,   10
    Or have so kingly cross'd the seas:
    Sufficeth it, in this we note the troth
    And more than common love you lend to us.
    So is it that mine honourable niece
    (For it beseems us now that it be known)
    Already is betroth'd to Balthazar:
    And by appointment and our condescent
    To-morrow are they to be marrièd.
    To this intent we entertain thyself,
    Thy followers, their pleasure, and our peace.   20
    Speak, men of Portingale, shall it be so?
    If ay, say so; if not, say flatly no.

Vic. Renownèd King, I come not, as thou think'st,
      With doubtful followers, unresolvèd men,
      But such as have upon thine articles
      Confirm'd thy motion, and contented me.
      Know, sovereign, I come to solemnise
      The marriage of thy belovèd niece,
      Fair Bel-imperia, with my Balthazar,
      With thee, my son; whom sith I live to see,   30
      Here take my crown, I give it her and thee;
      And let me live a solitary life,
      In ceaseless prayers,
      To think how strangely heav'n hath thee preserv'd.
King. See, brother, see, how nature strives in him!
      Come, worthy Viceroy, and accompany
      Thy friend [, to strive] with thine extremities:
      A place more private fits this princely mood.
Vic. Or here, or where your highness thinks it good.
                        Exeunt all but Castile and Lorenzo.
Cast. Nay, stay, Lorenzo, let me talk with you.   40
      See'st thou this entertainment of these kings?
Lor. I do, my lord, and joy to see the same.
Cast. And know'st thou why this meeting is?
Lor. For her, my lord, whom Balthazar doth love,
      And to confirm their promis'd marriage.
Cast. She is thy sister?
Lor.   Who, Bel-imperia? ay,
      My gracious lord, and this is the day,
      That I have long'd so happily to see.
Cast. Thou wouldst be loath that any fault of thine
      Should intercept her in her happiness?   50
Lor. Heavens will not let Lorenzo err so much.
Cast. Why then, Lorenzo, listen to my words:
      It is suspected, and reported too,
      That thou, Lorenzo, wrong'st Hieronimo,
      And in his suits towards his majesty
      Still keep'st him back, and seek'st to cross his suit.
Lor. That I, my lord——?

37 [*to strive*] (Manly).
46 *She is thy sister?* A rhetorical question from their father, leading on to 49–50

Cast. I tell thee, son, myself have heard it said,
    When (to my sorrow) I have been asham'd
    To answer for thee, though thou art my son.   60
    Lorenzo, know'st thou not the common love
    And kindness that Hieronimo hath won
    By his deserts within the court of Spain?
    Or see'st thou not the king my brother's care
    In his behalf, and to procure his health?
    Lorenzo, shouldst thou thwart his passions,
    And he exclaim against thee to the king,
    What honour were 't in this assembly,
    Or what a scandal were 't among the kings
    To hear Hieronimo exclaim on thee?   70
    Tell me—and look thou tell me truly too—
    Whence grows the ground of this report in court?
Lor. My lord, it lies not in Lorenzo's power
    To stop the vulgar, liberal of their tongues:
    A small advantage makes a water-breach,
    And no man lives that long contenteth all.
Cast. Myself have seen thee busy to keep back
    Him and his supplications from the king.
Lor. Yourself, my lord, hath seen his passions,
    That ill beseem'd the presence of a king: 80
    And for I pitied him in his distress,
    I held him thence with kind and courteous words,
    As free from malice to Hieronimo
    As to my soul, my lord.
Cast. Hieronimo, my son, mistakes thee then.
Lor. My gracious father, believe me, so he doth.
    But what's a silly man, distract in mind
    To think upon the murder of his son?
    Alas! how easy is it for him to err!
    But for his satisfaction and the world's,   90
    'Twere good, my lord, that Hieronimo and I
    Were reconcil'd, if he misconster me.
Cast. Lorenzo, thou hast said; it shall be so.
    Go one of you, and call Hieronimo.

94 *Go one of you:* calling to an off-stage attendant.

Enter BALTHAZAR *and* BEL-IMPERIA.

Bal. Come, Bel-imperia, Balthazar's content,
    My sorrow's ease and sovereign of my bliss,
    Sith heaven hath ordain'd thee to be mine:
    Disperse those clouds and melancholy looks,
    And clear them up with those thy sun-bright eyes,
    Wherein my hope and heaven's fair beauty lies.   100
Bel. My looks, my lord, are fitting for my love,
    Which, new-begun, can show no brighter yet.
Bal. New-kindled flames should burn as morning sun.
Bel. But not too fast, lest heat and all be done.
    I see my lord my father.
Bal.   Truce, my love;
    I'll go salute him.
Cast.   Welcome, Balthazar,
    Welcome, brave prince, the pledge of Castile's peace!
    And welcome, Bel-imperia!—How now, girl?
    Why com'st thou sadly to salute us thus?
    Content thyself, for I am satisfied: 110
    It is not now as when Andrea liv'd;
    We have forgotten and forgiven that,
    And thou art gracèd with a happier love.—
    But, Balthazar, here comes Hieronimo;
    I'll have a word with him.

Enter HIERONIMO *and a* Servant.

Hier. And where's the duke?
Serv.   Yonder.
Hier.   Even so.—
    What new device have they devisèd, trow?
    Pocas palabras! mild as the lamb!
    Is't I will be reveng'd?   No, I am not the man.—
Cast. Welcome, Hieronimo.   120
Lor. Welcome, Hieronimo.
Bal. Welcome, Hieronimo.
Hier. My lords, I thank you for Horatio.

102 *no brighter* Q2] brighter Q1.
118 *Pocas palabras:* few words (Spanish).

Cast. Hieronimo, the reason that I sent
    To speak with you, is this.
Hier.   What, so short?
    Then I'll be gone, I thank you for 't.
Cast. Nay, stay, Hieronimo!—go call him, son.
Lor. Hieronimo, my father craves a word with you.
Hier. With me, sir? why, my lord, I thought you had done.
Lor. [*aside.*] No; would he had!
Cast.   Hieronimo, I hear   130
    You find yourself aggrievèd at my son,
    Because you have not access unto the king;
    And say 'tis he that intercepts your suits.
Hier. Why, is not this a miserable thing, my lord?
Cast. Hieronimo, I hope you have no cause,
    And would be loath that one of your deserts
    Should once have reason to suspect my son,
    Considering how I think of you myself.
Hier. Your son Lorenzo! whom, my noble lord?
    The hope of Spain, mine honourable friend?   140
    Grant me the combat of them, if they dare:
                   Draws out his sword.

    I'll meet him face to face, to tell me so!
    These be the scandalous reports of such
    As love not me, and hate my lord too much:
    Should I suspect Lorenzo would prevent
    Or cross my suit, that lov'd my son so well?
    My lord, I am asham'd it should be said.
Lor. Hieronimo, I never gave you cause.
Hier. My good lord, I know you did not.
Cast.   There then pause;
    And for the satisfaction of the world,   150
    Hieronimo, frequent my homely house,
    The Duke of Castile, Cyprian's ancient seat;
    And when thou wilt, use me, my son, and it:
    But here, before Prince Balthazar and me,
    Embrace each other, and be perfect friends.
Hier. Ay, marry, my lord, and shall.
    Friends, quoth he? see, I'll be friends with you all:
    Especially with you, my lovely lord;

　　　　For divers causes it is fit for us
　　　　That we be friends: the world is suspicious,　　　　160
　　　　And men may think what we imagine not.
Bal. Why, this is friendly done, Hieronimo.
Lor. And thus, I hope, old grudges are forgot.
Hier. What else? it were a shame it should not be so.
Cast. Come on, Hieronimo, at my request;
　　　　Let us entreat your company to-day.　　　　*Exeunt.*
Hier. Your lordship's to command.—Pah! keep your way:
　　　　Chi mi fa più carezze che non suole,
　　　　Tradito mi ha, o tradir vuole.

　　　　　　　　　　　　　　　　　　　　　　　Exit.

[SCENE XV]

Ghost *and* Revenge.

Ghost. Awake, Erichtho! Cerberus, awake!
　　　　Solicit Pluto, gentle Proserpine!
　　　　To combat, Acheron and Erebus!
　　　　For ne'er, by Styx and Phlegethon, in hell
　　　　[Was I distress'd with outrage sore as this,]
　　　　Nor ferried Charon to the fiery lakes
　　　　Such fearful sights, as poor Andrea sees.
　　　　Revenge, awake!
Revenge. 　　　　　　Awake? for why?
Ghost. Awake, Revenge; for thou art ill-advis'd
　　　　To sleep—awake! what, thou art warn'd to watch!　　　　10
Revenge. Content thyself, and do not trouble me.
Ghost. Awake, Revenge, if love—as love hath had—
　　　　Have yet the power of prevalence in hell!
　　　　Hieronimo with Lorenzo is join'd in league,
　　　　And intercepts our passage to revenge:
　　　　Awake, Revenge, or we are woe-begone!
Revenge. Thus worldlings ground, what they have dream'd, upon.

163 *And thus* (Dodsley)] And that Q.
168–9 "Who pays me court he was not wont to pay me,/ He has betray'd me, or
　　　would fain betray me." (McIlwraith.)
5 *[Was I . . . as this,]:* Edwards's conjectural reconstruction.
16 *ground . . . upon:* "build upon what they have merely dreamed."

Content thyself, Andrea: though I sleep,
Yet is my mood soliciting their souls.
Sufficeth thee that poor Hieronimo   20
Cannot forget his son Horatio.
Nor dies Revenge, although he sleep awhile;
For in unquiet quietness is feign'd,
And slumb'ring is a common worldly wile.
Behold, Andrea, for an instance, how
Revenge hath slept, and then imagine thou,
What 'tis to be subject to destiny.

Enter a Dumb Show.

Ghost. Awake, Revenge; reveal this mystery.
Revenge. [Lo!] the two first the nuptial torches bore
        As brightly burning as the mid-day's sun;   30
        But after them doth Hymen hie as fast,
        Clothèd in sable and a saffron robe,
        And blows them out, and quencheth them with blood,
        As discontent that things continue so.
Ghost. Sufficeth me; thy meaning's understood,
        And thanks to thee and those infernal powers,
        That will not tolerate a lover's woe.
        Rest thee, for I will sit to see the rest.
Revenge. Then argue not, for thou hast thy request.

ACT IV

[SCENE I]

Enter BEL-IMPERIA *and* HIERONIMO.

Bel. Is this the love thou bear'st Horatio?
    Is this the kindness that thou counterfeits?
    Are these the fruits of thine incessant tears?
    Hieronimo, are these thy passions,
    Thy protestations and thy deep laments,
    That thou wert wont to weary men withal?
    O unkind father!　　O deceitful world!
    With what excuses canst thou shield thyself
    From this dishonour and the hate of men?
    Thus to neglect the loss and life of him   10
    Whom both my letters and thine own belief
    Assures thee to be causeless slaughterèd!
    Hieronimo, for shame, Hieronimo,
    Be not a history to after-times
    Of such ingratitude unto thy son:
    Unhappy mothers of such children then,
    But monstrous fathers to forget so soon
    The death of those, whom they with care and cost
    Have tender'd so, thus careless should be lost.
    Myself, a stranger in respect of thee,   20
    So lov'd his life, as still I wish their deaths.
    Nor shall his death be unreveng'd by me,
    Although I bear it out for fashion's sake:
    For here I swear, in sight of heaven and earth,
    Shouldst thou neglect the love thou shouldst retain,
    And give it over, and devise no more,
    Myself should send their hateful souls to hell,

---

8 *shield* (C)] show Q, which then prints a line I omit, "With what dishonour and the hate of men" (an accidental conflation of 8 and 9).

That wrought his downfall with extremest death.
Hier. But may it be that Bel-imperia
    Vows such revenge as she hath deign'd to say?   30
    Why, then I see that heaven applies our drift,
    And all the saints do sit soliciting
    For vengeance on those cursèd murderers.
    Madam, 'tis true, and now I find it so,
    I found a letter, written in your name,
    And in that letter, how Horatio died.
    Pardon, O pardon, Bel-imperia,
    My fear and care in not believing it;
    Nor think I thoughtless think upon a mean
    To let his death be unreveng'd at full.   40
    And here I vow—so you but give consent,
    And will conceal my resolution—
    I will ere long determine of their deaths
    That causeless thus have murderèd my son.
Bel. Hieronimo, I will consent, conceal,
    And ought that may effect for thine avail,
    Join with thee to revenge Horatio's death.
Hier. On, then; and whatsoever I devise,
    Let me entreat you, grace my practices,
    For why the plot's already in mine head.   50
    Here they are.

Enter BALTHAZAR *and* LORENZO.

Bal.   How now, Hieronimo?
    What, courting Bel-imperia?
Hier.   Ay, my lord;
    Such courting as (I promise you)
    She hath my heart, but you, my lord, have hers.
Lor. But now, Hieronimo, or never,
    We are to entreat your help.
Hier.   My help?
    Why, my good lords, assure yourselves of me;
    For you have giv'n me cause,

50 The rest of the scene has so much metrical irregularity that (as Edwards convincingly argues) it may be based on defective printer's copy.

Ay, by my faith have you!

Bal.   It pleas'd you,
At the entertainment of the ambassador,   60
To grace the king so much as with a show.
Now, were your study so well furnishèd,
As for the passing of the first night's sport
To entertain my father with the like,
Or any such-like pleasing motion,
Assure yourself, it would content them well.

Hier. Is this all?

Bal.   Ay, this is all.

Hier. Why then, I'll fit you: say no more.
When I was young, I gave my mind
And plied myself to fruitless poetry;   70
Which though it profit the professor naught,
Yet is it passing pleasing to the world.

Lor. And how for that?

Hier.   Marry, my good lord, thus:
(And yet methinks, you are too quick with us)
When in Toledo there I studièd,
It was my chance to write a tragedy:
See here, my lords—   *He shows them a book.*
Which, long forgot, I found this other day.
Now would your lordships favour me so much
As but to grace me with your acting it—   80
I mean each one of you to play a part—
Assure you it will prove most passing strange,
And wondrous plausible to that assembly.

Bal. What, would you have us play a tragedy?

Hier. Why, Nero thought it no disparagement,
And kings and emperors have ta'en delight
To make experience of their wits in plays.

Lor. Nay, be not angry, good Hieronimo;
The prince but ask'd a question.

Bal. In faith, Hieronimo, and you be in earnest,   90
I'll make one.

Lor.   And I another.

Hier. Now, my good lord, could you entreat
Your sister Bel-imperia to make one?

      For what's a play without a woman in it?

Bel. Little entreaty shall serve me, Hieronimo;
      For I must needs be employèd in your play.

Hier. Why, this is well: I tell you, lordings,
      It was determinèd to have been acted,
      By gentlemen and scholars too,
      Such as could tell what to speak.

Bal. And now it shall be play'd by princes and courtiers,   100
      Such as can tell how to speak:
      If, as it is our country manner,
      You will but let us know the argument.

Hier. That shall I roundly.   The chronicles of Spain
      Record this written of a knight of Rhodes:
      He was betroth'd, and wedded at the length,
      To one Perseda, an Italian dame,
      Whose beauty ravish'd all that her beheld,
      Especially the soul of Soliman,
      Who at the marriage was the chiefest guest.   110
      By sundry means sought Soliman to win
      Perseda's love, and could not gain the same.
      Then 'gan he break his passions to a friend,
      One of his bashaws, whom he held full dear;
      Her had this bashaw long solicited,
      And saw she was not otherwise to be won,
      But by her husband's death, this knight of Rhodes,
      Whom presently by treachery he slew.
      She, stirr'd with an exceeding hate therefore,
      As cause of this slew Soliman,   120
      And, to escape the bashaw's tyranny,
      Did stab herself: and this the tragedy.

Lor. O excellent!

Bel.   But say, Hieronimo,
      What then became of him that was the bashaw?

Hier. Marry, thus: mov'd with remorse of his misdeeds,
      Ran to a mountain-top, and hung himself.

Bal. But which of us is to perform that part?

Hier. O, that will I, my lords; make no doubt of it:
      I'll play the murderer, I warrant you
      For I already have conceited that.   130

Bal. And what shall I?

Hier. Great Soliman, the Turkish emperor.

Lor. And I?

Hier.　　　　Erastus, the knight of Rhodes.

Bel. And I?

Hier.　　　　Perseda, chaste and resolute.—

And here, my lords, are several abstracts drawn,
For each of you to note your parts,
And act it, as occasion's offer'd you.
You must provide [you with] a Turkish cap,
A black mustachio and a falchion;

Gives a paper to Balthazar.

You with a cross, like to a knight of Rhodes;　140

Gives another to Lorenzo.

And, madam, you must attire yourself

He giveth Bel-imperia another.

Like Phœbe, Flora, or the huntress,
Which to your discretion shall seem best.
And as for me, my lords, I'll look to one,
And, with the ransom that the viceroy sent,
So furnish and perform this tragedy,
As all the world shall say, Hieronimo
Was liberal in gracing of it so.

Bal. Hieronimo, methinks a comedy were better.

Hier. A comedy?　　　　　　　　　　　　　150

Fie! comedies are fit for common wits:
But to present a kingly troop withal,
Give me a stately-written tragedy;
Tragædia cothurnata, fitting kings,
Containing matter, and not common things.
My lords, all this must be perform'd,
As fitting for the first night's revelling.
The Italian tragedians were so sharp of wit,
That in one hour's meditation
They would perform anything in action.　160

Lor. And well it may; for I have seen the like

---

138 [*you with*] (C). Corrects the metre, and is necessary because of the "with" in 140.
154 *Tragædia cothurnata:* buskined tragedy.

In Paris 'mongst the French tragedians.
Hier. In Paris? mass, and well rememberèd!
    There's one thing more that rests for us to do.
Bal. What's that, Hieronimo? forget not anything.
Hier. Each one of us
    Must act his part in unknown languages,
    That it may breed the more variety:
    As you, my lord, in Latin, I in Greek,
    You in Italian, and for because I know   170
    That Bel-imperia hath practis'd the French,
    In courtly French shall all her phrases be.
Bel. You mean to try my cunning then, Hieronimo?
Bal. But this will be a mere confusion,
    And hardly shall we all be understood.
Hier. It must be so, for the conclusion
    Shall prove the invention and all was good:
    And I myself in an oration,
    And with a strange and wondrous show besides,
    That I will have there behind a curtain,   180
    Assure yourself, shall make the matter known:
    And all shall be concluded in one scene,
    For there's no pleasure ta'en in tediousness.
Bal. How like you this?
Lor.   Why, thus my lord:
    We must resolve to soothe his humours up.
Bal. On then, Hieronimo; farewell till soon.
Hier. You'll ply this gear?
Lor.   I warrant you.
                    Exeunt all but Hieronimo.
Hier.   Why so:
    Now shall I see the fall of Babylon,
    Wrought by the heav'ns in this confusion.
    And if the world like not this tragedy,   190
    Hard is the hap of old Hieronimo.   *Exit.*

---

188 *Babylon:* perhaps deliberately ambiguous, referring to his enemies' wicked-
    ness (Babylon as the type of iniquity in Revelation xviii) and the confusion
    of tongues in his play (the Tower of Babel, Genesis xi).

[SCENE II]

Enter ISABELLA *with a weapon.*

Isab. Tell me no more!—O monstrous homicides!
    Since neither piety nor pity moves
    The king to justice or compassion,
    I will revenge myself upon this place,
    Where thus they murder'd my belovèd son.

                                She cuts down the arbour.

    Down with these branches and these loathsome boughs
    Of this unfortunate and fatal pine:
    Down with them, Isabella; rent them up,
    And burn the roots from whence the rest is sprung.
    I will not leave a root, a stalk, a tree,   10
    A bough, a branch, a blossom, nor a leaf,
    No, not an herb within this garden-plot—
    Accursèd complot of my misery!
    Fruitless for ever may this garden be,
    Barren the earth, and blissless whosoe'er
    Imagines not to keep it unmanur'd!
    An eastern wind, commix'd with noisome airs,
    Shall blast the plants and the young saplings;
    The earth with serpents shall be pesterèd,
    And passengers, for fear to be infect,   20
    Shall stand aloof, and, looking at it, tell:
    " There, murder'd, died the son of Isabel."
    Ay, here he died, and here I him embrace:
    See, where his ghost solicits, with his wounds,
    Revenge on her that should revenge his death.
    Hieronimo, make haste to see thy son;
    For sorrow and despair hath cited me
    To hear Horatio plead with Rhadamanth:
    Make haste, Hieronimo, to hold excus'd
    Thy negligence in pursuit of their deaths   30
    Whose hateful wrath bereav'd him of his breath.—
    Ah, nay, thou dost delay their deaths,
    Forgives the murderers of thy noble son,
    And none but I bestir me—to no end!

And as I curse this tree from further fruit,
So shall my womb be cursèd for his sake;
And with this weapon will I wound the breast,
The hapless breast, that gave Horatio suck.

She stabs herself. [*Exit.*]

[SCENE III.]

Enter HIERONIMO; *he knocks up the curtain.*
Enter the DUKE OF CASTILE.

Cast. How now, Hieronimo, where's your fellows,
    That you take all this pain?
Hier. O sir, it is for the author's credit,
    To look that all things may go well.
    But, good my lord, let me entreat your grace,
    To give the king the copy of the play:
    This is the argument of what we show.
Cast. I will, Hieronimo.
Hier.   One thing more, my good lord.
Cast. What's that?
Hier.   Let me entreat your grace
    That, when the train are pass'd into the gallery,   10
    You would vouchsafe to throw me down the key.
Cast. I will, Hieronimo.   *Exit Castile.*
Hier. What, are you ready, Balthazar?
    Bring a chair and a cushion for the king.

Enter BALTHAZAR, *with a chair.*

    Well done, Balthazar! hang up the title:
    Our scene is Rhodes;—what, is your beard on?
Bal. Half on; the other is in my hand.
Hier. Despatch for shame; are you so long?   *Exit Balthazar.*
    Bethink thyself, Hieronimo,

---

11 *throw me down the key:* Though this action is precluded by the end of IV. iii and beginning of IV. iv, the request establishes that the royal spectators are to be considered as locked in, and its words show that they occupy the upper level. At 156–7 they can easily descend (during the struggle between Hieronimo and the attendants who "Break ope the doors") to the platform.

Recall thy wits, recount thy former wrongs   20
Thou hast receiv'd by murder of thy son,
And lastly, not least, how Isabel,
Once his mother and thy dearest wife,
All woe-begone for him, hath slain herself.
Behoves thee then, Hieronimo, to be reveng'd:
The plot is laid of dire revenge:
On, then, Hieronimo, pursue revenge,
For nothing wants but acting of revenge.

Exit Hieronimo.

[SCENE IV.]

Enter SPANISH KING, VICEROY, *the* DUKE OF CASTILE,
and their train.

King. Now, Viceroy, shall we see the tragedy
    Of Soliman, the Turkish emperor,
    Perform'd of pleasure by your son the prince,
    My nephew Don Lorenzo, and my niece.
Vic. Who? Bel-imperia?
King. Ay, and Hieronimo, our marshal,
    At whose request they deign to do't themselves:
    These be our pastimes in the court of Spain.
    Here, brother, you shall be the bookkeeper:
    This is the argument of that they show.   10
                    He giveth him a book.
    Gentlemen, this play of Hieronimo, in sundry languages, was
    thought good to be set down in English more largely, for the
    easier understanding to every public reader.

Enter BALTHAZAR, BEL-IMPERIA, *and* HIERONIMO.

Bal. Bashaw, that Rhodes is ours, yield heavens the honour,
    And holy Mahomet, our sacred prophet!
    And be thou grac'd with every excellence

---

10 *Publisher's Note:* Edwards satisfactorily explains the inconsistency over the
  "sundry languages" by postulating two versions, the one using these
  English speeches, the other mainly in mime with a few foreign phrases
  uttered.

That Soliman can give, or thou desire.
But thy desert in conquering Rhodes is less
Than in reserving this fair Christian nymph,
Perseda, blissful lamp of excellence,
Whose eyes compel, like powerful adamant,
The warlike heart of Soliman to wait.

King. See, Viceroy, that is Balthazar, your son,   20
    That represents the emperor Soliman:
    How well he acts his amorous passion!

Vic. Ay, Bel-imperia hath taught him that.

Cast. That's because his mind runs all on Bel-imperia.

Hier. Whatever joy earth yields betide your majesty.

Bal. Earth yields no joy without Perseda's love.

Hier. Let then Perseda on your grace attend.

Bal. She shall not wait on me, but I on her:
    Drawn by the influence of her lights, I yield.
    But let my friend, the Rhodian knight, come forth,   30
    Erasto, dearer than my life to me,
    That he may see Perseda, my belov'd.

Enter [LORENZO *as*] *Erasto.*

King. Here comes Lorenzo: look upon the plot,
    And tell me, brother, what part plays he?

Bel. Ah, my Erasto, welcome to Perseda.

Lor. Thrice happy is Erasto that thou liv'st;
    Rhodes' loss is nothing to Erasto's joy:
    Sith his Perseda lives, his life survives.

Bal. Ah, bashaw, here is love between Erasto
    And fair Perseda, sovereign of my soul.   40

Hier. Remove Erasto, mighty Soliman,
    And then Perseda will be quickly won.

Bal. Erasto is my friend; and while he lives,
    Perseda never will remove her love.

Hier. Let not Erasto live to grieve great Soliman.

Bal. Dear is Erasto in our princely eye.

Hier. But if he be your rival, let him die.

Bal. Why, let him die!—so love commandeth me.
    Yet grieve I that Erasto should so die.

Hier. Erasto, Soliman saluteth thee,   50

And lets thee wit by me his highness' will,
Which is, thou shouldst be thus employ'd.   Stab him.
Bel.   *Ay me!*
Erasto! see, Soliman, Erasto's slain!
Bal. *Yet liveth Soliman to comfort thee.*
Fair queen of beauty, let not favour die,
But with a gracious eye behold his grief,
That with Perseda's beauty is increas'd,
If by Perseda grief be not releas'd.
Bel. *Tyrant, desist soliciting vain suits;*
Relentless are mine ears to thy laments,   60
As thy butcher is pitiless and base,
Which seiẓ'd on my Erasto, harmless knight.
Yet by thy power thou thinkest to command,
And to thy power Perseda doth obey:
But, were she able, thus she would revenge
Thy treacheries on thee, ignoble prince: Stab him.
And on herself she would be thus reveng'd.   Stab herself.
King. Well said, old Marshal, this was bravely done!
Hier. But Bel-imperia plays Perseda well!
Vic. Were this in earnest, Bel-imperia,   70
    You would be better to my son than so.
King. But now what follows for Hieronimo?
Hier. Marry, this follows for Hieronimo:
    Here break we off our sundry languages,
    And thus conclude I in our vulgar tongue.
    Haply you think—but bootless are your thoughts—
    That this is fabulously counterfeit,
    And that we do as all tragedians do:
    To die to-day (for fashioning our scene)
    The death of Ajax or some Roman peer,   80
    And in a minute starting up again,
    Revive to please to-morrow's audience.
    No, princes; know I am Hieronimo,
    The hopeless father of a hapless son,
    Whose tongue is tun'd to tell his latest tale,
    Not to excuse gross errors in the play.
    I see, your looks urge instance of these words;
    Behold the reason urging me to this: *Shows his dead son.*

See here my show, look on this spectacle:
Here lay my hope, and here my hope hath end;   90
Here lay my heart, and here my heart was slain;
Here lay my treasure, here my treasure lost;
Here lay my bliss, and here my bliss bereft:
But hope, heart, treasure, joy, and bliss,
All fled, fail'd, died, yea, all decay'd with this.
From forth these wounds came breath that gave me life;
They murder'd me that made these fatal marks.
The cause was love, whence grew this mortal hate;
The hate, Lorenzo and young Balthazar;
The love, my son to Bel-imperia.   100
But night, the coverer of accursèd crimes,
With pitchy silence hush'd these traitors' harms,
And lent them leave, for they had sorted leisure
To take advantage in my garden-plot
Upon my son, my dear Horatio:
There merciless they butcher'd up my boy,
In black, dark night, to pale, dim, cruel death.
He shrieks: I heard (and yet, methinks, I hear)
His dismal outcry echo in the air.
With soonest speed I hasted to the noise,   110
Where hanging on a tree I found my son,
Through-girt with wounds, and slaughter'd as you see.
And griev'd I, think you, at this spectacle?
Speak, Portuguese, whose loss resembles mine:
If thou canst weep upon thy Balthazar,
'Tis like I wail'd for my Horatio.
And you, my lord, whose reconcilèd son
March'd in a net, and thought himself unseen,
And rated me for brainsick lunacy,
With " God amend that mad Hieronimo! "—   120
How can you brook our play's catastrophe?
And here behold this bloody handkercher,
Which at Horatio's death I weeping dipp'd
Within the river of his bleeding wounds:
It as propitious, see, I have reserv'd,
And never hath it left my bloody heart,
Soliciting remembrance of my vow

With these, O, these accursèd murderers:
Which now perform'd my heart is satisfied.
And to this end the bashaw I became   130
That might revenge me on Lorenzo's life,
Who therefore was appointed to the part,
And was to represent the knight of Rhodes,
That I might kill him more conveniently.
So, Viceroy, was this Balthazar, thy son,
That Soliman which Bel-imperia,
In person of Perseda, murderèd,
Solely appointed to that tragic part
That she might slay him that offended her.
Poor Bel-imperia miss'd her part in this: 140
For though the story saith she should have died,
Yet I of kindness, and of care to her,
Did otherwise determine of her end;
But love of him whom they did hate too much
Did urge her resolution to be such.—
And, princes, now behold Hieronimo,
Author and actor in this tragedy,
Bearing his latest fortune in his fist;
And will as resolute conclude his part,
As any of the actors gone before.   150
And, gentles, thus I end my play;
Urge no more words: I have no more to say.
                                He runs to hang himself.
King. O hearken, Viceroy!   Hold, Hieronimo!
    Brother, my nephew and thy son are slain!
Vic. We are betray'd; my Balthazar is slain!
    Break ope the doors; run, save Hieronimo.
                [*They break in and hold Hieronimo.*]
    Hieronimo,
    Do but inform the king of these events;
    Upon mine honour, thou shalt have no harm.
Hier. Viceroy, I will not trust thee with my life,   160
    Which I this day have offer'd to my son.
    Accursèd wretch!

156 *s.d.* Q4.

Why stay'st thou him that was resolv'd to die?
King. Speak, traitor! damnèd, bloody murderer, speak!
　　For now I have thee, I will make thee speak.
　　Why hast thou done this undeserving deed?
Vic. Why hast thou murderèd my Balthazar?
Cast. Why hast thou butcher'd both my children thus?
Hier. [*But are you sure they are dead?*
Cast. 　　　　　　　　　　　　*Ay, slave, too sure.*
Hier. *What, and yours too?*　　　　　　　　　170
Vic. *Ay, all are dead; not one of them survive.*
Hier. *Nay, then I care not; come, and we shall be friends,*
　　Let us lay our heads together:
　　See, here's a goodly noose will hold them all.
Vic. *O damnèd devil, how secure he is!*
Hier. *Secure? why, dost thou wonder at it?*
　　I tell thee, Viceroy, this day I have seen revenge,
　　And in that sight am grown a prouder monarch,
　　Than ever sat under the crown of Spain.
　　Had I as many lives as there be stars,　　　180
　　As many heavens to go to, as those lives,
　　I'd give them all, ay, and my soul to boot,
　　But I would see thee ride in this red pool.]
　　O, good words!
　　As dear to me was my Horatio,
　　As yours, or yours, or yours, my lord, to you.
　　My guiltless son was by Lorenzo slain,
　　And by Lorenzo and that Balthazar
　　Am I at last revengèd thoroughly,
　　Upon whose souls may heavens be yet aveng'd　190
　　With greater far than these afflictions.
Cast. But who were thy confederates in this?
Vic. That was thy daughter Bel-imperia;
　　For by her hand my Balthazar was slain:

166 *Why hast thou done this undeserving deed?* Another great inconsistency (after Hieronimo's long explanatory narrative of Horatio's murder), also explained by Edwards as evidence of alternative versions of the final scene: the version in which Hieronimo bites out his tongue rather than speak, and then kills Castile and himself with a penknife, has probably replaced a less sensational suicide.
183 *thee:* Revenge, in triumph.

I saw her stab him.

King.   Why speak'st thou not?

Hier. What lesser liberty can kings afford
    Than harmless silence? then afford it me.
    Sufficeth, I may not, nor I will not tell thee.

King. Fetch forth the tortures: traitor as thou art,
    I'll make thee tell.

Hier.   Indeed,   200
    Thou may'st torment me, as his wretched son
    Hath done in murdering my Horatio:
    But never shalt thou force me to reveal
    The thing which I have vow'd inviolate.
    And therefore, in despite of all thy threats,
    Pleas'd with their deaths, and eas'd with their revenge,
    First take my tongue, and afterwards my heart.

                              [*He bites out his tongue.*]

King. O monstrous resolution of a wretch!
    See, Viceroy, he hath bitten forth his tongue,
    Rather than to reveal what we requir'd.   210

Instead of ll. 195 (second half: "Why speak'st thou not") to 206, the Qq. from
    1602 onwards have the following passage (they have also put ll. 192–5,
    first half, before l. 184, changing "But" to "Speak,"):

> [Hier.] *Methinks, since I grew inward with revenge,*
> *I cannot look with scorn enough on death.*
>
> King. *What, dost thou mock us, slave? bring tortures forth.*
> Hier. *Do, do, do: and meantime I'll torture you.*
> *You had a son, as I take it; and your son*
> *Should ha' been married to your daughter:*
> *Ha, was it not so?—You had a son too,*
> *He was my liege's nephew; he was proud*
> *And politic; had he liv'd, he might have come*
> *To wear the crown of Spain (I think 'twas so):*
> *'Twas I that kill'd him; look you, this same hand,*
> *'Twas it that stabb'd his heart—do ye see this hand?*
> *For one Horatio, if you ever knew him: a youth,*
> *One that they hang'd up in his father's garden;*
> *One that did force your valiant son to yield,*
> *While your more valiant son did take him prisoner.*
> Vic. *Be deaf, my senses; I can hear no more.*
> King. *Fall, heav'n, and cover us with thy sad ruins.*
> Cast. *Roll all the world within thy pitchy cloud.*
> Hier. *Now do I applaud what I have acted.*
> *Nunc iners cadat manus!*
> *Now to express the rupture of my part,*

207 s.d. Q4.

Cast. Yet can he write.

King. And if in this he satisfy us not,
  We will devise th' extremest kind of death
  That ever was invented for a wretch.

      Then he makes signs for a knife to mend his pen.

Cast. O, he would have a knife to mend his pen.

Vic. Here, and advise thee that thou write the troth.

King. Look to my brother! save Hieronimo!

      He with a knife stabs the duke and himself.

  What age hath ever heard such monstrous deeds?
  My brother, and the whole succeeding hope
  That Spain expected after my decease!—   220
  Go, bear his body hence, that we may mourn
  The loss of our belovèd brother's death,
  That he may be entomb'd, whate'er befall;
  I am the next, the nearest, last of all.

Vic. And thou, Don Pedro, do the like for us:
  Take up our hapless son, untimely slain;
  Set me with him, and he with woeful me,
  Upon the main-mast of a ship unmann'd,
  And let the wind and tide haul me along
  To Scylla's barking and untamèd gulf,   230
  Or to the loathsome pool of Acheron,
  To weep my want for my sweet Balthazar:
  Spain hath no refuge for a Portingale.

    *The trumpets sound a dead march; the King of Spain
    mourning after his brother's body, and the King of
    Portingale bearing the body of his son.*   [*Exeunt.*]

[SCENE V.]

Ghost *and* Revenge.

Ghost. Ay, now my hopes have end in their effects,
  When blood and sorrow finish my desires:
  Horatio murder'd in his father's bower;
  Vild Serberine by Pedringano slain;

False Pedringano hang'd by quaint device;
Fair Isabella by herself misdone;
Prince Balthazar by Bel-imperia stabb'd;
The Duke of Castile and his wicked son
Both done to death by old Hieronimo;
My Bel-imperia fall'n, as Dido fell,   10
And good Hieronimo slain by himself:
Ay, these were spectacles to please my soul!—
Now will I beg at lovely Proserpine
That, by the virtue of her princely doom,
I may consort my friends in pleasing sort,
And on my foes work just and sharp revenge.
I'll lead my friend Horatio through those fields,
Where never-dying wars are still inur'd;
I'll lead fair Isabella to that train,
Where pity weeps, but never feeleth pain;   20
I'll lead my Bel-imperia to those joys,
That vestal virgins and fair queens possess;
I'll lead Hieronimo where Orpheus plays,
Adding sweet pleasure to eternal days.
But say, Revenge—for thou must help, or none—
Against the rest how shall my hate be shown?
Rev. This hand shall hale them down to deepest hell,
     Where none but Furies, bugs and tortures dwell.
Ghost. Then, sweet Revenge, do this at my request:
     Let me be judge, and doom them to unrest.   30
     Let loose poor Tityus from the vulture's gripe,
     And let Don Cyprian supply his room;
     Place Don Lorenzo on Ixion's wheel,
     And let the lover's endless pains surcease
     (Juno forgets old wrath, and grants him ease);
     Hang Balthazar about Chimæra's neck,
     And let him there bewail his bloody love,
     Repining at our joys that are above;
     Let Serberine go roll the fatal stone,
     And take from Sisyphus his endless moan;   40
     False Pedringano, for his treachery,
     Let him be dragg'd through boiling Acheron,
     And there live, dying still in endless flames,

Blaspheming gods and all their holy names.
Rev. Then haste we down to meet thy friends and foes:
To place thy friends in ease, the rest in woes;
For here though death hath end their misery,
I'll there begin their endless tragedy.   *Exeunt.*

45 *Then haste we down:* They may have entered in I. i from a trap (compare
Gorboduc, fourth dumb show), and, if so, now make their exit by it.

Arden of Feversham

[Dramatis Personae

THOMAS ARDEN, *Gentleman, of Feversham.*
FRANKLIN, *his Friend.*
MOSBIE.
CLARKE, *a Painter.*
ADAM FOWLE, *Landlord of the Flower-de-Luce.*
BRADSHAW, *a Goldsmith.*
MICHAEL, *Arden's Servant.*
GREENE.
RICHARD REEDE.
A SAILOR.
BLACK WILL } *Murderers.*
SHAKEBAG
A PRENTICE.
A FERRYMAN.
LORD CHEINY, *and his Men.*
MAYOR OF FEVERSHAM, *and Watch.*

ALICE, *Arden's Wife.*
SUSAN, *Mosbie's Sister.*]

Arden of Feversham

[SCENE I]

Enter ARDEN *and* FRANKLIN.

Franklin. Arden, cheer up thy spirits, and droop no more.
    My gracious Lord, the Duke of Somerset,
    Hath freely given to thee and to thy heirs,
    By letters patents from his Majesty,
    All the lands of the Abbey of Feversham.
    Here are the deeds,
    Seal'd and subscrib'd with his name and the king's:
    Read them, and leave this melancholy mood.
Arden. Franklin, thy love prolongs my weary life; 10
    And but for thee how odious were this life,
    That shows me nothing but torments my soul,
    And those foul objects that offend mine eyes;
    Which makes me wish that for this veil of heaven
    The earth hung over my head and cover'd me.
    Love-letters pass 'twixt Mosbie and my wife,
    And they have privy meetings in the town:
    Nay, on his finger did I spy the ring
    Which at our marriage-day the priest put on.
    Can any grief be half so great as this?
Franklin. Comfort thyself, sweet friend; it is not strange 20
    That women will be false and wavering.
Arden. Ay, but to dote on such a one as he
    Is monstrous, Franklin, and intolerable.
Franklin. Why, what is he?
Arden. A botcher, and no better at the first;
    Who, by base brokage getting some small stock,
    Crept into service of a nobleman,

2–5 The Duke of Somerset acted as Lord Protector (34) because Edward VI
was a minor. The abbeys had been dissolved, and their lands confiscated, by
the king's father, Henry VIII. Franklin is in the Duke's employ (ix, 105).

And by his servile flattery and fawning
Is now become the steward of his house,
And bravely jets it in his silken gown.   30
Franklin. No nobleman will countenance such a peasant.
Arden. Yes, the Lord Clifford, he that loves not me.
But through his favour let not him grow proud;
For were he by the Lord Protector back'd,
He should not make me to be pointed at.
I am by birth a gentleman of blood,
And that injurious ribald, that attempts
To violate my dear wife's chastity
(For dear I hold her love, as dear as heaven)
Shall on the bed which he thinks to defile   40
See his dissever'd joints and sinews torn,
Whilst on the planchers pants his weary body,
Smear'd in the channels of his lustful blood.
Franklin. Be patient, gentle friend, and learn of me
To ease thy grief and save her chastity:
Intreat her fair; sweet words are fittest engines
To raze the flint walls of a woman's breast.
In any case be not too jealous,
Nor make no question of her love to thee;
But, as securely, presently take horse,   50
And lie with me at London all this term;
For women, when they may, will not,
But, being kept back, straight grow outrageous.
Arden. Though this abhors from reason, yet I'll try it,
And call her forth, and presently take leave.
How, Alice!

Here enters ALICE.

Alice. Husband, what mean you to get up so early?
Summer nights are short, and yet you rise ere day.
Had I been wake, you had not risen so soon.

52 There are many imperfect lines in Q: I have emended when the original
line seemed recoverable, but I advise an intending producer to emend
freely, here reading either "For, Arden, women, when they may, will not"
or "For women, when they may, will not be naught".

Arden. Sweet love, thou know'st that we two, Ovid-like,   60
　　　　Have chid the morning when it 'gan to peep,
　　　　And often wish'd that dark night's purblind steeds
　　　　Would pull her by the purple mantle back,
　　　　And cast her in the ocean to her love.
　　　　But this night, sweet Alice, thou hast kill'd my heart:
　　　　I heard thee call on Mosbie in thy sleep.
Alice. 'Tis like I was asleep when I nam'd him,
　　　　For being awake he comes not in my thoughts.
Arden. Ay, but you started up, and suddenly,
　　　　Instead of him, caught me about the neck.   70
Alice. Instead of him? why, who was there but you?
　　　　And where but one is, how can I mistake?
Franklin. Arden, leave to urge her over-far.
Arden. Nay, love, there is no credit in a dream;
　　　　Let it suffice I know thou lovest me well.
Alice. Now I remember whereupon it came:
　　　　Had we no talk of Mosbie yesternight?
Franklin. Mistress Alice, I heard you name him once or twice.
Alice. And thereof came it, and therefore blame not me.
Arden. I know it did, and therefore let it pass.   80
　　　　I must to London, sweet Alice, presently.
Alice. But tell me, do you mean to stay there long?
Arden. No longer there till my affairs be done.
Franklin. He will not stay above a month at most.
Alice. A month? ay me! Sweet Arden, come again
　　　　Within a day or two, or else I die.
Arden. I cannot long be from thee, gentle Alice.
　　　　Whilst Michael fetch our horses from the field,
　　　　Franklin and I will down unto the quay;
　　　　For I have certain goods there to unload.   90
　　　　Meanwhile prepare our breakfast, gentle Alice;
　　　　For yet ere noon we'll take horse and away.
　　　　　　　　　　　　　　　Exeunt Arden and Franklin.
Alice. Ere noon he means to take horse and away!

60 *Ovid-like:* alluding to his poem (*Amores* I. xiii, memorably quoted in
Faustus' last soliloquy) asking the dawn to delay.
61 *Have chid* (A. H. Bullen, ed. *Arden of Feversham*, 1887.)] Have often
chid Q (caught from 62).

Sweet news is this.   O that some airy spirit
Would in the shape and likeness of a horse
Gallop with Arden 'cross the ocean,
And throw him from his back into the waves!
Sweet Mosbie is the man that hath my heart:
And he usurps it, having nought but this,
That I am tied to him by marriage.   100
Love is a god, and marriage is but words;
And therefore Mosbie's title is the best.
Tush! whether it be or no, he shall be mine,
In spite of him, of Hymen, and of rites.

Here enters ADAM *of the Flower-de-luce.*

And here comes Adam of the Flower-de-luce;
I hope he brings me tidings of my love.
—How now, Adam, what is the news with you?
Be not afraid; my husband is now from home.
Adam. He whom you wot of, Mosbie, Mistress Alice,
    Is come to town, and sends you word by me   110
    In any case you may not visit him.
Alice. Not visit him?
Adam. No, nor take no knowledge of his being here.
Alice. But tell me, is he angry or displeas'd?
Adam. Should seem so, for he is wondrous sad.
Alice. Were he as mad as raving Hercules,
    I'll see him, I; and were thy house of force,
    These hands of mine should raze it to the ground,
    Unless that thou wouldst bring me to my love.
Adam. Nay, and you be so impatient, I'll be gone.   120
Alice. Stay, Adam, stay; thou wert wont to be my friend.
    Ask Mosbie how I have incurr'd his wrath;
    Bear him from me these pair of silver dice,
    With which we play'd for kisses many a time,
    And when I lost, I won, and so did he;—
    Such winning and such losing Jove send me!
    And bid him, if his love do not decline,
    Come this morning but along my door,

---

116 *raving Hercules:* the subject of one of Seneca's plays. Compare *Midsummer Night's Dream*, I. ii. 25–34.

And as a stranger but salute me there:
This may he do without suspect or fear.   130
Adam. I'll tell him what you say, and so farewell.   *Exit Adam.*
Alice. Do, and one day I'll make amends for all.—
I know he loves me well, but dares not come,
Because my husband is so jealous,
And these my narrow-prying neighbours blab,
Hinder our meetings when we would confer.
But, if I live, that block shall be remov'd,
And, Mosbie, thou that comes to me by stealth,
Shalt neither fear the biting speech of men,
Nor Arden's looks; as surely shall he die   140
As I abhor him and love only thee.

Here enters MICHAEL.

How now, Michael, whither are you going?
Michael: To fetch my master's nag.
    I hope you'll think on me.
Alice. Ay, but, Michael, see you keep your oath,
And be as secret as you are resolute.
Michael. I'll see he shall not live above a week.
Alice. On that condition, Michael, here is my hand:
None shall have Mosbie's sister but thyself.
Michael. I understand the painter here hard by   150
    Hath made report that he and Sue is sure.
Alice. There's no such matter, Michael; believe it not.
Michael. But he hath sent a dagger sticking in a heart,
    With a verse or two stolen from a painted cloth,
    The which I hear the wench keeps in her chest.
    Well, let her keep it! I shall find a fellow
    That can both write and read and make rhyme too.
    And if I do—well, I say no more:
    I'll send from London such a taunting letter
    As she shall eat the heart he sent with salt   160
    And fling the dagger at the painter's head.
Alice. What needs all this?   I say that Susan's thine.
Michael. Why, then I say that I will kill my master,

---

160 *As she shall* (N. Delius, ed. *Arden of Feversham*, 1855.)] As shall Q.

Or anything that you will have me do.

Alice. But, Michael, see you do it cunningly.

Michael. Why, say I should be took, I'll ne'er confess
    That you know anything; and Susan, being a maid,
    May beg me from the gallows of the shrieve.

Alice. Trust not to that, Michael.

Michael. You cannot tell me, I have seen it, I.   170
    But, mistress, tell her, whether I live or die,
    I'll make her more worth than twenty painters can;
    For I will rid mine elder brother away,
    And then the farm of Bolton is mine own.
    Who would not venture upon house and land,
    When he may have it for a right down blow?

Here enters MOSBIE.

Alice. Yonder comes Mosbie.   Michael, get thee gone,
    And let not him nor any know thy drifts.   *Exit Michael.*
    Mosbie, my love!

Mosbie. Away, I say, and talk not to me now.   180

Alice. A word or two, sweet heart, and then I will.
    'Tis yet but early days, thou needs not fear.

Mosbie. Where is your husband?

Alice. 'Tis now high water, and he is at the quay.

Mosbie. There let him be; henceforward know me not.

Alice. Is this the end of all thy solemn oaths?
    Is this the fruit thy reconcilement buds?
    Have I for this given thee so many favours,
    Incurr'd my husband's hate, and, out alas!
    Made shipwreck of mine honour for thy sake?   190
    And dost thou say " henceforward know me not "?
    Remember, when I lock'd thee in my closet,
    What were thy words and mine; did we not both
    Decree to murder Arden in the night?
    The heavens can witness, and the world can tell,
    Before I saw that falsehood look of thine,
    'Fore I was tangled with thy 'ticing speech,
    Arden to me was dearer than my soul,—

174 *Bolton:* probably Boughton under Blean, near Faversham. I have retained
    all the English place-names as in Q.

And shall be still: base peasant, get thee gone,
And boast not of thy conquest over me,   200
Gotten by witchcraft and mere sorcery!
For what hast thou to countenance my love,
Being descended of a noble house,
And match'd already with a gentleman
Whose servant thou may'st be!—and so farewell.

Mosbie. Ungentle and unkind Alice, now I see
That which I ever fear'd, and find too true:
A woman's love is as the lightning-flame,
Which even in bursting forth consumes itself.
To try thy constancy have I been strange;   210
Would I had never tried, but liv'd in hope!

Alice. What need'st thou try me whom thou ne'er found false?

Mosbie. Yet pardon me, for love is jealous.

Alice. So lists the sailor to the mermaid's song,
So looks the traveller to the basilisk:
I am content for to be reconcil'd,
And that, I know, will be mine overthrow.

Mosbie. Thine overthrow? first let the world dissolve.

Alice. Nay, Mosbie, let me still enjoy thy love,
And happen what will, I am resolute.   220
My saving husband hoards up bags of gold
To make our children rich, and now is he
Gone to unload the goods that shall be thine,
And he and Franklin will to London straight.

Mosbie. To London, Alice? if thou'lt be rul'd by me,
We'll make him sure enough for coming there.

Alice. Ah, would we could!

Mosbie. I happen'd on a painter yesternight,
The only cunning man of Christendom;
For he can temper poison with his oil,   230
That whoso looks upon the work he draws
Shall, with the beams that issue from his sight,
Suck venom to his breast and slay himself.
Sweet Alice, he shall draw thy counterfeit,

222 *our children:* In Holinshed, after Arden's murder, "After supper, Mistress Arden caused her daughter to play on the virginals." In the play, where they do not appear as characters, they may be prospective.

That Arden may by gazing on it perish.
Alice. Ay, but Mosbie, that is dangerous,
  For thou, or I, or any other else,
  Coming into the chamber where it hangs, may die.
Mosbie. Ay, but we'll have it cover'd with a cloth
  And hung up in the study for himself.   240
Alice. It may not be, for when the picture's drawn,
  Arden, I know, will come and show it me.
Mosbie. Fear not; we'll have that shall serve the turn.
  This is the painter's house; I'll call him forth.
Alice. But, Mosbie, I'll have no such picture, I.
Mosbie. I pray thee leave it to my discretion.
  How, Clarke!

     Here enters CLARKE.

  Oh, you are an honest man of your word! you serv'd me
    well.
Clarke. Why, sir, I'll do it for you at any time,
  Provided, as you have given your word,   250
  I may have Susan Mosbie to my wife.
  For, as sharp-witted poets, whose sweet verse
  Make heavenly gods break off their nectar draughts
  And lay their ears down to the lowly earth,
  Use humble promise to their sacred Muse,
  So we that are the poets' favourites
  Must have a love; ay, Love is the painter's muse,
  That makes him frame a speaking countenance,
  A weeping eye that witnesses heart's grief.
  Then tell me, Master Mosbie, shall I have her? 260
Alice. 'Tis pity but he should; he'll use her well.
Mosbie. Clarke, here's my hand: my sister shall be thine.
Clarke. Then, brother, to requite this courtesy,
  You shall command my life, my skill, and all.
Alice. Ah, that thou couldst be secret.
Mosbie. Fear him not; leave; I have talk'd sufficient.
Clarke. You know not me that ask such questions.
  Let it suffice I know you love him well,
  And fain would have your husband made away:
  Wherein, trust me, you show a noble mind,   270

That rather than you'll live with him you hate,
You'll venture life, and die with him you love.
The like will I do for my Susan's sake.

Alice. Yet nothing could inforce me to the deed
But Mosbie's love.   Might I without control
Enjoy thee still, then Arden should not die:
But seeing I cannot, therefore let him die.

Mosbie. Enough, sweet Alice; thy kind words makes me melt.
Your trick of poison'd pictures we dislike;
Some other poison would do better far.   280

Alice. Ay, such as might be put into his broth,
And yet in taste not to be found at all.

Clarke. I know your mind, and here I have it for you.
Put but a dram of this into his drink,
Or any kind of broth that he shall eat,
And he shall die within an hour after.

Alice. As I am a gentlewoman, Clarke, next day
Thou and Susan shall be marrièd.

Mosbie. And I'll make her dowry more than I'll talk of, Clarke.

Clarke. Yonder's your husband.   Mosbie, I'll be gone.   290

Here enters ARDEN *and* FRANKLIN.

Alice. In good time see where my husband comes.
Master Mosbie, ask him the question yourself.   *Exit Clarke.*

Mosbie. Master Arden, being at London yesternight,
The Abbey lands whereof you are now possess'd
Were offer'd me on some occasion
By Greene, one of Sir Antony Ager's men:
I pray you, sir, tell me, are not the lands yours?
Hath any other interest herein?

Arden. Mosbie, that question we'll decide anon.
Alice, make ready my breakfast, I must hence.   300
                                                  Exit Alice.

As for the lands, Mosbie, they are mine
By letters patents from his Majesty.
But I must have a mandate for my wife;
They say you seek to rob me of her love:
Villain, what makes thou in her company?
She's no companion for so base a groom.

Mosbie. Arden, I thought not on her, I came to thee;
    But rather than I pocket up this wrong——
Franklin. What will you do, sir?
Mosbie. Revenge it on the proudest of you both.   310
                    Then Arden draws forth Mosbie's sword.
Arden. So, sirrah; you may not wear a sword,
    The statute makes against artificers;
    I warrant that I do.   Now use your bodkin,
    Your Spanish needle, and your pressing iron,
    For this shall go with me; and mark my words,
    You, goodman botcher, 'tis to you I speak:
    The next time that I take thee near my house,
    Instead of legs I'll make thee crawl on stumps.
Mosbie. Ah, Master Arden, you have injur'd me:
    I do appeal to God and to the world.   320
Franklin. Why, canst thou deny thou wert a botcher once?
Mosbie. Measure me what I am, not what I was.
Arden. Why, what art thou now but a velvet drudge,
    A cheating steward, and base-minded peasant?
Mosbie. Arden, now thou hast belch'd and vomited
    The rancorous venom of thy mis-swoll'n heart,
    Hear me but speak: as I intend to live
    With God and his elected saints in heaven,
    I never meant more to solicit her;
    And that she knows, and all the world shall see.   330
    I lov'd her once;—sweet Arden, pardon me,
    I could not choose, her beauty fir'd my heart!
    But time hath quench'd these over-raging coals;
    And, Arden, though I now frequent thy house,
    'Tis for my sister's sake, her waiting-maid,
    And not for hers.   Mayest thou enjoy her long:
    Hell-fire and wrathful vengeance light on me,
    If I dishonour her or injure thee.
Arden. Mosbie, with these thy protestations
    The deadly hatred of my heart's appeased,   340
    And thou and I'll be friends, if this prove true.
    As for the base terms I gave thee late,

312 *the statute:* a law of Edward III requiring every man to be equipped
    according to his social position.

Forget them, Mosbie: I had cause to speak,
When all the knights and gentlemen of Kent
Make common table-talk of her and thee.

Mosbie. Who lives that is not touch'd with slanderous tongues?

Franklin. Then, Mosbie, to eschew the speech of men,
Upon whose general bruit all honour hangs,
Forbear his house.

Arden. Forbear it! nay, rather frequent it more: 350
The world shall see that I distrust her not.
To warn him on the sudden from my house
Were to confirm the rumour that is grown.

Mosbie. By my faith, sir, you say true,
And therefore will I sojourn here a while,
Until our enemies have talk'd their fill;
And then, I hope, they'll cease, and at last confess
How causeless they have injur'd her and me.

Arden. And I will lie at London all this term
To let them see how light I weigh their words.   360

Here enters ALICE.

Alice. Husband, sit down; your breakfast will be cold.

Arden. Come, Master Mosbie, will you sit with us?

Mosbie. I cannot eat, but I'll sit for company.

Arden. Sirrah Michael, see our horse be ready.

Alice. Husband, why pause ye? why eat you not?

Arden. I am not well; there's something in this broth
That is not wholesome: didst thou make it, Alice?

Alice. I did, and that's the cause it likes not you.

Then she throws down the broth on the ground.
There's nothing that I do can please your taste;
You were best to say I would have poison'd you.   370
I cannot speak or cast aside my eye,
But he imagines I have stepp'd awry.
Here's he that you cast in my teeth so oft:
Now will I be convinc'd or purge myself.

364 *Michael:* No entry has been given for him. Perhaps he is off-stage, but more probably he appears with Alice and the breakfast, goes out and returns here, and is thus on stage for his marked exit at 417. I do not think he is present when Arden quarrels with Mosbie.

I charge thee speak to this mistrustful man,
Thou that wouldst see me hang, thou, Mosbie, thou:
What favour hast thou had more than a kiss
At coming or departing from the town?

Mosbie. You wrong yourself and me to cast these doubts:
Your loving husband is not jealous.   380

Arden. Why, gentle Mistress Alice,
Cannot I be ill but you'll accuse yourself?
Franklin, thou hast a box of mithridate;
I'll take a little to prevent the worst.

Franklin. Do so, and let us presently take horse;
My life for yours, ye shall do well enough.

Alice. Give me a spoon, I'll eat of it myself.
Would it were full of poison to the brim!
Then should my cares and troubles have an end.
Was ever silly woman so tormented?   390

Arden. Be patient, sweet love; I mistrust not thee.

Alice. God will revenge it, Arden, if thou dost;
For never woman lov'd her husband better
Than I do thee.

Arden. I know it, sweet Alice; cease to complain,
Lest that in tears I answer thee again.

Franklin. Come, leave this dallying, and let us away.

Alice. Forbear to wound me with that bitter word;
Arden shall go to London in my arms.

Arden. Loth am I to depart, yet I must go.   400

Alice. Wilt thou to London, then, and leave me here?
Ah, if thou love me, gentle Arden, stay.
Yet, if thy business be of great import,
Go, if thou wilt, I'll bear it as I may;
But write from London to me every week,
Nay, every day, and stay no longer there
Than thou must needs, lest that I die for sorrow.

Arden. I'll write unto thee every other tide,
And so farewell, sweet Alice, till we meet next.

Alice. Farewell, husband, seeing you'll have it so;   410
And, Master Franklin, seeing you take him hence,
In hope you'll hasten him home, I'll give you this.
                        And then she kisseth him.

Franklin. And if he stay, the fault shall not be mine.
    Mosbie, farewell, and see you keep your oath.
Mosbie. I hope he is not jealous of me now.
Arden. No, Mosbie, no; hereafter think of me
    As of your dearest friend, and so farewell.

                              Exeunt Arden, Franklin, and Michael.

Alice. I am glad he is gone; he was about to stay,
    But did you mark me then how I brake off?
Mosbie. Ay, Alice, and it was cunningly perform'd.   420
    But what a villain is this painter Clarke!
Alice. Was it not a goodly poison that he gave?
    Why, he's as well now as he was before.
    It should have been some fine confection
    That might have given the broth some dainty taste:
    This powder was too gross and populous.
Mosbie. But had he eaten but three spoonfuls more,
    Then had he died, and our love continu'd.
Alice. Why, so it shall, Mosbie, albeit he live.
Mosbie. It is unpossible, for I have sworn   430
    Never hereafter to solicit thee,
    Or, whilst he lives, once more importune thee.
Alice. Thou shalt not need, I will importune thee.
    What, shall an oath make thee forsake my love?
    As if I have not sworn as much myself
    And given my hand unto him in the church!
    Tush, Mosbie, oaths are words, and words is wind,
    And wind is mutable: then, I conclude,
    'Tis childishness to stand upon an oath.
Mosbie. Well provèd, Mistress Alice; yet by your leave   440
    I'll keep mine unbroken whilst he lives.
Alice. Ay, do, and spare not, his time is but short;
    For if thou beest as resolute as I,
    We'll have him murder'd as he walks the streets.
    In London many alehouse ruffians keep,
    Which, as I hear, will murder men for gold.
    They shall be soundly fee'd to pay him home.

                    Here enters GREENE.

Mosbie. Alice, what's he that comes yonder? knowest thou him?

Alice, Mosbie, be gone: I hope 'tis one that comes
    To put in practice our intended drifts.   *Exit Mosbie.*
Greene. Mistress Arden, you are well met.   451
    I am sorry that your husband is from home,
    Whenas my purpos'd journey was to him:
    Yet all my labour is not spent in vain,
    For I suppose that you can full discourse
    And flat resolve me of the thing I seek.
Alice. What is it, Master Greene?   If that I may
    Or can with safety, I will answer you.
Greene. I heard your husband hath the grant of late,
    Confirm'd by letters patents from the king,   460
    Of all the lands of the Abbey of Feversham,
    Generally intitl'd, so that all former grants
    Are cut off; whereof I myself had one;
    But now my interest by that is void.
    This is all, Mistress Arden; is it true or no?
Alice. True, Master Greene; the lands are his in state,
    And whatsoever leases were before
    Are void for term of Master Arden's life;
    He hath the grant under the Chancery seal.
Greene. Pardon me, Mistress Arden, I must speak,   470
    For I am touch'd.   Your husband doth me wrong
    To wring me from the little land I have.
    My living is my life, only that [land]
    Resteth remainder of my portion.
    Desire of wealth is endless in his mind,
    And he is greedy-gaping still for gain;
    Nor cares he though young gentlemen do beg,
    So he may scrape and hoard up in his pouch.
    But, seeing he hath taken my lands, I'll value life
    As careless as he is careful for to get: 480
    And tell him this from me, I'll be reveng'd,
    And so as he shall wish the Abbey lands
    Had rested still within their former state.
Alice. Alas, poor gentleman, I pity you,
    And woe is me that any man should want!

472 *To wring me from:* not transposition but 16th-century usage.
473 [*land*] (C).

          God knows 'tis not my fault; but wonder not
          Though he be hard to others, when to me—
          Ah, Master Greene, God knows how I am us'd.
Greene. Why, Mistress Arden, can the crabbèd churl
          Use you unkindly? respects he not your birth,   490
          Your honourable friends, nor what you brought?
          Why, all Kent knows your parentage and what you are.
Alice. Ah, Master Greene, be it spoken in secret here,
          I never live good day with him alone:
          When he is at home, then have I froward looks,
          Hard words and blows to mend the match withal;
          And though I might content as good a man,
          Yet doth he keep in every corner trulls;
          And [being] weary with his trugs at home,
          Then rides he straight to London; there, forsooth,   500
          He revels it among such filthy ones
          As counsels him to make away his wife.
          Thus live I daily in continual fear,
          In sorrow, so despairing of redress
          As every day I wish with hearty prayer
          That he or I were taken forth the world.
Greene. Now trust me, Mistress Alice, it grieveth me
          So fair a creature should be so abus'd.
          Why, who would have thought the civil sir so sullen?
          He looks so smoothly. Now, fie upon him, churl!   510
          And if he live a day, he lives too long.
          But frolic, woman! I shall be the man
          Shall set you free from all this discontent;
          And if the churl deny my interest
          And will not yield my lease into my hand,
          I'll pay him home, whatever hap to me.
Alice. But speak you as you think?
Greene. Ay, God's my witness, I mean plain dealing,
          For I had rather die than lose my land.
Alice. Then, Master Greene, be counsellèd by me: 520
          Indanger not yourself for such a churl,
          But hire some cutter for to cut him short,

499 [*being*] (C).

And here's ten pound to wager them withal;
When he is dead, you shall have twenty more,
And the lands whereof my husband is possess'd
Shall be intitl'd as they were before.

Greene. Will you keep promise with me?

Alice. Or count me false and perjur'd whilst I live.

Greene. Then here's my hand, I'll have him so dispatch'd.
I'll up to London straight, I'll thither post,   530
And never rest till I have compass'd it.
Till then farewell.

Alice. Good fortune follow all your forward thoughts.
And whosoever doth attempt the deed,
A happy hand I wish, and so farewell.—   *Exit Greene.*
All this goes well: Mosbie, I long for thee
To let thee know all that I have contriv'd.

Here enters MOSBIE *and* CLARKE.

Mosbie. How, now, Alice, what's the news?

Alice. Such as will content thee well, sweetheart.

Mosbie. Well, let them pass a while, and tell me, Alice,   540
How have you dealt and temper'd with my sister?
What, will she have my neighbour Clarke, or no?

Alice. What, Master Mosbie, let him woo himself!
Think you that maids look not for fair words?
Go to her, Clarke; she's all alone within;
Michael my man is clean out of her books.

Clarke. I thank you, Mistress Arden, I will in;
And if fair Susan and I can make a gree,
You shall command me to the uttermost,
As far as either goods or life may stretch.   *Exit Clarke.*

Mosbie. Now, Alice, let's hear thy news.   551

Alice. They be so good that I must laugh for joy,
Before I can begin to tell my tale.

Mosbie. Let's hear them, that I may laugh for company.

Alice. This morning, Master Greene, Dick Greene I mean,
From whom my husband had the Abbey land,
Came hither, railing, for to know the truth

544 *fair:* a disyllable, like "hire", 567.

    Whether my husband had the lands by grant.
    I told him all, whereat he storm'd amain
    And swore he would cry quittance with the churl,   560
    And, if he did deny his interest,
    Stab him, whatsoever did befall himself.
    Whenas I saw his choler thus to rise,
    I whetted on the gentleman with words;
    And, to conclude, Mosbie, at last we grew
    To composition for my husband's death.
    I gave him ten pound for to hire knaves,
    By some device to make away the churl;
    When he is dead, he should have twenty more
    And repossess his former lands again.   570
    On this we 'greed, and he is ridden straight
    To London, [for] to bring his death about.
Mosbie. But call you this good news?
Alice. Ay, sweetheart, be they not?
Mosbie. 'Twere cheerful news to hear the churl were dead;
    But trust me, Alice, I take it passing ill
    You would be so forgetful of our state
    To make recount of it to every groom.
    What! to acquaint each stranger with our drifts,
    Chiefly in case of murder, why, 'tis the way   580
    To make it open unto Arden's self
    And bring thyself and me to ruin both.
    Forewarn'd, forearm'd; who threats his enemy,
    Lends him a sword to guard himself withal.
Alice. I did it for the best.
Mosbie. Well, seeing 'tis done, cheerly let it pass.
    You know this Greene; is he not religious?
    A man, I guess, of great devotion?
Alice. He is.

587–635 Sturgess points out the inconsistency between Clarke's reluctance
here and his earlier readiness, and thinks this Italianate episode may be a
late addition. The crucifix seems here intended to remove the accessory
Greene (587–91)—who is therefore most incongruously declared to
be very religious—while at x. 77–81 it is intended for Arden. Scene i
would play better with a cut from 586 to 636 (which may indeed be its
original form); but to cut x. 46–103 involves sacrificing two good
speeches for Alice and Mosbie.

Mosbie. Then, sweet Alice, let it pass: I have a drift   590
    Will quiet all, whatever is amiss.

Here enters CLARKE *and* SUSAN.

Alice. How now, Clarke? have you found me false?
    Did I not plead the matter hard for you?
Clarke. You did.
Mosbie. And what? will't be a match?
Clarke. A match? Ay, faith, sir: ay, the day is mine.
    The painter lays his colours to the life,
    His pencil draws no shadows in his love.
    Susan is mine.
Alice. You make her blush.   600
Mosbie. What, sister, is it Clarke must be the man?
Susan. It resteth in your grant; some words are pass'd,
    And haply we be grown unto a match,
    If you be willing that it shall be so.
Mosbie. Ah, Master Clarke, it resteth at my grant:
    You see my sister's yet at my dispose,
    But, so you'll grant me one thing I shall ask,
    I am content my sister shall be yours.
Clarke. What is it, Master Mosbie?
Mosbie. I do remember once in secret talk   610
    You told me how you could compound by art
    A crucifix impoison'd,
    That whoso look upon it should wax blind
    And with the scent be stifled, that ere long
    He should die poison'd that did view it well.
    I would have you make me such a crucifix,
    And then I'll grant my sister shall be yours.
Clarke. Though I am loth, because it toucheth life,
    Yet, rather or I'll leave sweet Susan's love,
    I'll do it, and with all the haste I may.   620
    But for whom is it?
Alice. Leave that to us.   Why, Clarke, is it possible
    That you should paint and draw it out yourself,
    The colours being baleful and impoison'd,
    And no ways prejudice yourself withal?
Mosbie. Well question'd, Alice; Clarke, how answer you that?

Clarke. Very easily: I'll tell you straight
    How I do work of these impoison'd drugs.
    I fasten on my spectacles so close
    As nothing can any way offend my sight;   630
    Then, as I put a leaf within my nose,
    So put I rhubarb to avoid the smell,
    And softly as another work I paint.
Mosbie. 'Tis very well; but against when shall I have it?
Clarke. Within this ten days.
Mosbie.   'Twill serve the turn.
    Now, Alice, let's in and see what cheer you keep.
    I hope, now Master Arden is from home,
    You'll give me leave to play your husband's part.
Alice. Mosbie, you know, who's master of my heart,
    He well may be the master of the house.   640
                                    Exeunt.

[SCENE II]

Enter GREENE *and* BRADSHAW.

Bradshaw. See you them that comes yonder, Master Greene?
Greene. Ay, very well: do you know them?

Here enters BLACK WILL *and* SHAKEBAG.

Bradshaw. The one I know not, but he seems a knave
    Chiefly for bearing the other company;
    For such a slave, so vile a rogue as he,
    Lives not again upon the earth.
    Black Will is his name.   I tell you, Master Greene,
    At Boulogne he and I were fellow-soldiers,
    Where he play'd such pranks
    As all the camp fear'd him for his villainy.   10
    I warrant you he bears so bad a mind
    That for a crown he'll murder any man.
Greene [*aside*]. The fitter is he for my purpose, marry!
Will. How now, fellow Bradshaw?   Whither away so early?

---

8 *Boulogne:* pronounced "Bullen" ("Bulloine", Q).

Bradshaw. O Will, times are chang'd: no fellows now,
    Though we were once together in the field;
    Yet thy friend to do thee any good I can.

Will. Why, Bradshaw, was not thou and I fellow-soldiers at
    Boulogne, where I was a corporal, and thou but a base
    mercenary groom? No fellows now! because you are a
    goldsmith and have a little plate in your shop! You were
    glad to call me " fellow Will," and with a curtsey to the
    earth, " One snatch, good corporal," when I stole the half
    ox from John the victualler, and domineer'd with it amongst
    good fellows in one night.   25

Bradshaw. Ay, Will, those days are past with me.

Will. Ay, but they be not past with me, for I keep that same
    honourable mind still. Good neighbour Bradshaw, you
    are too proud to be my fellow; but were it not that I see
    more company coming down the hill, I would be fellows
    with you once more, and share crowns with you too. But
    let that pass, and tell me whither you go.   32

Bradshaw. To London, Will, about a piece of service,
    Wherein haply thou may'st pleasure me.

Will. What is it?

Bradshaw. Of late Lord Cheiny lost some plate,
    Which one did bring and sold it at my shop,
    Saying he serv'd Sir Antony Cooke.
    A search was made, the plate was found with me,
    And I am bound to answer at the 'size.   40
    Now, Lord Cheiny solemnly vows,
    If law will serve him, he'll hang me for his plate.
    Now I am going to London upon hope
    To find the fellow. Now, Will, I know
    Thou art acquainted with such companions.

Will. What manner of man was he?

Bradshaw. A lean-faced writhen knave,
    Hawk-nos'd and very hollow-ey'd,
    With mighty furrows in his stormy brows;
    Long hair down his shoulders curl'd;   50
    His chin was bare, but on his upper lip
    A mutchado, which he wound about his ear.

Will. What apparel had he?

Bradshaw. A watchet satin doublet all to-torn,
    The inner side did bear the greater show;
    A pair of thread-bare velvet hose, seam-rent,
    A worsted stocking rent above the shoe,
    A livery cloak, but all the lace was off;
    'Twas bad, but yet it serv'd to hide the plate.

Will. Sirrah Shakebag, canst thou remember since we trolled the
    bowl at Sittingburgh, where I broke the tapster's head of
    the Lion with a cudgel stick?   62

Shakebag. Ay, very well, Will.

Will. Why, it was with the money that the plate was sold for.
    Sirrah Bradshaw, what wilt thou give him that can tell
    thee who sold thy plate?

Bradshaw. Who, I pray thee, good Will?

Will. Why, 'twas one Jack Fitten. He's now in Newgate for
    stealing a horse, and shall be arraigned the next 'size.

Bradshaw. Why then, let Lord Cheiny seek Jack Fitten forth,
    For I'll back and tell him who robb'd him of his plate.   71
    This cheers my heart; Master Greene, I'll leave you,
    For I must to the Isle of Sheppey with speed.

Green. Before you go, let me intreat you
    To carry this letter to Mistress Arden of Feversham
    And humbly recommend me to herself.

Bradshaw. That will I, Master Greene, and so farewell.
    Here, Will, there's a crown for thy good news.

                                      Exit Bradshaw.

Will. Farewell, Bradshaw; I'll drink no water for thy sake
    whilst this lasts.—Now, gentleman, shall we have your
    company to London?   81

Greene, Nay, stay, sirs:
    A little more I needs must use your help,
    And in a matter of great consequence,
    Wherein if you'll be secret and profound,
    I'll give you twenty angels for your pains.

---

75 *this letter:* In Holinshed, the letter is written after engaging Black Will,
    and runs, "We have got a man for our purpose, we may thank my brother
    Bradshaw." At viii. 157–9, for dramatic economy, the letter gives Alice
    the latest news, "We have missed of our purpose at London, but shall
    perform it by the way."

Will. How? twenty angels? give my fellow George Shakebag
    and me twenty angels? And if thou'lt have thy own father
    slain, that thou may'st inherit his land, we'll kill him.

Shakebag. Ay, thy mother, thy sister, thy brother, or all thy
    kin.   90

Greene. Well, this it is: Arden of Feversham
    Hath highly wrong'd me about the Abbey land,
    That no revenge but death will serve the turn.
    Will you two kill him? here's the angels down,
    And I will lay the platform of his death.

Will. Plat me no platforms; give me the money, and I'll stab
    him as he stands pissing against a wall, but I'll kill him.

Shakebag. Where is he?

Greene. He is now at London, in Aldersgate Street.

Shakebag. He's dead as if he had been condemned by an Act of
    Parliament, if once Black Will and I swear his death.   101

Greene. Here is ten pound,
    And when he is dead, ye shall have twenty more.

Will. My fingers itches to be at the peasant. Ah, that I might
    be set a-work thus through the year, and that murder would
    grow to an occupation, that a man might [follow] without
    danger of law:—zounds, I warrant I should be warden of
    the company! Come, let us be going, and we'll bait at
    Rochester, where I'll give thee a gallon of sack to handsel the
    match withal.   110

                                                    Exeunt.

[SCENE III]

Here enters MICHAEL.

Michael. I have gotten such a letter as will touch the painter.
    And thus it is:

Here enters ARDEN *and* FRANKLIN *and hears* MICHAEL *read
this letter.*

" My duty remembered, Mistress Susan, hoping in God you be

106 [*follow*] (Bullen), "follow it" (A. F. Hopkinson, *Shakespeare's Doubtful
    Plays*, 1898.)

in good health, as I Michael was at the making hereof.
This is to certify you that as the turtle true, when she hath
lost her mate, sitteth alone, so I, mourning for your absence,
do walk up and down Paul's till one day I fell asleep and
lost my master's pantofles. Ah, Mistress Susan, abolish
that paltry painter, cut him off by the shins with a frowning look of your crabbed countenance, and think upon
Michael, who, drunk with the dregs of your favour, will
cleave as fast to your love as a plaster of pitch to a galled
horse-back. Thus hoping you will let my passions pene-
trate, or rather impetrate mercy of your meek hands, I end.
            " Yours, Michael, or else not Michael."
Arden. Why, you paltry knave,
   Stand you here loitering, knowing my affairs,
   What haste my business craves to send to Kent?
Franklin. Faith, friend Michael, this is very ill,
   Knowing your master hath no more but you,   20
   And do ye slack his business for your own?
Arden. Where is the letter, sirrah? let me see it.
                    Then he gives him the letter.
   See, Master Franklin, here's proper stuff:
   Susan my maid, the painter, and my man,
   A crew of harlots, all in love, forsooth;
   Sirrah, let me hear no more of this,
   Nor for thy life once write to her a word.

    Here enters GREENE, WILL, *and* SHAKEBAG.

   Wilt thou be married to so base a trull?
   'Tis Mosbie's sister: come I once at home,
   I'll rouse her from remaining in my house.   30
   Now, Master Franklin, let us go walk in Paul's;
   Come, but a turn or two, and then away.   *Exeunt.*
Greene. The first is Arden, and that's his man,
   The other is Franklin, Arden's dearest friend.
Will. Zounds, I'll kill them all three.
Greene. Nay, sirs, touch not his man in any case;

15 *Yours, Michael, or else not Michael:* meaning that he will die unless he
    wins her hand.
27 *Nor* (E. Jacob, ed. *Arden of Feversham,* 1770.)] Now Q.

But stand close, and take you fittest standing,
And at his coming forth speed him:
To the Nag's Head, there is this coward's haunt.
But now I'll leave you till the deed be done.   *Exit Greene.*

Shakebag. If he be not paid his own, ne'er trust Shakebag.   41

Will. Sirrah Shakebag, at his coming forth I'll run him through,
and then to the Blackfriars, and there take water and away.

Shakebag. Why, that's the best; but see thou miss him not.

Will. How can I miss him, when I think on the forty angels I
must have more?

Here enters a PRENTICE.

Prentice. 'Tis very late; I were best shut up my stall, for here
will be old filching, when the press comes forth of Paul's.
    *Then lets he down his window, and it breaks Black Will's
    head.*

Will. Zounds, draw, Shakebag, draw! I am almost killed.

Prentice. We'll tame you, I warrant.   50

Will. Zounds, I am tame enough already.

Here enters ARDEN, FRANKLIN, *and* MICHAEL.

Arden. What troublesome fray or mutiny is this?

Franklin. 'Tis nothing but some brabbling paltry fray,
Devis'd to pick men's pockets in the throng.

Arden. Is't nothing else? come, Franklin, let us away.   *Exeunt.*

Will. What 'mends shall I have for my broken head?

Prentice. Marry, this 'mends, that if you get you not away all the
sooner, you shall be well beaten and sent to the Counter.
            Exit Prentice.

Will. Well, I'll be gone, but look to your signs, for I'll pull them
down all. Shakebag, my broken head grieves me not so
much as by this means Arden hath escaped. I had a glimpse of
him and his companion.   61

Here enters GREENE.

Greene. Why, sirs, Arden's as well as I; I met him and Franklin
going merrily to the ordinary. What, dare you not do it?

Will. Yes, sir, we dare do it; but, were my consent to give
again, we would not do it under ten pound more. I value

every drop of my blood at a French crown. I have had
ten pound to steal a dog, and we have no more here to kill
a man; but that a bargain is a bargain, and so forth, you
should do it yourself.   70

Greene. I pray thee, how came thy head broke?

Will. Why, thou seest it is broke, dost thou not?

Shakebag. Standing against a stall, watching Arden's coming,
a boy let down his shop-window, and broke his head;
whereupon arose a brawl, and in the tumult Arden escaped
us and passed by unthought on. But forbearance is no
acquittance; another time we'll do it, I warrant thee.

Greene. I pray thee, Will, make clean thy bloody brow,
    And let us bethink us on some other place
    Where Arden may be met with handsomely.   80
    Remember how devoutly thou hast sworn
    To kill the villain; think upon thine oath.

Will. Tush, I have broken five hundred oaths!
    But wouldst thou charm me to effect this deed,
    Tell me of gold, my resolution's fee;
    Say thou seest Mosbie kneeling at my knees,
    Offering me service for my high attempt,
    And sweet Alice Arden, with a lap of crowns,
    Comes with a lowly curtsey to the earth,
    Saying, "Take this but for thy quarterage,
    Such yearly tribute will I answer thee."   90
    Why, this would steel soft-mettled cowardice,
    With which Black Will was never tainted with.
    I tell thee, Greene, the forlorn traveller,
    Whose lips are glued with summer's parching heat,
    Ne'er long'd so much to see a running brook
    As I to finish Arden's tragedy.
    Seest thou this gore that cleaveth to my face?
    From hence ne'er will I wash this bloody stain,
    Till Arden's heart be panting in my hand.   100

Greene. Why, that's well said; but what saith Shakebag?

Shakebag. I cannot paint my valour out with words:
    But, give me place and opportunity,

---

72 *Why,* . . . *not?* i.e. "Well, it *is* broken, no matter how."
93 Q's final "with", though redundant, is idiomatic. Some editors read "yet".

Such mercy as the starven lioness,
When she is dry-suck'd of her eager young,
Shows to the prey that next encounters her,
On Arden so much pity would I take.

Greene. So should it fare with men of firm resolve.
And now, sirs, seeing [that] this accident
Of meeting him in Paul's hath no success,   110
Let us bethink us on some other place
Whose earth may swallow up this Arden's blood.

Here enters MICHAEL.

See, yonder comes his man: and wot you what?
The foolish knave is in love with Mosbie's sister,
And for her sake, whose love he cannot get
Unless Mosbie solicit his suit,
The villain hath sworn the slaughter of his master.
We'll question him, for he may stead us much.—
How now, Michael, whither are you going?

Michael. My master hath new supp'd,   120
And I am going to prepare his chamber.

Greene. Where supp'd Master Arden?

Michael. At the Nag's Head, at the eighteen pence ordinary.
How now, Master Shakebag? what, Black Will! God's
dear lady, how chance your face is so bloody?

Will. Go to, sirrah, there is a chance in it; this sauciness in you
will make you be knocked.

Michael. Nay, and you be offended, I'll be gone.

Greene. Stay, Michael, you may not 'scape us so.
Michael, I know you love your master well.   130

Michael. Why, so I do; but wherefore urge you that?

Greene. Because I think you love your mistress better.

Michael. So think not I: but say, i'faith, what if I should?

Shakebag. Come, to the purpose: Michael, we hear
You have a pretty love in Feversham.

Michael. Why, have I two or three, what's that to thee?

Will. You deal too mildly with the peasant. Thus it is:
'Tis known to us [that] you love Mosbie's sister;

133 "say" and "i'faith" do not both seem necessary, and spoil the metre. Was
the second a correction of the first?

We know besides that you have ta'en your oath
To further Mosbie to your mistress' bed,   140
And kill your master for his sister's sake.
Now, sir, a poorer coward than yourself
Was never foster'd in the coast of Kent:
How comes it then that such a knave as you
Dare swear a matter of such consequence?

Greene. Ah, Will——

Will. Tush, give me leave, there's no more but this:
Sith thou hast sworn, we dare discover all;
And hadst thou [ruth,] or should'st thou utter it,
We have devis'd a complot under hand,   150
Whatever shall betide to any of us,
To send thee roundly to the devil of hell.
And therefore thus: I am the very man,
Marked in my birth-hour by the destinies,
To give an end to Arden's life on earth;
Thou but a member but to whet the knife
Whose edge must search the closet of his breast:
Thy office is but to appoint the place,
And train thy master to his tragedy;
Mine to perform it when occasion serves.   160
Then be not nice, but here devise with us
How and what way we may conclude his death.

Shakebag. So shalt thou purchase Mosbie for thy friend,
And by his friendship gain his sister's love.

Greene. So shall thy mistress be thy favourer,
And thou disburden'd of the oath thou made.

Michael. Well, gentlemen, I cannot but confess,
Sith you have urg'd me so apparently,
That I have vow'd my master Arden's death;
And he whose kindly love and liberal hand   170
Doth challenge nought but good deserts of me,
I will deliver over to your hands.
This night come to his house at Aldersgate:
The doors I'll leave unlock'd against you come.
No sooner shall ye enter through the latch,
Over the threshold to the inner court,

148 [*ruth*] (C).

But on your left hand shall you see the stairs
That leads directly to my master's chamber:
There take him and dispose him as ye please.
Now it were good we parted company;   180
What I have promisèd, I will perform.

Will. Should you deceive us, 'twould go wrong with you.

Michael. I will accomplish all I have reveal'd.

Will. Come, let's go drink: choler makes me as dry as a dog.

         Exeunt Will, Greene, and Shakebag.   Manet Michael.

Michael. Thus feeds the lamb securely on the down,
Whilst through the thicket of an arbour brake
The hunger-bitten wolf o'erpries his haunt
And takes advantage [for] to eat him up.
Ah, harmless Arden, how, how hast thou misdone,
That thus thy gentle life is levell'd at?   190
The many good turns that thou hast done to me
Now must I quittance with betraying thee.
I that should take the weapon in my hand
And buckler thee from ill-intending foes,
Do lead thee with a wicked fraudful smile,
As unsuspected, to the slaughter-house.
So have I sworn to Mosbie and my mistress,
So have I promis'd to the slaughtermen;
And should I not deal currently with them,
Their lawless rage would take revenge on me.   200
Tush, I will spurn at mercy for this once:
Let pity lodge where feeble women lie,
I am resolv'd, and Arden needs must die.

                               Exit Michael.

[SCENE IV]

Here enters ARDEN *and* FRANKLIN.

Arden. No, Franklin, no: if fear or stormy threats,
If love of me or care of womanhood,
If fear of God or common speech of men,

189 *how, how:* Probably correct: it makes clear that the rhetorical question is not
an exclamation of reproach.

Who mangle credit with their wounding words,
And couch dishonour as dishonour buds,
Might 'join repentance in her wanton thoughts,
No question then but she would turn the leaf
And sorrow for her dissolution;
But she is rooted in her wickedness,
Perverse and stubborn, not to be reclaim'd;   10
Good counsel is to her as rain to weeds,
And reprehension makes her vice to grow
As Hydra's head that plenish'd by decay.
Her faults, methink, are painted in my face,
For every searching eye to overread;
And Mosbie's name, a scandal unto mine,
Is deeply trenchèd in my blushing brow.
Ah, Franklin, Franklin, when I think on this,
My heart's grief rends my other powers
Worse than the conflict at the hour of death.   20

Franklin. Gentle Arden, leave this sad lament:
She will amend, and so your griefs will cease;
Or else she'll die, and so your sorrows end.
If neither of these two do haply fall,
Yet let your comfort be that others bear
Your woes, twice doubled all, with patience.

Arden. My house is irksome; there I cannot rest.

Franklin. Then stay with me in London; go not home.

Arden. Then that base Mosbie doth usurp my room
And makes his triumph of my being thence.   30
At home or not at home, where'er I be,
Here, here it lies, ah Franklin, here it lies
That will not out till wretched Arden dies.

Here enters MICHAEL.

Franklin. Forget your griefs a while; here comes your man.

---

5 *couch* Q3 (1633)] cooch Q1. "Embroider with gold thread laid flat on the
surface" (OED 4b, cited by Sturgess).
13 *plenish'd* (Warnke and Proescholdt)] perisht Q. The Hydra had nine heads,
each being replaced by two fresh ones as Hercules cut them off.
19 *my other powers:* Read either "my body's other powers" or "My other vital
powers"?
32 *Here, here it lies:* at his heart. Compare *The Spanish Tragedy*, III. vi. 16.

Arden. What a'clock is't, sirrah?

Michael. Almost ten.

Arden. See, see, how runs away the weary time!
Come, Master Franklin, shall we go to bed?

Exeunt Arden and Michael.   Manet Franklin.

Franklin. I pray you, go before: I'll follow you.
—Ah, what a hell is fretful jealousy!   40
What pity-moving words, what deep-fetch'd sighs,
What grievous groans and overlading woes
Accompanies this gentle gentleman!
Now will he shake his care-oppressèd head,
Then fix his sad eyes on the sullen earth,
Asham'd to gaze upon the open world;
Now will he cast his eyes up towards the heavens,
[As] looking that ways for redress of wrong:
Sometimes he seeketh to beguile his grief
And tells a story with his careful tongue;   50
Then comes his wife's dishonour in his thoughts
And in the middle cutteth off his tale,
Pouring fresh sorrow on his weary limbs.
So woe-begone, so inly charg'd with woe,
Was never any liv'd and bare it so.

Here enters MICHAEL.

Michael. My master would desire you come to bed.

Franklin. Is he himself already in his bed?

Exit Franklin.   Manet Michael.

Michael. He is, and fain would have the light away.
—Conflicting thoughts, encampèd in my breast,
Awake me with the echo of their strokes,   60
And I, a judge to censure either side,
Can give to neither wishèd victory.
My master's kindness pleads to me for life
With just demand, and I must grant it him:
My mistress she hath forc'd me with an oath,
For Susan's sake, the which I may not break,
For that is nearer than a master's love:

That grim-fac'd fellow, pitiless Black Will,
And Shakebag, stern in bloody stratagem,
—Two rougher ruffians never lived in Kent—   70
Have sworn my death, if I infringe my vow,
A dreadful thing to be consider'd of.
Methinks I see them with their bolter'd hair
Staring and grinning in thy gentle face,
And in their ruthless hands their daggers drawn,
Insulting o'er thee with a peck of oaths,
Whilst thou submissive, pleading for relief,
Art mangled by their ireful instruments.
Methinks I hear them ask where Michael is,
And pitiless Black Will cries: " Stab the slave!   80
The peasant will detect the tragedy! "
The wrinkles in his foul death-threat'ning face
Gapes open wide, like graves to swallow men.
My death to him is but a merriment,
And he will murder me to make him sport.
He comes, he comes! ah, Master Franklin, help!
Call up the neighbours, or we are but dead!

Here enters FRANKLIN *and* ARDEN.

Franklin. What dismal outcry calls me from my rest?
Arden. What hath occasion'd such a fearful cry?
    Speak, Michael: hath any injur'd thee?   90
Michael. Nothing, sir; but as I fell asleep
    Upon the threshold, leaning to the stairs,
    I had a fearful dream that troubled me,
    And in my slumber thought I was beset
    With murderer thieves that came to rifle me.
    My trembling joints witness my inward fear:
    I crave your pardons for disturbing you.
Arden. So great a cry for nothing I ne'er heard.
    What, are the doors fast lock'd and all things safe?
Michael. I cannot tell; I think I lock'd the doors.   100
Arden. I like not this, but I'll go see myself.—
    Ne'er trust me but the doors were all unlock'd:

73 *bolter'd* (Sturgess)] bolstred Q.

This negligence not half contenteth me.
Get you to bed, and if you love my favour,
Let me have no more such pranks as these.
Come, Master Franklin, let us go to bed.
Franklin. Ay, by my faith; the air is very cold.
Michael, farewell; I pray thee dream no more.   *Exeunt.*

[SCENE V]

Here enters WILL, GREENE, *and* SHAKEBAG.

Shakebag. Black night hath hid the pleasures of the day,
And sheeting darkness overhangs the earth,
And with the black fold of her cloudy robe
Obscures us from the eyesight of the world,
In which sweet silence such as we triumph.
The lazy minutes linger on their time,
[As] loth to give due audit to the hour,
Till in the watch our purpose be complete,
And Arden sent to everlasting night.
Greene, get you gone, and linger here about,   10
And at some hour hence come to us again,
Where we will give you instance of his death.
Greene. Speed to my wish, whose will so e'er says no;
And so I'll leave you for an hour or two.   *Exit Greene.*
Will. I tell thee, Shakebag, would this thing were done:
I am so heavy that I can scarce go;
This drowsiness in me bodes little good.
Shakebag. How now, Will, become a precisian?
Nay then, let's go sleep, when bugs and fears
Shall kill our courages with their fancy's work.   20
Will. Why, Shakebag, thou mistakes me much,
And wrongs me too in telling me of fear.
Were't not a serious thing we go about,
It should be slipp'd till I had fought with thee,
To let thee know I am no coward, I.

7 [*As*] (Jacob).

I tell thee, Shakebag, thou abusest me.

Shakebag. Why, thy speech bewray'd an inly kind of fear,
    And savour'd of a weak relenting spirit.
    Go forward now in that we have begun,
    And afterwards attempt me when thou darest.   30

Will. And if I do not, heaven cut me off!
    But let that pass, and show me to this house,
    Where thou shalt see I'll do as much as Shakebag.

Shakebag. This is the door; but soft, methinks 'tis shut.
    The villain Michael hath deceivèd us.

Will. Soft, let me see; Shakebag, 'tis shut indeed.
    Knock with thy sword, perhaps the slave will hear.

Shakebag. It will not be; the white-livered peasant
    Is gone to bed, and laughs us both to scorn.

Will. And he shall buy his merriment as dear   40
    As ever coistrel bought so little sport:
    Ne'er let this sword assist me when I need,
    But rust and canker after I have sworn,
    If I, the next time that I meet the hind,
    Lop not away his leg, his arm, or both.

Shakebag. And let me never draw a sword again,
    Nor prosper in the twilight, cockshut light,
    When I would fleece the wealthy passenger,
    But lie and languish in a loathsome den,
    Hated and spit at by the goers-by,   50
    And in that death may die unpitièd,
    If I, the next time that I meet the slave,
    Cut not the nose from off the coward's face
    And trample on it for this villainy.

Will. Come, let's go seek out Greene: I know he'll swear.

Shakebag. He were a villain, and he would not swear.
    'Twould make a pedant swear amongst his boys,
    That ne'er durst say before but " yea " and " no,"
    To be thus flouted of a coisterel.

Will. Shakebag, let's seek out Greene, and in the morning   60

---

57 *pedant* (C)] pesant Q. I adopt Sturgess's conjecture, since a schoolmaster
    would be found "among his boys" and might well scrupulously observe
    Christ's command "Swear not at all . . . But let your communication be,
    Yea, yea; nay, nay" (Matthew v. 34, 37).

At the alehouse butting Arden's house
Watch the out-coming of that prick-ear'd cur,
And then let me alone to handle him.   *Exeunt.*

[SCENE VI]

Here enters ARDEN, FRANKLIN, *and* MICHAEL.

Arden. Sirrah, get you back to Billingsgate
And learn what time the tide will serve our turn;
Come to us in Paul's.   First go make the bed,
And afterwards go hearken for the flood.   *Exit Michael.*
Come, Master Franklin, you shall go with me.
This night I dream'd that, being in a park,
A toil was pitch'd to overthrow the deer,
And I upon a little rising hill
Stood whistly watching for the herd's approach.
Even there, methoughts, a gentle slumber took me,   10
And summon'd all my parts to sweet repose;
But in the pleasure of this golden rest
An ill-thew'd foster had remov'd the toil,
And rounded me with that beguiling snare
Which late, methought, was pitch'd to cast the deer.
With that he blew an evil-sounding horn,
And at the noise another herdman came,
With falchion drawn, and bent it at my breast,
Crying aloud, " Thou art the game we seek! "
With this I wak'd and trembled every joint,   20
Like one obscurèd in a little bush,
That sees a lion foraging about,
And, when the dreadful forest-king is gone,
He pries about with timorous suspect
Throughout the thorny casements of the brake,
And will not think his person dangerless,
But quakes and shivers, though the cause be gone:
So, trust me, Franklin, when I did awake,

14 *snare* (C)] home Q. I regard "home" as an error deriving from "horne"
   (Q's spelling) two lines later.

I stood in doubt whether I wak'd or no:
Such great impression took this fond surprise.   30
God grant this vision bedeem me any good.
Franklin. This fantasy doth rise from Michael's fear,
Who being awakèd with the noise he made,
His troubled senses yet could take no rest;
And this, I warrant you, procur'd your dream.
Arden. It may be so, God frame it to the best:
But oftentimes my dreams presage too true.
Franklin. To such as note their nightly fantasies,
Some one in twenty may incur belief;
But use it not, 'tis but a mockery.   40
Arden. Come, Master Franklin; we'll now walk in Paul's
And dine together at the ordinary,
And by my man's direction draw to the quay,
And with the tide go down to Feversham.
Say, Master Franklin, shall it not be so?
Franklin. At your good pleasure, sir; I'll bear you company.
                                                        Exeunt.

[SCENE VII]

Here enters MICHAEL *at one door.*

Here enters GREENE, WILL, *and* SHAKEBAG *at another door.*

Will. Draw, Shakebag, for here's that villain Michael.
Greene. First, Will, let's hear what he can say.
Will. Speak, milksop slave, and never after speak.
Michael. For God's sake, sirs, let me excuse myself:
For here I swear, by heaven and earth and all,
I did perform the utmost of my task,
And left the doors unbolted and unlock'd.
But see the chance: Franklin and my master
Were very late conferring in the porch,
And Franklin left his napkin where he sat   10
With certain gold knit in it, as he said.

---

30 Compare *Richard III*, I. iv. 63: "Such terrible impression made my dream."
Clarence's prophetic dream probably inspired Arden's.

Being in bed, he did bethink himself,
And coming down he found the doors unshut:
He lock'd the gates, and brought away the keys,
For which offence my master rated me.
But now I am going to see what flood it is,
For with the tide my master will away;
Where you may front him well on Rainham Down,
A place well fitting such a stratagem.

Will. Your excuse hath somewhat mollified my choler.   20
    Why now, Greene, 'tis better now nor e'er it was.

Greene. But, Michael, is this true?

Michael. As true as I report it to be true.

Shakebag. Then, Michael, this shall be your penance,
    To feast us all at the Salutation,
    Where we will plot our purpose thoroughly.

Greene. And, Michael, you shall bear no news of this tide,
    Because they two may be in Rainham Down
    Before your master.

Michael. Why, I'll agree to anything you'll have me,   30
    So you will except of my company.   *Exeunt.*

[SCENE VIII]

Here enters MOSBIE.

Mosbie. Disturbèd thoughts drives me from company
    And dries my marrow with their watchfulness;
    Continual trouble of my moody brain
    Feebles my body by excess of drink,
    And nips me as the bitter north-east wind
    Doth check the tender blossoms in the spring.
    Well fares the man, howe'er his cates do taste,
    That tables not with foul suspicion;
    And he but pines amongst his delicates,

---

4 *drink:* If correct, this word is presumably metaphorical; but the metaphor
would be so uncharacteristically elliptical that I incline to read "grief" or
"dread".

Whose troubled mind is stuff'd with discontent.   10
My golden time was when I had no gold;
Though then I wanted, yet I slept secure;
My daily toil begat me night's repose,
My night's repose made daylight fresh to me.
But since I climb'd the top-bough of the tree
And sought to build my nest among the clouds,
Each gentlest airy gale doth shake my bed
And makes me dread my downfall to the earth.
But whither doth contemplation carry me?
The way I seek to find, where pleasure dwells,   20
Is hedg'd behind me that I cannot back,
But needs must on, although to danger's gate.
Then, Arden, perish thou by that decree;
For Greene doth ear the land and weed thee up
To make my harvest nothing but pure corn.
And for his pains I'll hive him up a while,
And after smother him to have his wax:
Such bees as Greene must never live to sting.
Then is there Michael and the painter too,
Chief actors too in Arden's overthrow;   30
Who when they shall see me sit in Arden's seat,
They will insult upon me for my meed,
Or fright me by detecting of his end.
I'll none of that, for I can cast a bone
To make these curs pluck out each other's throat,
And then am I sole ruler of mine own.
Yet Mistress Arden lives; but she's myself,
And holy church-rites makes us two but one.
But what for that?   I may not trust you, Alice:
You have supplanted Arden for my sake,   40
And will extirpen me to plant another.
'Tis fearful sleeping in a serpent's bed,
And I will cleanly rid my hands of her.

17 *gentlest airy* (P. A. McElwaine, in *Notes and Queries*, 1910.)] gentle
   stary Q.
26 *hive* (Delius)] heaue Q.
30 *too in* (C)] to Q (the usual spelling of "too", *e.g.* 29).
43 *s.d.* Alice is carrying the prayer-book of 116–22.

Here enters ALICE.

But here she comes, and I must flatter her.
—How now, Alice? what, sad and passionate?
Make me partaker of thy pensiveness:
Fire divided burns with lesser force.

Alice. But I will dam that fire in my breast
Till by the force thereof my heart consume.
Ah, Mosbie!   50

Mosbie. Such deep pathaires, like to a cannon's burst
Discharg'd against a ruinated wall,
Breaks my relenting heart in thousand pieces.
Ungentle Alice, thy sorrow is my sore;
Thou know'st it well, and 'tis thy policy
To forge distressful looks to wound a breast
Where lies a heart that dies when thou art sad.
It is not love that loves to anger love.

Alice. It is not love that loves to murder love.

Mosbie. How mean you that?   60

Alice. Thou knowest how dearly Arden lovèd me.

Mosbie. And then?

Alice. And then—conceal the rest, for 'tis too bad,
Lest that my words be carried with the wind,
And publish'd in the world to both our shames.
I pray thee, Mosbie, let our springtime wither;
Our harvest else will yield but loathsome weeds.
Forget, I pray thee, what hath pass'd betwixt us,
For now I blush and tremble at the thoughts.

Mosbie. What, are you chang'd?   70

Alice. Ay, to my former happy life again,
From title of an odious strumpet's name:
Honest Arden's wife, not Arden's honest wife.
Ha, Mosbie! 'tis thou has rifled me of that,
And made me slanderous to all my kin;
Even in my forehead is thy name ingraven,

49 *heart* (C)] part Q (in error for "hart", so spelled 53, 57].
73 *Honest Arden's wife* (C)] To honest Ardens wife Q. "To" has been inter-
  polated as the supposed consequence of "From" in 72, thus giving the
  wrong sense.

A mean artificer, that low-born name.
I was bewitch'd: woe worth the hapless hour
And all the causes that enchanted me!

Mosbie. Nay, if thou ban, let me breathe curses forth,   80
And if you stand so nicely at your fame,
Let me repent the credit I have lost.
I have neglected matters of import
That would have stated me above thy state,
Forslow'd advantages, and spurn'd at time:
Ay, Fortune's right hand Mosbie hath forsook
To take a wanton giglot by the left.
I left the marriage of an honest maid,
Whose dowry would have weigh'd down all thy wealth,
Whose beauty and demeanour far exceeded thee: 90
This certain good I lost for changing bad,
And wrack'd my credit in thy company.
I was bewitch'd,—that is no theme of thine—
And thou unhallow'd has enchanted me.
But I will break thy spells and exorcisms,
And put another sight upon these eyes
That show'd my heart a raven for a dove.
Thou art not fair, I view'd thee not till now;
Thou art not kind, till now I knew thee not;
And now the rain hath beaten off thy gilt,   100
Thy worthless copper shows thee counterfeit.
It grieves me not to see how foul thou art,
But mads me that I ever thought thee fair.
Go, get thee gone, a copesmate for thy hinds;
I am too good to be thy favourite.

Alice. Ay, now I see, and too soon find it true,
Which often hath been told me by my friends,
That Mosbie loves me not but for my wealth,
Which too incredulous I ne'er believ'd.
Nay, hear me speak, Mosbie, a word or two;   110
I'll bite my tongue if it speak bitterly.
Look on me, Mosbie, or I'll kill myself:
Nothing shall hide me from thy stormy look.

92 *wrack'd* (C)] wrapt Q. "Ruined my reputation."
103 *I ever* (C)] euer I Q.

If thou cry war, there is no peace for me;
I will do penance for offending thee,
And burn this prayer-book, where I here see
The holy word that had converted me.
See, Mosbie, I will tear away the leaf,
And all the leaves, and in this golden cover
Shall thy sweet phrases and thy letters dwell;   120
And thereon will I chiefly meditate,
And hold no other sect but such devotion.
Wilt thou not look? is all thy love o'erwhelm'd?
Wilt thou not hear? what malice stops thine ears?
Why speaks thou not? what silence ties thy tongue?
Thou hast been sighted as the eagle is,
And heard as quickly as the fearful hare,
And spoke as smoothly as an orator,
When I have bid thee hear or see or speak,
And art thou sensible in none of these?   130
Weigh all thy good turns with this little fault,
And I deserve not Mosbie's muddy looks.
A fount once troubl'd is not thicken'd still:
Be clear again, I'll ne'er more trouble thee.

Mosbie. O no, I am a base artificer:
My wings are feather'd for a lowly flight.
Mosbie? fie, no! not for a thousand pound.
Make love to you? why, 'tis unpardonable;
We beggars must not breathe where gentles are.

Alice. Sweet Mosbie is as gentle as a king,   140
And I too blind to judge him otherwise.
Flowers do sometimes spring in fallow lands,
Weeds in gardens, roses grow on thorns;
So, whatsoe'er my Mosbie's father was,
Himself [is] valued gentle by his worth.

---

116 *see* (C)] vse Q.
118 *leaf* (C)] leaues Q. Alice points (116) to a passage (doubtless in the marriage
     service) and then tears out the leaf (but not "all the leaves": 119–20 is a
     figurative way of saying that she regards Mosbie's love-letters more highly
     than the prayer-book).
133 *A fount once troubl'd* (W. Headlam, in *The Athenaeum*, 26 December 1903.)]
     A fence of trouble Q.

Mosbie. Ah, how you women can insinuate,
  And clear a trespass with your sweet-set tongue!
  I will forget this quarrel, gentle Alice,
  Provided I'll be tempted so no more.

Here enters BRADSHAW.

Alice. Then with thy lips seal up this new-made match.   150
Mosbie. Soft, Alice, for here comes somebody.
Alice. How now, Bradshaw, what's the news with you?
Bradshaw. I have little news, but here's a letter
  That Master Greene importun'd me to give you.
Alice. Go in, Bradshaw; call for a cup of beer;
  'Tis almost supper-time, thou shalt stay with us.
              Exit [*Bradshaw*].

Then she reads the letter.

" We have missed of our purpose at London, but shall per-
 form it by the way. We thank our neighbour Bradshaw.—
 Yours, Richard Greene."
  How likes my love the tenor of this letter?   160
Mosbie. Well, were his date expirèd and complete.
Alice. Ah, would it were! Then comes my happy hour:
  Till then my bliss is mix'd with bitter gall.
  Come, let us in to shun suspicion.
Mosbie. Ay, to the gates of death to follow thee.   *Exeunt.*

[SCENE IX]

Here enters GREENE, WILL, *and* SHAKEBAG.

Shakebag. Come, Will, see thy tools be in a readiness.
  Is not thy powder dank, or will thy flint strike fire?
Will. Then ask me if my nose be on my face,
  Or whether my tongue be frozen in my mouth.
  Zounds, here's a coil!
  You were best swear me on the inter'gatories

---

161 *expirèd and complete* (C)] compleat and expired Q. A transposition error.

How many pistols I have took in hand,
Or whether I love the smell of gunpowder,
Or dare abide the noise the dag will make,
Or will not wink at flashing of the fire.   10
I pray thee, Shakebag, let this answer thee,
That I have took more purses in this down
Than e'er thou handledst pistols in thy life.
Shakebag. Ay, haply thou has pick'd more in a throng:
But, should I brag what booties I have took,
I think the overplus that's more than thine
Would mount to a greater sum of money
Than either thou or all thy kin are worth.
Zounds, I hate them as I hate a toad
That carry a muscado in their tongue,   20
And scarce a hurting weapon in their hand.
Will. O Greene, intolerable!
It is not for mine honour to bear this.
Why, Shakebag, I did serve the king at Boulogne,
And thou canst brag of nothing that thou hast done.
Shakebag. Why, so can Jack of Feversham,
That sounded for a fillip on the nose,
When he that gave it him holloed in his ear,
And he suppos'd a cannon-bullet hit him.

Then they fight.

Greene. I pray you, sirs, list to Æsop's talk: 30
Whilst two stout dogs were striving for a bone,
There comes a cur and stole it from them both;
So, while you stand striving on these terms of manhood,
Arden escapes us, and deceives us all.
Shakebag. Why, he begun.
Will.   And thou shalt find I'll end;
I do but slip it until better time:
But, if I do forget——
        Then he kneels down and holds up his hands to heaven.
Greene. Well, take your fittest standings, and once more

---

26 *Jack of Feversham:* presumably a bragging local coward, invented by the
dramatist for the nonce.

Lime [me] your twigs to catch this wary bird.
I'll leave you, and at your dag's discharge   40
Make towards, like the longing water-dog
That coucheth till the fowling-piece be off,
Then seizeth on the prey with eager mood.
Ah, might I see him stretching forth his limbs,
As I have seen them beat their wings ere now!
Shakebag. Why, that thou shalt see, if he come this way.
Greene. Yes, that he doth, Shakebag, I warrant thee:
But brawl not when I am gone in any case.
But, sirs, be sure to speed him when he comes,
And in that hope I'll leave you for an hour.   50
                                        Exit Greene.

Here enters ARDEN, FRANKLIN, *and* MICHAEL.

Michael. 'Twere best that I went back to Rochester:
The horse halts downright; it were not good
He travelled in such pain to Feversham;
Removing of a shoe may haply help it.
Arden. Well, get you back to Rochester; but, sirrah, see
Ye overtake us ere we come to Rainham Down,
For it will be very late ere we get home.
Michael [aside]. Ay, God he knows, and so doth Will and Shakebag,
That thou shalt never go further than that down;
And therefore have I prick'd the horse on purpose,   60
Because I would not view the massacre.   *Exit Michael.*
Arden. Come, Master Franklin, onwards with your tale.
Franklin. I do assure you, sir, you task me much:
A heavy blood is gather'd at my heart,
And on the sudden is my wind so short
As hindereth the passage of my speech;
So fierce a qualm yet ne'er assailèd me.
Arden. Come, Master Franklin, let us go on softly:
The annoyance of the dust or else some meat
You ate at dinner cannot brook with you.   70
I have been often so, and soon amended.
Franklin. Do you remember where my tale did leave?

39 *Lime* [*me*[(C)] Lime Q. *weary:* "wearisome".

Arden. Ay, where the gentleman did check his wife.

Franklin. She being reprehended for the fact,
 Witness produc'd that took her with the deed,
 Her glove brought in which there she left behind,
 And many other assurèd arguments,
 Her husband ask'd her whether it were not so.

Arden. Her answer then? I wonder how she look'd,
 Having forsworn it with such vehement oaths,   80
 And at the instant so approv'd upon her.

Franklin. First did she cast her eyes down to the earth,
 Watching the drops that fell amain from thence;
 Then softly draws she forth her handkercher,
 And modestly she wipes her tear-stain'd face;
 Then hemm'd she out, to clear her voice should seem,
 And with a majesty address'd herself
 To encounter all their accusations.—
 Pardon me, Master Arden, I can no more;
 This fighting at my heart makes short my wind.   90

Arden. Come, we are almost now at Rainham Down:
 Your pretty tale beguiles the weary way;
 I would you were in state to tell it out.

Shakebag. Stand close, Will, I hear them coming.

    Here enters LORD CHEINY *with his men.*

Will. Stand to it, Shakebag, and be resolute.

L. Cheiny. Is it so near night as it seems,
 Or will this black-fac'd evening have a shower?
 —What, Master Arden! you are well met,
 I have long'd this fortnight's day to speak with you:
 You are a stranger, man, in the Isle of Sheppey.   100

Arden. Your honour's always! bound to do you service.

L. Cheiny. Come you from London, and ne'er a man with
   you?

Arden. My man's coming after,
 But here's my honest friend that came along with me.

L. Cheiny. My Lord Protector's man I take you to be.

Franklin. Ay, my good lord, and highly bound to you.

L. Cheiny. You and your friend come home and sup with
   me.

Arden. I beseech your honour pardon me;
    I have made a promise to a gentleman,
    My honest friend, to meet him at my house;   110
    The occasion is great, or else would I wait on you.
L. Cheiny. Will you come to-morrow and dine with me,
    And bring your honest friend along with you?
    I have divers matters to talk with you about.
Arden. To-morrow we'll wait upon your honour.
L. Cheiny. One of you stay my horse at the top of the hill.
    —What, Black Will! for whose purse wait you?
    Thou wilt be hang'd in Kent, when all is done.
Will. Not hang'd, God save your honour;
    I am your bedesman, bound to pray for you.   120
L. Cheiny. I think thou ne'er said'st prayer in all thy life.
    One of you give him a crown:—
    And, sirrah, leave this kind of life;
    If thou beest tainted for a penny-matter,
    And come in question, surely thou wilt truss.
    —Come, Master Arden, let us be going;
    Your way and mine lies four mile together.
                    Exeunt.   Manet Black Will and Shakebag.
Will. The devil break all your necks at four miles' end!
    Zounds, I could kill myself for very anger!
    His lordship chops me in,   130
    Even when my dag was levell'd at his heart.
    I would his crown were molten down his throat.
Shakebag. Arden, thou hast wondrous holy luck.
    Did ever man escape as thou hast done?
    Well, I'll discharge my pistol at the sky,
    For by this bullet Arden might not die.

                Here enters GREENE.

Greene. What, is he down? is he despatch'd?
Shakebag. Ay, in health towards Feversham, to shame us all.
Greene. The devil he is! why, sirs, how escap'd he?
Shakebag. When we were ready to shoot,   140
    Comes my Lord Cheiny to prevent his death.
Greene. The Lord of Heaven hath preserv'd him.

Will. Preserv'd a fig! The Lord Cheiny hath preserv'd him,
　　　And bids him to a feast to his house at Shorlow.
　　　But by the way once more I'll meet with him,
　　　And, if all the Cheinies in the world say no,
　　　I'll have a bullet in his breast to-morrow.
　　　Therefore come, Greene, and let us to Feversham.
Greene. Ay, and excuse ourselves to Mistress Arden:
　　　O, how she'll chafe when she hears of this!　　　150
Shakebag. Why, I'll warrant you she'll think we dare not do it.
Will. Why, then, let us go, and tell her all the matter,
　　　And plot the news to cut him off to-morrow.　　　*Exeunt.*

[SCENE X]

Here enters ARDEN *and his wife,* FRANKLIN, *and* MICHAEL.

Arden. See how the hours, the guardant of heaven's gate,
　　　Have by their toil remov'd the darksome clouds,
　　　That Sol may well discern the trampled pace
　　　Wherein he wont to guide his golden car;
　　　The season fits; come, Franklin, let's away.
Alice. I thought you did pretend some special hunt,
　　　That made you thus cut short the time of rest.
Arden. It was no chase that made me rise so early,
　　　But, as I told thee yesternight, to go
　　　To the Isle of Sheppey, there to dine with my Lord Cheiny;
　　　For so his honour late commanded me.　　　11
Alice. Ay, such kind husbands seldom want excuses;
　　　Home is a wild cat to a wandering wit.
　　　The time hath been,—would God it were not past,—
　　　That honour's title nor a lord's command
　　　Could once have drawn you from these arms of mine.
　　　But my deserts or your desires decay,
　　　Or both; yet if true love may seem desert,

143 *Preserv'd a fig!* "A fig [Italian *fica*] for the notion that he has been divinely
　　　preserved!" Sturgess adopts M. P. Jackson's suggestion "The Lord of
　　　Heaven a fig!"
3 *discern* Q3] deserue Q.
17 *desires* (Warnke and Proescholdt)] deserues Q.

I merit still to have thy company.

Franklin. Why, I pray you, sir, let her go along with us; 20
    I am sure his honour will welcome her
    And us the more for bringing her along.

Arden. Content; sirrah, saddle your mistress' nag.

Alice. No, begg'd favour merits little thanks;
    If I should go, our house would run away,
    Or else be stolen; therefore I'll stay behind.

Arden. Nay, see how mistaking you are! I pray thee, go.

Alice. No, no, not now.

Arden. Then let me leave thee satisfied in this,
    That time nor place nor persons alter me, 30
    But that I hold thee dearer than my life.

Alice. That will be seen by your quick return.

Arden. And that shall be ere night, and if I live.
    Farewell, sweet Alice, we mind to sup with thee.

                                  Exit Alice.

Franklin. Come, Michael, are our horses ready?

Michael. Ay, your horse are ready, but I am not ready, for I
    have lost my purse, with six and thirty shillings in it, with
    taking up of my master's nag.

Franklin. Why, I pray you, let us go before,
    Whilst he stays behind to seek his purse. 40

Arden. Go to, sirrah, see you follow us to the Isle of Sheppey
    To my Lord Cheiny's, where we mean to dine.

              Exeunt Arden and Franklin. Manet Michael.

Michael. So, fair weather after you, for before you lies Black
    Will and Shakebag in the broom close, too close for you.
    They'll be your ferrymen to [your] long home.

            Here enters the Painter.

But who is this? the painter, my corrival, that would
    needs win Mistress Susan.

Clarke. How now, Michael? how doth my mistress and all at
    home?

Michael. Who, Susan Mosbie? she is your mistress, too?

Clarke. Ay, how doth she and all the rest? 50

45 [your] *long* (C)] long Q.

Michael. All's well but Susan; she is sick.

Clarke. Sick? Of what disease?

Michael. Of a great fever.

Clarke. A fear of what?

Michael. A great fever.

Clarke. A fever? God forbid!

Michael. Yes, faith, and of a lurden, too, as big as yourself.

Clarke. O, Michael, the spleen prickles you. Go to, you carry
　　an eye over Mistress Susan.

Michael. Ay, faith, to keep her from the painter.　　　　60

Clarke. Why more from a painter than from a serving-creature
　　like yourself?

Michael. Because you painters make but a painting table of a
　　pretty wench, and spoil her beauty with blotting.

Clarke. What mean you by that?

Michael. Why, that you painters paint lambs in the lining of
　　wenches' petticoats, and we serving-men put horns to them
　　to make them become sheep.

Clarke. Such another word will cost you a cuff or a knock.

Michael. What, with a dagger made of a pencil? Faith, 'tis
　　too weak, and therefore thou too weak to win Susan.　　71

Clarke. Would Susan's love lay upon this stroke.

　　　　　　　　　　　　Then he breaks Michael's head.

　　　Here enters MOSBIE, GREENE, *and* ALICE.

Alice. I'll lay my life, this is for Susan's love.
　　Stay'd you behind your master to this end?
　　Have you no other time to brabble in
　　But now when serious matters are in hand?—

　　　　　　　　　　　　　　　[*Exit Michael.*]

　　Say, Clarke, hast thou done the thing thou promisèd?

Clarke. Ay, here it is; the very touch is death.

Alice. Then this, I hope, if all the rest do fail,
　　Will catch Master Arden,　　　　　　　　　80

53 *fever* (Delius)] feare Q. The humour, such as it is, of Clarke's question is the
　　humour of mis-hearing. The compositor has over-corrected Michael's line
　　by looking ahead to Clarke's. The two speeches may be a "gag" evolved
　　during performances.
57 *lurden:* Michael plays upon "lurden", an idler, and "fever-lurden", a debili-
　　tating fever (so called from the former word).

And make him wise in death that liv'd a fool.
Why should he thrust his sickle in our corn,
Or what hath he to do with thee, my love,
Or govern me that am to rule myself?
Forsooth, for credit sake, I must leave thee!
Nay, he must leave to live that we may love,
May love, may live; for what is life but love?
And love shall last as long as life remains,
And life shall end before my love depart.

Mosbie. Why, what is love without true constancy?   90
Like to a pillar built of many stones,
Yet neither with good mortar well compact
Nor cement [for] to fasten it in the joints,
But that it shakes with every blast of wind,
And, being touch'd, straight falls unto the earth,
And buries all his haughty pride in dust.
No, let our love be rocks of adamant,
Which time nor place nor tempest can asunder.

Greene. Mosbie, leave protestations now,
And let us bethink us what we have to do.   100
Black Will and Shakebag I have plac'd
I' the broom close watching Arden's coming;
Let's to them and see what they have done.   *Exeunt.*

[SCENE XI]

Here enters ARDEN *and* FRANKLIN.

Arden. Oh, ferryman, where art thou?

Here enters the FERRYMAN.

Ferryman. Here, here, go before to the boat, and I will follow
you.
Arden. We have a great haste; I pray thee, come away.

87 *May love, may live* (C)] May liue, may loue Q.
93 *Nor cement [for] to* (C)] Nor semell to Q1, Q2. Nor cement to Q3. "Semel"
is fine wheat flour or a cake made from it (OED); here an error for
"cement" (commonly spelled with initial s, and accented on the first
syllable, in 16th century).

Ferryman. Fie, what a mist is here!

Arden. This mist, my friend, is mystical,
        Like to a good companion's smoky brain,
        That was half drown'd with new ale overnight.

Ferryman. 'Twere pity but his skull were opened to make more
        chimney room.

Franklin. Friend, what's thy opinion of this mist?   10

Ferryman. I think 'tis like to a curst wife in a little house, that
        never leaves her husband till she have driven him out at
        doors with a wet pair of eyes; then looks he as if his house
        were afire, or some of his friends dead.

Arden. Speaks thou this of thine own experience?

Ferryman. Perhaps, ay; perhaps, no: for my wife is as other
        women are, that is to say, governed by the moon.

Franklin. By the moon? how, I pray thee?

Ferryman. Nay, thereby lies a bargain, and you shall not have
        it fresh and fasting.   20

Arden. Yes, I pray thee, good ferryman.

Ferryman. Then for this once let it be midsummer moon, but
        yet my wife has another moon.

Franklin. Another moon?

Ferryman. Ay, and it hath influences and eclipses.

Arden. Why, then, by this reckoning you sometimes play the
        man in the moon?

Ferryman. Ay, but you had not best to meddle with that moon,
        lest I scratch you by the face with my bramble-bush.

Arden. I am almost stifled with this fog; come, let's away.   30

Franklin. And, sirrah, as we go, let us have some more of your
        bold yeomanry.

Ferryman. Nay, by my troth, sir, but flat knavery.   *Exeunt.*

22 *midsummer moon:* when people go mad (OED).
23 *another moon:* her sexual parts.

[SCENE XII]

Here enters WILL *at one door, and* SHAKEBAG *at another.*

Shakebag. O, Will, where art thou?

Will. Here, Shakebag, almost in hell's mouth, where I cannot see my way for smoke.

Shakebag. I pray thee speak still that we may meet by the sound, for I shall fall into some ditch or other, unless my feet see better than my eyes.

Will. Didst thou ever see better weather to run away with another man's wife, or play with a wench at pot-finger?

Shakebag. No; this were a fine world for chandlers, if this weather would last; for then a man should never dine nor sup without candle-light. But, sirrah Will, what horses are those that passed?   12

Will. Why, didst thou hear any?

Shakebag. Ay, that I did.

Will. My life for thine, 'twas Arden and his companion, and then all our labour's lost.

Shakebag. Nay, say not so, for if it be they, they may haply lose their way as we have done, and then we may chance meet with them.

Will. Come, let us go on like a couple of blind pilgrims.   20

Then Shakebag falls into a ditch.

Shakebag. Help, Will, help, I am almost drowned.

Here enters the FERRYMAN.

Ferryman. Who's that that calls for help?

Will. 'Twas none here, 'twas thou thyself.

Ferryman. I came to help him that called for help.

Why, how now? who is this that's in the ditch?

You are well enough served to go without a guide such weather as this.

Will. Sirrah, what companies hath passed your ferry this morning?

---

8 *pot-finger:* "pop-finger" (OED pot, 3, cites Withals, *Dictionary*, "A potte made in the mouthe, with one finger, as children used to doo, *scloppus*"). Here with sexual innuendo.

Ferryman. None but a couple of gentlemen, that went to dine
    at my Lord Cheiny's.   31

Will. Shakebag, did not I tell thee as much?

Ferryman. Why, sir, will you have any letters carried to them?

Will. No, sir; get you gone.

Ferryman. Did you ever see such a mist as this?

Will. No, nor such a fool as will rather be hocked than get
    his way.

Ferryman. Why, sir, this is no Hock-Monday; you are deceived.
    —What's his name, I pray you, sir?

Shakebag. His name is Black Will.   40

Ferryman. I hope to see him one day hanged upon a hill.

                                          Exit Ferryman.

Shakebag. See how the sun hath clear'd the foggy mist,
    Now we have miss'd the mark of our intent.

           Here enters GREENE, MOSBIE, *and* ALICE.

Mosbie. Black Will and Shakebag, what make you here?
    What, is the deed done? is Arden dead?

Will. What could a blinded man perform in arms?
    Saw you not how till now the sky was dark,
    That neither horse nor man could be discern'd?
    Yet did we hear their horses as they pass'd.

Greene. Have they escap'd you, then, and pass'd the ferry?   50

Shakebag. Ay, for a while; but here we two will stay,
    And at their coming back meet with them once more.
    Zounds, I was ne'er so toil'd in all my life
    In following so slight a task as this.

Mosbie. How cam'st thou so beray'd?

Will. With making false footing in the dark;
    He needs would follow them without a guide.

Alice. Here's to pay for a fire and good cheer:
    Get you to Feversham to the Flower-de-luce,
    And rest yourselves until some other time.   60

Greene. Let me alone; it most concerns my state.

---

38 *Hock-Monday:* the second Monday after Easter, on which, by old custom,
    ropes are used to stop passers-by and secure them until they pay for their
    release (OED).

61 *Let me alone . . . my state:* "Leave that [payment] to me; it is my affair."

Will. Ay, Mistress Arden, this will serve the turn,
    In case we fall into a second fog.

                      Exeunt Greene, Will, and Shakebag.

Mosbie. These knaves will never do it, let us give it over.
Alice. First tell me how you like my new device:
    Soon, when my husband is returning back,
    You and I both marching arm in arm,
    Like loving friends, we'll meet him on the way,
    And boldly beard and brave him to his teeth.
    When words grow hot and blows begin to rise,   70
    I'll call those cutters forth your tenement,
    Who, in a manner to take up the fray,
    Shall wound my husband Hornsby to the death.
Mosbie. Ah, fine device! why, this deserves a kiss.   *Exeunt.*

[SCENE XIII]

Here enters DICK REEDE *and a* SAILOR.

Sailor. Faith, Dick Reede, it is to little end:
    His conscience is too liberal, and he too niggardly
    To part from any thing may do thee good.
Reede. He is coming from Shorlow as I understand;
    Here I'll intercept him, for at his house
    He never will vouchsafe to speak with me.
    If prayers and fair entreaties will not serve,
    Or make no battery in his flinty breast,

Here enters FRANKLIN, ARDEN, *and* MICHAEL.

    I'll curse the carle, and see what that will do.
    See where he comes to further my intent!—
    Master Arden, I am now bound to the sea;   10
    My coming to you was about the plot of ground
    Which wrongfully you detain from me.
    Although the rent of it be very small,
    Yet will it help my wife and children,

73 *Hornsby:* Cuckold (a nonce-coinage, by analogy with "Mosbie").

Which here I leave in Feversham, God knows,
Needy and bare: for Christ's sake, let them have it!
Arden. Franklin, hearest thou this fellow speak?
That which he craves I dearly bought of him,
Although the rent of it was ever mine.—   20
Sirrah, you that ask these questions,
If with thy clamorous impeaching tongue
Thou rail on me, as I have heard thou dost,
I'll lay thee up so close a twelve-month's day,
As thou shalt neither see the sun nor moon.
Look to it, for, as surely as I live,
I'll banish pity if thou use me thus.
Reede. What, wilt thou do me wrong and threat me too?
Nay, then, I'll tempt thee, Arden, do thy worst.
God, I beseech thee, show some miracle   30
On thee or thine, in plaguing thee for this.
That plot of ground which thou detains from me,
I speak it in an agony of spirit,
Be ruinous and fatal unto thee!
Either there be butcher'd by thy dearest friends,
Or else be brought for men to wonder at,
Or thou or thine miscarry in that place,
Or there run mad and end thy cursèd days!
Franklin. Fie, bitter knave, bridle thine envious tongue;
For curses are like arrows shot upright,   40
Which falling down light on the shooter's head.
Reede. Light where they will! Were I upon the sea,
As oft I have in many a bitter storm,
And saw a dreadful southern flaw at hand,
The pilot quaking at the doubtful storm,
And all the sailors praying on their knees,
Even in that fearful time would I fall down,
And ask of God, whate'er betide of me,
Vengeance on Arden or some misevent
To show the world what wrong the carle hath done.   50
This charge I'll leave with my distressful wife,

43 *storm:* Perhaps, since the storm is approaching (44–5), this should be "stour"
(time of stress, OED 3, in common literary use about 1590); "storme"
may be caught from 45. Yet "bitter storm" is satisfactory in itself.

    My children shall be taught such prayers as these;
    And thus I go, but leave my curse with thee.

                    Exeunt Reede and Sailor.

Arden. It is the railingest knave in Christendom,
    And oftentimes the villain will be mad;
    It greatly matters not what he says,
    But I assure you I ne'er did him wrong.
Franklin. I think so, Master Arden.
Arden. Now that our horses are gone home before,
    My wife may haply meet me on the way.   60
    For God knows she is grown passing kind of late,
    And greatly chang'd from the old humour
    Of her wonted frowardness,
    And seeks by fair means to redeem old faults.
Franklin. Happy the change that alters for the best!
    But see in any case you make no speech
    Of the cheer we had at my Lord Cheiny's,
    Although most bounteous and liberal,
    For that will make her think herself more wrong'd,
    In that we did not carry her along;   70
    For sure she griev'd that she was left behind.
Arden. Come, Franklin, let us strain to mend our pace,
    And take her unawares playing the cook;

        Here enters ALICE *and* MOSBIE.

    For I believe she'll strive to mend our cheer.
Franklin. Why, there's no better creatures in the world,
    Than women are when they are in good humours.
Arden. Who is that?   Mosbie? what, so familiar?
    Injurious strumpet, and thou ribald knave,
    Untwine those arms.
Alice. Ay, with a sugar'd kiss let them untwine.   80
Arden. Ah, Mosbie! perjur'd beast! bear this and all!
Mosbie. And yet no hornèd beast; the horns are thine.
Franklin. O monstrous! Nay, then 'tis time to draw.
Alice. Help, help! they murder my husband.

84 *s.d.* In the fight (as Will narrates, xiv. 54–68) Franklin wounds Shakebag,
    and Arden wounds Mosbie.

Here enters WILL *and* SHAKEBAG.

Shakebag. Zounds, who injures Master Mosbie? Help, Will!
    I am hurt.
Mosbie. I may thank you, Mistress Arden, for this wound.
                  Exeunt Mosbie, Will, and Shakebag.
Alice. Ah, Arden, what folly blinded thee?
    Ah, jealous harebrain man, what hast thou done!
    When we, to welcome thee, intending sport,
    Came lovingly to meet thee on thy way,   90
    Thou drew'st thy sword, enrag'd with jealousy,
    And hurt thy friend whose thoughts were free from harm:
    All for a worthless kiss and joining arms,
    Both done but merrily to try thy patience.
    Ah me unhappy that devis'd the jest,
    Which, though begun in sport, yet ends in blood!
Franklin. Marry, God defend me from such a jest!
Alice. Couldst thou not see us friendly smile on thee,
    When we join'd arms, and when I kiss'd his cheek?
    Hast thou not lately found me over-kind?   100
    Didst thou not hear me cry " they murder thee "?
    Call'd I not help to set my husband free?
    No, ears and all were witch'd; ah me accurs'd
    To link in liking with a frantic man!
    Henceforth I'll be thy slave, no more thy wife,
    For with that name I never shall content thee.
    If I be merry, thou straightways thinks me light;
    If sad, thou sayest the sullens trouble me;
    If well attir'd, thou thinks I will be gadding;
    If homely, I seem sluttish in thine eye: 110
    Thus am I still, and shall be while I die,
    Poor wench, abus'd by thy misgovernment!
Arden. But is it for truth that neither thou nor he
    Intendedst malice in your misdemeanour?
Alice. The heavens can witness of our harmless thoughts,
Arden. Then pardon me, sweet Alice, and forgive this fault!

89 *thee,* **i**ntending (F. E. Schelling, *Typical Elizabethan Plays,* 1926)] thy
    intended Q.
95 *Ah me* (C; conj. Sturgess.)] And me Q. Compare 103.

Forget but this and never see the like.
Impose me penance, and I will perform it,
For in thy discontent I find a death,
A death tormenting more than death itself.   120
Alice. Nay, hadst thou lov'd me as thou dost pretend,
Thou wouldst have mark'd the speeches of thy friend,
Who going wounded from the place, he said
His skin was pierc'd only through my device;
And if sad sorrow taint thee for this fault,
Thou wouldst have follow'd him, and seen him dress'd,
And cried him mercy whom thou has misdone:
Ne'er shall my heart be eas'd till this be done.
Arden. Content thee, sweet Alice, thou shalt have thy will,
Whate'er it be.   For that I injur'd thee,   130
And wrong'd my friend, shame scourgeth my offence;
Come thou thyself, and go along with me,
And be a mediator 'twixt us two.
Franklin. Why, Master Arden! know you what you do?
Will you follow him that hath dishonour'd you?
Alice. Why, canst thou prove I have been disloyal?
Franklin. Why, Mosbie taunt your husband with the horn.
Alice. Ay, after he had revilèd him
By the injurious name of perjured beast:
He knew no wrong could spite a jealous man   140
More than the hateful naming of the horn.
Franklin. Suppose 'tis true, yet is it dangerous
To follow him whom he hath lately hurt.
Alice. A fault confess'd is more than half amends;
But men of such ill spirit as yourself
Work crosses and debates 'twixt man and wife.
Arden. I pray thee, gentle Franklin, hold thy peace:
I know my wife counsels me for the best.
I'll seek out Mosbie where his wound is dress'd,
And salve this hapless quarrel if I may.   150
                              Exeunt Arden and Alice.
Franklin. He whom the devil drives must go perforce,

137 *taunt your* (Sturgess)] traunt you Q. Used for "taunted", for the metre.
138 *he:* Metre, here and at xiv. 71, calls for "Arden".
150 *this* (Jacob)] his Q.

Poor gentleman, how soon he is bewitch'd!
And yet, because his wife is the instrument,
His friends must not be lavish in their speech.

Exit Franklin.

[SCENE XIV]

Here enters WILL, SHAKEBAG, *and* GREENE.

Will. Sirrah Greene, when was I so long in killing a man?

Greene. I think we shall never do it; let us give it over.

Shakebag. Nay, zounds! we'll kill him, though we be hanged at
his door for our labour.

Will. Thou knowest, Greene, that I have lived in London this
twelve years, where I have made some go upon wooden
legs for taking the wall on me; divers with silver noses
for saying " There goes Black Will! " I have cracked as
many blades as thou hast done nuts.

Greene. O monstrous lie!   10

Will. Faith, in a manner I have.   The bawdy-houses have paid
me tribute; there durst not a whore set up, unless she have
agreed with me first for opening her shop-windows.   For a
cross word of a tapster I have pierced one barrel after
another with my dagger, and held him by the ears till all
his beer hath run out.   In Thames Street a brewer's cart
was like to have run over me: I made no more ado, but
went to the clerk and cut all the notches off his tallies and
beat them about his head.   I and my company have taken
the constable from his watch, and carried him about the
fields on a coltstaff.   I have broken a sergeant's head with
his own mace, and bailed whom I list with my sword and
buckler.   All the tenpenny-alehouses would stand every
morning with a quart-pot in his hand, saying, " Will it
please your worship drink? "   He that had not done so,
had been sure to have had his sign pulled down and his
lattice borne away the next night.   To conclude, what
have I not done? yet cannot do this; doubtless, he is preserved by miracle.

Here enters ALICE *and* MICHAEL.

Greene. Hence, Will! here comes Mistress Arden.
Alice. Ah, gentle Michael, art thou sure they're friends?   30
Michael. Why, I saw them when they both shook hands.
When Mosbie bled, he even wept for sorrow,
And rail'd on Franklin that was cause of all.
No sooner came the surgeon in at doors,
But my master took to his purse and gave him money,
And, to conclude, sent me to bring you word
That Mosbie, Franklin, Bradshaw, Adam Fowle,
With divers of his neighbours and his friends,
Will come and sup with you at our house this night.   40
Alice. Ah, gentle Michael, run thou back again,
And, when my husband walks into the fair,
Bid Mosbie steal from him and come to me;
And this night shall thou and Susan be made sure.
Michael. I'll go tell him.
Alice. And as thou goest, tell John cook of our guests,
And bid him lay it on, spare for no cost.   *Exit Michael.*
Will. Nay, and there be such cheer, we will bid ourselves.—
Mistress Arden, Dick Greene and I do mean to sup with you.
Alice. And welcome shall you be. Ah, gentlemen,   50
How miss'd you of your purpose yesternight?
Greene. 'Twas' long of Shakebag, that unlucky villain.
Shakebag. Thou dost me wrong; I did as much as any.
Will. Nay then, Mistress Alice, I'll tell you how it was:
When he should have lock'd with both his hilts,
He in a bravery flourish'd o'er his head;
With that comes Franklin at him lustily,
And hurts the slave; with that he slinks away.
Now his way had been to have come hand and feet,
one and two round at his costard; he like a fool bears his
sword-point half a yard out of danger. I lie here, for my
life; if the devil come, and he have no more strength than
fence, he shall never beat me from this ward. I'll stand
to it, a buckler in a skilful hand is as good as a castle; nay,

59–65 This reads like an actor's interpolation, since it disconnects "this" (66)
from its antecedent (58).

'Tis better than a sconce, for I have tried it.
Mosbie, perceiving this, began to faint:
With that comes Arden with his arming sword,
And thrust him through the shoulder in a trice.
Alice. Ay, but I wonder why you both stood still.
Will. Faith, I was so amaz'd, I could not strike.   70
Alice. Ah, sirs, had he yesternight been slain,
For every drop of his detested blood
I would have cramm'd an angel in thy fist,
And kiss'd thee, too, and hugg'd thee in my arms.
Will. Patient yourself, we cannot help it now.
Greene and we two will dog him through the fair,
And stab him in the crowd, and steal away.

Here enters MOSBIE.

Alice. It is unpossible; but here comes he
That will, I hope, invent some surer means.
Sweet Mosbie, hide thy arm, it kills my heart.   80
Mosbie. Ay, Mistress Arden, this is your favour.
Alice. Ah, say not so; for when I saw thee hurt,
I could have took the weapon thou let'st fall,
And run at Arden; for I have sworn
That these mine eyes, offended with his sight,
Shall never close till Arden's be shut up.
This night I rose and walk'd about the chamber,
And twice or thrice I thought to have murder'd him.
Mosbie. What, in the night? then had we been undone.
Alice. Why, how long shall he live?   90
Mosbie. Faith, Alice, no longer than this night.—
Black Will and Shakebag, will you two perform
The complot that I have laid?
Will. Ay, or else think me as a villain.
Greene. And rather than you shall want, I'll help myself.
Mosbie. You, Master Greene, shall single Franklin forth,
And hold him with a long tale of strange news,
That he may not come home till supper-time.

67 *arming sword:* military sword (OED arming, 1b).
73 *have cramm'd an angel* (C)] cramme in Angels Q. Balances "every drop"
and corrects the metre.

> I'll fetch Master Arden home, and we like friends
> Will play a game or two at tables here.   100

Alice. But what of all this? how shall he be slain?

Mosbie. Why, Black Will and Shakebag lock'd within the
>   counting-house
> Shall, at a certain watchword given, rush forth.

Will. What shall the watchword be?

Mosbie. "Now I can take you"; that shall be the word:
> But come not forth before in any case.

Will. I warrant you.   But who shall lock me in?

Alice. That will I do; thou'st keep the key thyself.

Mosbie. Come, Master Greene, go you along with me.
> See all things ready, Alice, against we come.   110

Alice. Take no care for that; send you him home

>   *Exeunt Mosbie and Greene.*

> And if he e'er go forth again, blame me.
> Come, Black Will, that in mine eyes art fair;
> Next unto Mosbie do I honour thee;
> Instead of fair words and large promises
> My hands shall play you golden harmony:
> How like you this? say, will you do it, sirs?

Will. Ay, and that bravely, too.   Mark my device:
> Place Mosbie, being a stranger, in a chair,
> And let your husband sit upon a stool,   120
> That I may come behind him cunningly,
> And with a towel pull him to the ground,
> Then stab him till his flesh be as a sieve;
> That done, bear him behind the Abbey,
> That those that find him murder'd may suppose
> Some slave or other kill'd him for his gold.

Alice. A fine device! you shall have twenty pound,
> And, when he is dead, you shall have forty more,
> And, lest you might be suspected staying here,
> Michael shall saddle you two lusty geldings;   130
> Ride whither you will, to Scotland, or to Wales,
> I'll see you shall not lack, where'er you be.

Will. Such words would make one kill a thousand men!

---

105 *Now I can take you* (C)] Now I take you Q. Metre, Holinshed ("Now may
I take you, sir, if I will"), and consistency with 233, require the correction
.

Give me the key; which is the counting-house?

Alice. Here would I stay and still encourage you,
But that I know how resolute you are.

Shakebag. Tush, you are too faint-hearted; we must do it.

Alice. But Mosbie will be there, whose very looks
Will add unwonted courage to my thought,
And make me the first that shall adventure on him.   140

Will. Tush, get you gone; 'tis we must do the deed.
When this door opens next, look for his death.

[Will and Shakebag withdraw.]

Alice. Ah, would he now were here that it might open!
I shall no more be clos'd in Arden's arms,
That like the snakes of black Tisiphone
Sting me with their embracings! Mosbie's arms
Shall compass me, and, were I made a star,
I would have none other spheres but those.
There is no nectar but in Mosbie's lips!
Had chaste Diana kiss'd him, she like me   150
Would grow love-sick, and from her watery bower
Fling down Endymion and snatch him up:
Then blame not me that slay a silly man
Not half so lovely as Endymion.

Here enters MICHAEL.

Michael. Mistress, my master is coming hard by.

Alice. Who comes with him?

Michael. Nobody but Mosbie.

Alice. That's well, Michael. Fetch in the tables, and when
thou hast done, stand before the counting-house door.

Michael. Why so?   160

Alice. Black Will is lock'd within to do the deed.

Michael. What, shall he die to-night?

Alice. Ay, Michael.

Michael. But shall not Susan know it?

Alice. Yes, for she'll be as secret as ourselves.

Michael. That's brave. I'll go fetch the tables.

Alice. But, Michael, hark to me a word or two:

145 *Tisiphone:* one of the Furies.

When my husband is come in, lock the street-door;
He shall be murder'd or the guests come in.

Exit Michael.

Here enters ARDEN *and* MOSBIE [, MICHAEL *following*].

Husband, what mean you to bring Mosbie home?   170
Although I wish'd you to be reconcil'd,
'Twas more for fear of you than love of him.
Black Will and Greene are his companions,
And they are cutters, and may cut you short:
Therefore I thought it good to make you friends.
But wherefore do you bring him hither now?
You have given me my supper with his sight.
Mosbie. Master Arden, methinks your wife would have me gone.
Arden. No, good Master Mosbie; women will be prating.
Alice, bid him welcome; he and I are friends.   180
Alice. You may enforce me to it, if you will;
But I had rather die than bid him welcome.
His company hath purchas'd me ill friends,
And therefore will I ne'er frequent it more.
Mosbie [*aside*]. Oh, how cunningly she can dissemble!
Arden. Now he is here, you will not serve me so.
Alice. I pray you be not angry or displeas'd;
I'll bid him welcome, seeing you'll have it so.
You are welcome, Master Mosbie; will you sit down?
Mosbie. I know I am welcome to your loving husband;   190
But for yourself, you speak not from your heart.
Alice. And if I do not, sir, think I have cause.
Mosbie. Pardon me, Master Arden; I'll away.
Arden. No, good Master Mosbie.
Alice. We shall have guests enough, though you go hence.
Mosbie. I pray you, Master Arden, let me go.
Arden. I pray thee, Mosbie, let her prate her fill.
Alice. The doors are open, sir, you may be gone.
Michael [*aside*]. Nay, that's a lie, for I have lock'd the doors.
Arden. Sirrah, fetch me a cup of wine, I'll make them friends.
And, gentle Mistress Alice, seeing you are so stout,   201

177 *given me my supper:* "taken away my appetite."
183–4 Anticipates 210, 213, and so is perhaps an actor's interpolation.

You shall begin.   Frown not, I'll have it so.

Alice. I pray you meddle with that you have to do.

Arden. Why, Alice! how can I do too much for him
     Whose life I have endanger'd without cause?

Alice. 'Tis true; and, seeing 'twas partly through my means,
     I am content to drink to him for this once.
     Here, Master Mosbie! and I pray you, henceforth
     Be you as strange to me as I to you.
     Your company hath purchas'd me ill friends,   210
     And I for you, God knows, have undeserv'd
     Been evil spoken of in every place;
     Therefore henceforth frequent my house no more.

Mosbie. I'll see your husband in despite of you.
     Yet, Arden, I protest to thee by heaven,
     Thou ne'er shalt see me more after this night.
     I'll go to Rome rather than be forsworn.

Arden. Tush, I'll have no such vows made in my house.

Alice. Yes, I pray you, husband, let him swear;
     And, on that condition, Mosbie, pledge me here.   220

Mosbie. Ay, as willingly as I mean to live.

Arden. Come, Alice, is our supper ready yet?

Alice. It will by then you have play'd a game at tables.

Arden. Come, Master Mosbie, what shall we play for?

Mosbie. Three games for a French crown, sir, and please you.

Arden. Content.

            Then they play at the tables. [*Will looks forth.*]

Will. —Can he not take him yet? what a spite is that!

Alice. —Not yet, Will; take heed he see thee not.

Will. —I fear he will spy me as I am coming.

Michael. —To prevent that, creep betwixt my legs.   230

Mosbie. One ace, or else I lose the game.

Arden. Marry, sir, there's two for failing.

Mosbie. Ah, Master Arden, " now I can take you."

            Then Will pulls him down with a towel.

Arden. Mosbie! Michael! Alice! what will you do?

Will. Nothing but take you up, sir, nothing else.

---

212 *evil* (C)] ill Q (unmetrical and influenced by 210).

231 *ace:* a "one" on the dice. Backgammon is played with a pair of dice. Mosbie
    now throws two "ones" at the same throw.

Mosbie. There's for the pressing iron you told me of.

[Stabs him.]

Shakebag. And there's for the ten pound in my sleeve.

[Stabs him.]

Alice. What, groans thou? nay, then give me the weapon!
Take this for hindering Mosbie's love and mine.

[Stabs him.]

Michael. O, mistress!   240

Will. Ah, that villain will betray us all.

Mosbie. Tush, fear him not; he will be secret.

Michael. Why, dost thou think I will betray myself?

Shakebag. In Southwark dwells a bonny northern lass,
The widow Chambley; I'll to her house now,
And if she will not give me harborough,
I'll make booty of the quean even to her smock.

Will. Shift for yourselves; we two will leave you now.

Alice. First lay the body in the counting-house.

Then they lay the body in the counting-house.

Will. We have our gold; Mistress Alice, adieu;   250
Mosbie, farewell, and Michael, farewell too.   *Exeunt.*

Enter SUSAN.

Susan. Mistress, the guests are at the doors.
Hearken, they knock: what, shall I let them in?

Alice. Mosbie, go thou and bear them company.   *[Exit Mosbie.*
And, Susan, fetch water and wash away this blood.

Susan. The blood cleaveth to the ground and will not out.

Alice. But with my nails I'll scrape away the blood.—
The more I strive, the more the blood appears!

Susan. What's the reason, Mistress, can you tell?

Alice. Because I blush not at my husband's death.   260

Here enters MOSBIE.

Mosbie. How now, what's the matter? is all well?

Alice. Ay, well, if Arden were alive again.
In vain we strive, for here his blood remains.

236 *pressing iron:* recalling i. 314. Mosbie uses an actual pressing-iron here in
    Holinshed (which doubtless inspired i. 314), but surely uses his sword in
    the play.

Mosbie. Why, strew rushes on it, can you not?
This wench doth nothing: fall unto the work.
Alice. 'Twas thou that made me murder him.
Mosbie. What of that?
Alice. Nay, nothing, Mosbie, so it be not known.
Mosbie. Keep thou it close, and 'tis unpossible.
Alice. Ah, but I cannot! was he not slain by me?   270
My husband's death torments me at the heart.
Mosbie. It shall not long torment thee, gentle Alice;
I am thy husband, think no more of him.

> *Here enters* ADAM FOWLE *and* BRADSHAW.

Bradshaw. How now, Mistress Arden? what ail you weep?
Mosbie. Because her husband is abroad so late.
A couple of ruffians threaten'd him yesternight,
And she, poor soul, is afraid he should be hurt.
Adam. Is't nothing else? tush, he'll be here anon.

> *Here enters* GREENE.

Greene. Now, Mistress Arden, lack you any guests?
Alice. Ah, Master Greene, did you see my husband lately?   280
Greene. I saw him walking behind the Abbey even now.

> *Here enters* FRANKLIN.

Alice. I do not like this being out so late.
Master Franklin, where did you leave my husband?
Franklin. Believe me I saw him not since morning.
Fear you not, he'll come anon; meantime
You may do well to bid his guests sit down.
Alice. Ay, so they shall; Master Bradshaw, sit you there;
I pray you, be content, I'll have my will.
Master Mosbie, sit you in my husband's seat.
Michael. —Susan, shall thou and I wait on them?   290
Or, and thou say'st the word, let us sit down too.
Susan. —Peace, we have other matters now in hand.
I fear me, Michael, all will be bewray'd.
Michael. —Tush, so it be known that I shall marry thee in the
morning, I care not though I be hanged ere night.
But to prevent the worst, I'll buy some ratsbane.

Susan. —Why, Michael, wilt thou poison thyself?

Michael. —No, but my mistress, for I fear she'll tell.

Susan. —Tush, Michael, fear not her, she's wise enough.

Mosbie. Sirrah Michael, give's a cup of beer.—   300

    Mistress Arden, here's to your husband.

Alice. My husband!

Franklin. What ails you, woman, to cry so suddenly?

Alice. Ah, neighbours, a sudden qualm came over my heart;

    My husband's being forth torments my mind.

    I know something's amiss, he is not well;

    Or else I should have heard of him ere now.

Mosbie [aside]. She will undo us through her foolishness.

Greene. Fear not, Mistress Arden, he's well enough.

Alice. Tell not me; I know he is not well: 310

    He was not wont for to stay thus late.

    Good Master Franklin, go and seek him forth,

    And if you find him, send him home to me,

    And tell him what a fear he hath put me in.

Franklin [aside]. I like not this; I pray God all be well.—

    I'll seek him out, and find him if I can.

                  Exeunt Franklin, Mosbie, and Greene.

Alice. —Michael, how shall I do to rid the rest away?

Michael. —Leave that to my charge, let me alone.—

    'Tis very late, Master Bradshaw,

    And there are many false knaves abroad,   320

    And you have many narrow lanes to pass.

Bradshaw. Faith, friend Michael, and thou sayest true.

    Therefore I pray thee light's forth and lend's a link.

                  Exeunt Bradshaw, Adam, and Michael.

Alice. Michael, bring them to the doors, but do not stay;

    You know I do not love to be alone.

    Go, Susan, and bid thy brother come:

    But wherefore should he come?   Here is nought but fear;

    Stay, Susan, stay, and help to counsel me.

Susan. Alas, I counsel? fear frights away my wits.

               Then they open the counting-house door,

                       and look upon Arden.

Alice. See, Susan, where thy quondam master lies,   330

    Sweet Arden, smear'd in blood and filthy gore.

Susan. My brother, you, and I shall rue this deed.
Alice. Come, Susan, help to lift his body forth,
    And let our salt tears be his obsequies.

Here enters MOSBIE *and* GREENE.

Mosbie. How now, Alice, whither will you bear him?
Alice. Sweet Mosbie, art thou come?   Then weep that will:
    I have my wish in that I joy thy sight.
Greene. Well, it 'hoves us to be circumspect.
Mosbie. Ay, for Franklin thinks that we have murder'd him.
Alice. Ay, but he cannot prove it for his life.   340
    We'll spend this night in dalliance and in sport.

Here enters MICHAEL.

Michael. O mistress, the Mayor and all the watch
    Are coming towards our house with glaives and bills.
Alice. Make the door fast; let them not come in.
Mosbie. Tell me, sweet Alice, how shall I escape?
Alice. Out at the back-door, over the pile of wood,
    And for one night lie at the Flower-de-luce.
Mosbie. That is the next way to betray myself.
Greene. Alas, Mistress Arden, the watch will take me here,
    And cause suspicion, where else would be none.   350
Alice. Why, take that way that Master Mosbie doth;
    But first convey the body to the fields.
                    Then they bear the body into the fields.
Mosbie. Until to-morrow, sweet Alice, now farewell:
    And see you confess nothing in any case.
Greene. Be resolute, Mistress Alice, betray us not,
    But cleave to us as we will stick to you.
                    Exeunt Mosbie and Greene.
Alice. Now, let the judge and juries do their worst:
    My house is clear, and now I fear them not.
Susan. As we went, it snowèd all the way,
    Which makes me fear our footsteps will be spied.   360
Alice. Peace, fool, the snow will cover them again.

352 *But first . . . the fields:* not a command to Greene but to Michael and Susan
    ("first": "the first thing to do is"), whose absence is covered by 353–8.

Susan. But it had done before we came back again.
Alice. Hark, hark, they knock! go, Michael, let them in.

Here enters the MAYOR *and the* Watch.

How now, Master Mayor, have you brought my husband
    home?
Mayor. I saw him come into your house an hour ago.
Alice. You are deceiv'd; it was a Londoner.
Mayor. Mistress Arden, know you not one that is call'd Black
    Will?
Alice. I know none such: what mean these questions?
Mayor. I have the Council's warrant to apprehend him.
Alice [*aside*]. I am glad it is no worse.—   370
    Why, Master Mayor, think you I harbour any such?
Mayor. We are inform'd that here he is;
    And therefore pardon us, for we must search.
Alice. Ay, search, and spare you not, through every room:
    Were my husband at home, you would not offer this.

Here enters FRANKLIN.

Master Franklin, what mean you come so sad?
Franklin. Arden, thy husband and my friend, is slain.
Alice. Ah, by whom? Master Franklin, can you tell?
Franklin. I know not; but behind the Abbey
    There he lies murder'd in most piteous case.   380
Mayor. But, Master Franklin, are you sure 'tis he?
Franklin. I am too sure; would God I were deceiv'd.
Alice. Find out the murderers, let them be known.
Franklin. Ay, so they shall: come you along with us.
Alice. Wherefore?
Franklin. Know you this hand-towel and this knife?
Susan. —Ah, Michael, thorough this thy negligence
    Thou hast betrayèd and undone us all.
Michael. —I was so afraid I knew not what I did:
    I thought I had thrown them both into the well.   390
Alice. It is the pig's blood we had to supper.
    But wherefore stay you? find out the murderers.
Mayor. I fear me you'll prove one of them yourself.
Alice. I one of them? what mean such questions?

Franklin. I fear me he was murder'd in this house
    And carried to the fields; for from that place
    Backwards and forwards may you see
    The print of many feet within the snow.
    And look about this chamber where we are,
    And you shall find part of his guiltless blood;   400
    For in his slipshoe did I find some rushes,
    Which argueth he was murder'd in this room.
Mayor. Look in the place where he was wont to sit.
    See, see, his blood! it is too manifest.
Alice. It is a cup of wine that Michael shed.
Michael. Ay, truly.
Franklin. It is his blood, which, strumpet, thou hast shed.
    But if I live, thou and thy 'complices
    Which have conspir'd and wrought his death shall rue it.
Alice. Ah, Master Franklin, God and heaven can tell   410
    I lov'd him more than all the world beside.
    But bring me to him, let me see his body.
Franklin. Bring that villain and Mosbie's sister too;
    And one of you go to the Flower-de-luce,
    And seek for Mosbie, and apprehend him too.   *Exeunt.*

[SCENE XV]

Here enters SHAKEBAG *solus.*

Shakebag. The widow Chambley in her husband's days I kept;
    And now he's dead, she is grown so stout
    She will not know her old companions.
    I came thither, thinking to have had
    Harbour as I was wont,
    And she was ready to thrust me out at doors;
    But whether she would or no, I got me up,
    And as she follow'd me, I spurn'd her down the stairs,
    And broke her neck, and cut her tapster's throat,
    And now I am going to fling them in the Thames.   10
    I have the gold; what care I though it be known?
    I'll cross the water and take sanctuary.   *Exit Shakebag.*

[SCENE XVI]

Here enters the MAYOR, MOSBIE, ALICE, FRANKLIN,
MICHAEL, *and* SUSAN.

Mayor. See, Mistress Arden, where your husband lies;
  Confess this foul fault and be penitent.
Alice. Arden, sweet husband, what shall I say?
  The more I sound his name, the more he bleeds;
  This blood condemns me, and in gushing forth
  Speaks as it falls, and asks me why I did it.
  Forgive me, Arden: I repent me now,
  And, would my death save thine, thou shouldst not die.
  Rise up, sweet Arden, and enjoy thy love,
  And frown not on me when we meet in heaven: 10
  In heaven I'll love thee, though on earth I did not.
Mayor. Say, Mosbie, what made thee murder him?
Franklin. Study not for an answer; look not down;
  His purse and girdle found at thy bed's head
  Witness sufficiently thou didst the deed;
  It bootless is to swear thou didst it not.
Mosbie. I hir'd Black Will and Shakebag, ruffians both,
  And they and I have done this murderous deed.
  But wherefore stay we? Come and bear me hence.
Franklin. Those ruffians shall not escape; I will up to London,
  And get the Council's warrant to apprehend them.   21
                                                Exeunt.

[SCENE XVII]

Here enters WILL.

Will. Shakebag, I hear, hath taken sanctuary,
  But I am so pursued with hues and cries
  For petty robberies that I have done,

11 *I'll* (H. Tyrrell, *The Doubtful Plays of Shakspere,* 1851.)] I Q.
17–18 The first line passes as truth in the theatre because of the second.

That I can come unto no sanctuary.
Therefore must I in some oyster-boat
At last be fain to go aboard some hoy,
And so to Flushing.   There is no staying here.
At Sittingburgh the watch was like to take me,
And had not I with my buckler cover'd my head,
And run full blank at all adventures,   10
I am sure I had ne'er gone further than that place;
For the constable had twenty warrants to apprehend me,
Besides that, I robb'd him and his man once at Gadshill.
Farewell, England; I'll to Flushing now.

Exit Will.

[SCENE XVIII]

Here enters the MAYOR, MOSBIE, ALICE, MICHAEL, SUSAN,
and BRADSHAW.

Mayor. Come, make haste, and bring away the prisoners.
Bradshaw. Mistress Arden, you are now going to God,
    And I am by the law condemn'd to die
    About a letter I brought from Master Greene.
    I pray you, Mistress Arden, speak the truth:
    Was I ever privy to your intent or no?
Alice. What should I say?   You brought me such a letter,
    But I dare swear thou knew'st not the contents.
    Leave now to trouble me with worldly things,
    And let me meditate upon my saviour Christ,   10
    Whose blood must save me for the blood I shed.
Mosbie. How long shall I live in this hell of grief?
    Convey me from the presence of that strumpet.
Alice. Ah, but for thee I had never been [a] strumpet.
    What cannot oaths and protestations do,
    When men have opportunity to woo?
    I was too young to sound thy villainies,
    But now I find it and repent too late.
Susan. Ah, gentle brother, wherefore should I die?
    I knew not of it till the deed was done.   20

Mosbie. For thee I mourn more than for myself;
    But let it suffice, I cannot save thee now.
Michael. And if your brother and my mistress
    Had not promis'd me you in marriage,
    I had ne'er given consent to this foul deed.
Mayor. Leave to accuse each other now,
    And listen to the sentence I shall give.
    Bear Mosbie and his sister to London straight,
    Where they in Smithfield must be executed;
    Bear Mistress Arden unto Canterbury,   30
    Where her sentence is she must be burnt;
    Michael and Bradshaw in Feversham must suffer death.
Alice. Let my death make amends for all my sins.
Mosbie. Fie upon women! this shall be my song;
    But bear me hence, for I have liv'd too long.
Susan. Seeing no hope on earth, in heaven is my hope.
Michael. Faith, I care not, seeing I die with Susan.
Bradshaw. My blood be on his head that gave the sentence.
Mayor. To speedy execution with them all!   *Exeunt.*

[*EPILOGUE.*]

Here enters FRANKLIN.

Franklin. Thus have you seen the truth of Arden's death.
    As for the ruffians, Shakebag and Black Will,
    The one took sanctuary, and, being sent for out,
    Was murderèd in Southwark as he pass'd
    To Greenwich, where the Lord Protector lay.
    Black Will was burn'd in Flushing on a stage;
    Greene was hang'd at Osbridge in Kent;
    The painter fled and how he died we know not.
    But this above the rest is to be noted:
    Arden lay murder'd in that plot of ground   10
    Which he by force and violence held from Reede;
    And in the grass his body's print was seen

Two years and more after the deed was done.
Gentlemen, we hope you'll pardon this naked tragedy,
Wherein no filèd points are foisted in
To make it gracious to the ear or eye;
For simple truth is gracious enough,
And needs no other points of glozing stuff.   [*Exit.*]

Glossary

Glossary

abstract, summary
abuse, deceive, insult
accident, incident
adrad, dreading
advise, consider
aggress, advance
aglet, tag of a lace
agnise, learn
ambages, circumlocutions
ancient, ensign
angel, gold coin
answer, repay
apparently, plainly
appeal, accuse
apply, agree with, assist
approve, prove
argument, proof
artificer, workman
attempt, attack

bait, take refreshment
ballace, ballast
ban, curse
bashaw, Turkish nobleman
basilisk, fabulous reptile with deadly eye
battle, body of troops
bedesman, prayer-man, pensioner
behight, promise
beray, defile
bewray, reveal
bod (*bode*), remained
boltered, tangled, matted
boot, help
botcher, tailor who mends clothes
bound, commission
bow, bend
brabble, brawl
braid, start
bravely, showily
bravery, ostentation
bring, be with you to, be even with you

brokage, secondhand dealing
brook, digest, endure
bruit, rumour
buckler, shield
budget, bag
bug, bugbear
buss, kiss
butting, abutting, adjoining
by, aby, pay for
by and by, immediately

capcase, bag
carbines, cavalry with firearms
carle, churl
cast, contrived
cates, food, dainties
check, chide
cheer, countenance, entertainment
clepe, call
close with, agree with; come to grips with
closely, secretly
clout, cloth, bundle
cockshut, twilight
coil, disturbance
coiled, beaten
coistrel, knave
colour, pretence
colours of device, heraldic banners
coltstaff, pole for carrying a tub
commends, greetings
companion, fellow, knave
complot, plot
conceit, idea, fancy, opinion
conceived, possessed
condescent, consent
condition, station
conveyance, artful contrivance
convince, convict, conquer
copesmate, companion
cornet, troop of cavalry
corregidor, advocate

costard, head (apple)
cottons, this gear, this affair goes well
couch, lie down, embroider
countenance, be in keeping with
countermured, doubly walled
courage, vigour, ambition
coy, reserved
crabbed, ill-natured
cry creak, confess defeat
cunning, skilful
curious, intricate
currently, truly
curst, shrewish
cutter, cutthroat
Counter, prison in London
counterfeit, portrait

dag, heavy pistol
daunt, subdue
defend, forbid
demean, behave
derive, pass (receive) by inheritance
despite, spite
despoil, lay bare
detect, reveal
devocate, ?demand money ?derogate
    (deprive of rights)
dilate, show
ding, dash
discover, reveal
dissolution, dissoluteness
distain, stain, disgrace
doom, judgment
dote, behave madly
drift, design
ducat, European gold coin
during, enduring

ear, plough
eke, also
engine, instrument
enjoin, join
enlarge, set free
entreat, treat
erst, formerly
exasperate, make worse, provoke
except of, excuse
extirpen, root out
extremities, strong feelings

fact, deed, crime
failing, for, to ensure sufficiency
falchion, curved sword

fall, befall
fatch, fetch, device
favour, beauty, kindness, token
fear, frighten
fence, fencing skill
festination, haste
fet, fetched
filed, polished
fine, in, in the end
flaw, squall
flight, fright
flood, tide
fond, foolish
force, of, fortified
foreset, of, deliberately
forslow, delay
foster, forester
frames, buildings
fretful, gnawing
front, forehead
froward, stubborn

gage, pledge
gear, thing, clothing
giglot, harlot
Gis, by, by Jesus
give back, draw back
glaive, halbert
glozing, specious
graft, grafted, emplanted
graved, entombed
gree, agreement
gripe, grip, griffin, vulture
grudge, reluctance
guard, border of garment
guardant, guards
guerdon, reward

hability, means
haggard, untamed (hawk)
halt, limp
hand, under, secretly
handsel, wish good luck (with present)
hap, chance
happily, perhaps
harborough, harbour, refuge
harquebus, long gun
hateful, full of hate
heat, haste, violence
hest, command
hight, named
hind, servant
hocked, hamstrung

Glossary

283

holidam, holy thing
host, be with you at, be even with you
humours, passions

ignomy, dishonour
ill-thewed, ill-natured
impeach, accuse
impetrate, procure
inexplicable, indissoluble
infect, corrupt
infective, infectious
injurious, insulting
instance, proof
insult, triumph over
intend, express
intent, purpose
intentive, attentive
inter'gatory, question to be answered on oath
intreat, treat
inure, accustom
irk, annoy
iwis, in truth

jack, knave
jet, strut
jill, wench
'join, enjoin
jug, wench

keep, dwell
kind, nature, kindred
kindness, human nature
kindship, kindness

Lakin, by, by our Lady
largess, bounty
lay up, send to prison
lean from, avoid
leese, lose
let, hinder
lewd, base
lift, steal
lime, spread with bird-lime
list, like
lob, lout
lurden, idler, debilitating fever

march, border
matted, dull
meed, reward
mell, meddle
mend, amend

merely, entirely
misconster, misconstrue, misunderstand
misdeem, suspect
miss, misdeed
mistrust, forebode
mithridate, antidote to poison
mo, more
moiety, half
motion, proposal, entertainment
muscado, musket
mutchado, moustache

ne, nor
next, nearest
nice, scrupulous, particular
nill, will not

old, great
ordinary, eating-tavern
outrage, violence
overshot, be, go too far
overthrow, fall down

pace, path
painted cloth, ornamental wall-hanging
pantofles, slippers
parasite, flatterer
passenger, passer-by
passing, very
patch, fool
pathaire, passionate outburst
Paul's, St Paul's Cathedral
pencil, paintbrush
pined, afflicted
plain, complain
plancher, floorboard
platform, plan
plausible, worthy of applause
point, ornamental tag
poniard, dagger
populous, crude
post, in, in haste
pouchmouth, thicklips
practice, plot
precisian, puritan
prefer, promote
present, immediate
prest, ready, at hand
pretend, intend, claim
prevent, anticipate
prise, value, price
prosecute, continue

protract, delay
purblind, quite blind

quaint, artful
quarterage, quarterly allowance
quean, wench
quick, living
quill, reed-pipe
quital, requital
quittance, repay

raked, covered
rampier, rampart
random, act without restraint
rate, chide
reaching, far-reaching
reave, bereave
reck, care for
record, sing, witness
recourse, flow
recure, restore
rede, counsel
reduce, bring under control
remit, pardon
repine, discontent
repugn, oppose
respect, motive
retort, throw back
round, bring round, whisper
roundly, directly
rout, mob
ruth, pity

sain, said
sconce, fort
score on the post, get drink on credit
scummer, shallow ladle
seam-rent, split at the seams
secretary, privy councillor
secure, confident
seld, seldom
senseless, unfeeling
sensible, able to feel
shift, manage
shrieve, sheriff
shrow, shrew
silly, weak, innocent
sith, sithens, since
sit beside, go without
skilless, irrational
sleight, stratagem
slip, put off
slipshoe, slipper

smug, neat, decent
soothe, flatter, confirm
sort, company
sort, allot, choose
sound, swoon
square, shape
stage, scaffold
standing, vantage-point
state, in, by law, in a condition
stern, rudder
stick, hesitate
still, always
stoop to lure, come down to keeper's fist
store, many
success, outcome
sufferance, suffering, submission
suggestion, accusation
surcease, cease
sure, betrothed

table, painter's canvas
tables, backgammon
taint, accuse
take the wall of, push from the wall
take up, catch
tallies, pieces of wood notched to record accounts
temper, make fit
tender, cherish
testy, furious
tentive, attentive
thoughtful, anxious
through-girt, pierced through
tickle, precarious
Titan, the sun-god
to-torn, badly torn
towardness, willingness
toy, trifle
trace, track, walk about
trade, way
train, treachery
trick, adorn
troll, send round
trug, wench
trull, wench
truss, breeches, hang
turn off, hang

unkindly, unnatural
unskilful, without judgment
unvalued, beyond price
ure, use

vild, vile

wager, pay
want, lack
watch, part of the night
watchet, pale blue
wealth, well-being
whenas, when
whilom, formerly
whipstalk, whipstock
whistly, silently
wield, govern

wight, creature
wist, knew
wit, know
words of course, ceremonial phrases
wreak, avenge
writhe, twist
wroke, avenged
wry, perverted

yielden, yielded
yeomanry, countryman's talk